D0576256

ILLUSTRATED HISTORY OF NORTH AMERICAN RAILROADS

18
18
823
823
UNION PACIFIC
823

ILLUSTRATED HISTORY OF

NORTH AMERICAN

RAILROADS

ARTHUR TAYLER

CHARTWELL
BOOKS, INC.

A QUINTET BOOK

Published by Chartwell Books, Inc.
A Division of Book Sales, Inc.
114 Northfield Avenue
Edison, New Jersey 08837

This edition produced for sale in the U.S.A., Its
territories and dependencies only.

ISBN 0-7858-0564-8

Reprinted 1997, 1999, 2002

This book was designed and produced by
Quintet Publishing Limited
6 Blundell Street
London N7 9BH

Creative Director: Richard Dewing
Designer: Peter Laws
Senior Editor: Anna Briffa
Editor: Kit Coppard

Typeset in Great Britain by
Central Southern Typesetters, Eastbourne
Manufactured in Singapore by Eray Scan Pte Ltd
Printed in China by Leefung-Asco Printers Ltd

ACKNOWLEDGMENTS

Thanks are due to many friends and former colleagues for support and information. Particular mention must be made of the help received from The American Society of Mechanical Engineers, The Library of the Institution of Mechanical Engineers, The Electro-Motive Division of General Motors, General Electric, New Sulzer Diesel Limited, Baltimore & Ohio Museum, and many more.

CONTENTS

Introduction

This book is a general review of North American railroad history as seen by an outside observer. It is divided into five main groups: the era from birth to maturity, 1830–1870; steady growth and consolidation up to the beginning of the 20th century; the era of steam development and domination, electrification as an alternative for heavy haul, up to 1935; the change to diesel traction and the beginnings of road and air competition; the post-War-era decline, renaissance, regrouping and restructuring leading to the healthy state of the much smaller but effective industry of the present day.

In the beginning industrial growth was dependent on canals and other forms of water transport while stage coaches provided transport for passengers and mail. The first railroads were built by canal companies, and the first passenger trains adopted stage-coach-type bodies on railroad wheels with locomotives imported from Britain. It soon became clear that British construction methods were too expensive and unsuited to the needs of a rapidly developing country. The American railroad began to emerge and was constructed as cheaply as possible while the locomotives were manufactured locally to suit specific requirements. Railroads spread rapidly opening up a host of new opportunities for the development of natural resources.

CP Limited

Many more railroads, both great and small, were built carrying passengers and freight to previously undeveloped territories. Locomotives developed along well-defined lines, increasing in size and power yet retaining the characteristics of earlier years, that is to say simplicity, reliability, and ease of maintenance. Cars had long ridden on trucks and passenger amenities were improved; continuous automatic brakes were introduced and perfected.

By the early part of the 20th century, the tractive

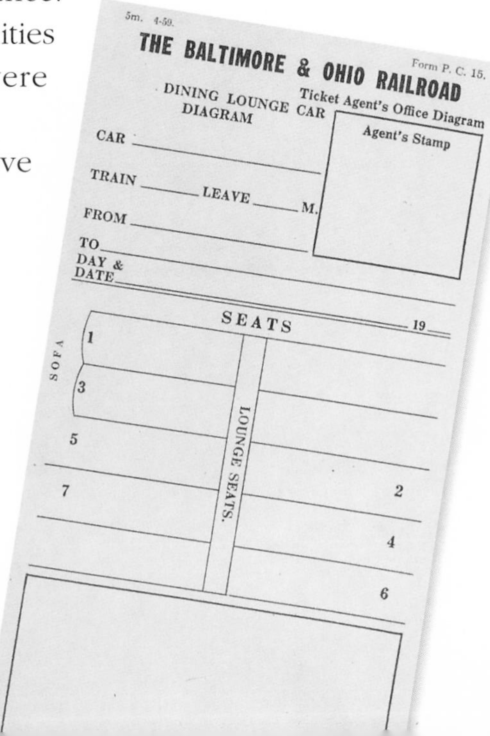
5m. 4-59.
THE BALTIMORE & OHIO RAILROAD
Form P. C. 15.
DINING LOUNGE CAR DIAGRAM
Ticket Agent's Office Diagram
Agent's Stamp
CAR
TRAIN LEAVE M.
FROM
TO
DAY & DATE
SEATS 19
SOFA
1
3
5
7
LOUNGE SEATS.
2
4
6

capacity of locomotives had reached the point where more sophistication was necessary. American locomotives grew in both size and weight; train speeds and train weights, particularly freight, were increased. Locomotive and car builders were able to satisfy not only the needs of the United States but were healthy exporters too.

Coal was predominant in the eastern part of the United States and with large deposits of oil, many steam locomotives used oil as their staple fuel. The rapid development of the internal combustion engine soon saw the introduction of compression-ignition engines to rail traction. The ability to run vast distances without attention and the increasing reliability of diesel engines soon saw the rapid introduction of diesel locomotives, even to the detriment of many electrified lines. In the same period the steam locomotive reached its zenith. The War in Europe and the Far East found railroads hard pressed.

Dan Pope Collection

Meanwhile other forms of transport were developing rapidly, particularly air travel which became economic in terms of time between large centers of population. The private car had already reduced the pressure on commuting and modern roads were being built at a fast pace. Rail travel became less popular. Many formerly viable railroads had to retract their operation, shed some traffic, and combine with others to survive. Steam locomotives disappeared from the scene altogether and the diesel engine reigned supreme – almost – except where traffic density made electrification viable. Today railroads still have their place but changes are occurring involving takeovers and mergers. The 21st century may see a resurgence in the more environmentally-friendly railroads.

American railroads and the industry which supported them served the country well. At first they were lightly built and this was to cost them dearly later, as practically every main line built had to be expensively rebuilt. Nevertheless had it not been for these railroad pioneers America as an industrial nation would probably have developed much more slowly.

CHAPTER ONE

THE EARLY YEARS

The first commercial railways were laid down in Britain in the early 1820s. The potential of railways did not escape the notice of United States citizens, and as early as 1825 William Strickland made a study for the Pennsylvania Society for the Promotion of Internal Improvement. Others sent to study pioneer British lines in the latter part of the decade were Horatio Allen of the Delaware & Hudson Canal Company, and George W. Whistler, Jonathan Knight and Ross Winans for the Baltimore & Ohio Railroad. Horatio Allen and Ross Winans both attended the Rainhill trials near Liverpool, England in 1829 when, on October 26, George Stephenson's *Rocket* was awarded the first prize. The reports received from these men were to have a strong influence on the construction of the early United States railroads.

It is difficult to think of any country which benefited more from railroads than the United States, and the assertion by Edward Pease, backer of the Stockton & Darlington Railway, might have applied equally to the United States: "Let the country but make the railways and the railways will make the country." The 50 years following the end of the Civil War in 1865 saw a nationwide transformation that was made possible by the railroads. Yet in a further 40 years a revolution in transport and travel would bring the American railroads to their knees!

February 28, 1827 is one of the most important dates in the history of railroads in the United States. It was the day on which the state of Maryland granted a charter to the promoters of what was to become the Baltimore & Ohio Railroad. The aim was to reach the Ohio River and funnel commerce into Baltimore, MD. The original route, which was surveyed with the help of the U.S. Army, included the splendid Carrollton Viaduct. On July 4, 1828 the foundation stone was laid by Charles Carroll; then in his 92nd year, Carroll was at that time the last survivor of the signatories of the American Declaration of Independence. He lived to see the railroad completed as far as Point of Rocks, which lay 73 miles southwest of Baltimore.

Some historians hold that the Granite Railway in Quincy, MA, a horse-worked, iron-faced timber track, which received its charter on April 3, 1826 and opened later the same year, was the first railroad in the United States. Be that as it may, the Baltimore & Ohio RR was the very first common carrier, and also the first to offer scheduled freight and passenger services to the general public.

August 28, 1830 was another red-letter day. Peter Cooper, an industrialist and inventor, had constructed a small experimental steam-driven locomotive, the *Tom Thumb*, at his Canton Iron Works in Baltimore. The first part of the Baltimore & Ohio railroad had a 14-mile stretch of double-track, iron-faced wood road between

B & O Railroad Museum

ABOVE ROSS WINANS WAS SENT TO ENGLAND TO STUDY PIONEER BRITISH RAILWAYS. ON HIS RETURN TO THE UNITED STATES HE WAS ONE OF THE FIRST TO RECOMMEND STEAM LOCOMOTIVES.

B & O Railroad Museum

ABOVE A REPLICA OF PETER COOPER'S *TOM THUMB*, AN OPEN CAR BUILT IN 1927 FOR THE BALTIMORE & OHIO CENTENARY.

B & O Railroad Museum

RIGHT PETER COOPER, THE INVENTOR OF *TOM THUMB*.

RIGHT Carrollton Viaduct of the Baltimore & Ohio line. The first stone was laid by Charles Carroll in his 92nd year.

B & O Railroad Museum

BELOW Baltimore & Ohio Carrollton Viaduct with replicas of *Tom Thumb* and the rival horse-drawn car for the Baltimore & Ohio centennial *Fair of the Iron Horse* in 1927. In the background is the latest 4–8–2 No. 5000.

California State Railroad Museum

LEFT CHARLES CARROLL OF CARROLLTON LAID THE FIRST STONE OF THE BALTIMORE & OHIO CARROLLTON VIADUCT ON JULY 4, 1828. HE WAS AT THAT TIME THE LAST SURVIVING SIGNATORY OF THE DECLARATION OF INDEPENDENCE.

B & O Railroad Museum

Baltimore and Ellicott's Mills worked by horses. Peter Cooper staged a race between *Tom Thumb*, drawing a car-load of directors, and a horse-drawn car. The draft for the boiler of his little locomotive was provided by a belt-driven fan, and in the race the belt would not stay in place, so steam pressure was lost. On this occasion the horse won, but the contest certainly served to convince a lot of people of the potential practicability of steam as motive power.

Motive power was at first imported from Britain, and the firm of Foster, Rastrick & Company of Stourbridge, England built the first steam locomotive, the *Stourbridge Lion* costing $2,914, to the order of Horatio Allen for the Delaware & Hudson Canal Company. This was delivered in August 1829 for use on a coal line they were building over the 11 miles from Carbondale to Honesdale, PA. Even at 7 tons it was too heavy for the lightly-laid timber and iron road, and in particular was deemed unsuitable for a wooden trestle over Lackawaxen Creek. Although Allen himself drove over the trestle and back at 10 miles per hour (some say 20 mph!), many people thought it too dangerous.

Improvements were made to the track, and *Stourbridge Lion* was given a second try, but its 7 tons of unsprung weight led to derailments and it was laid aside at Honesdale. In 1849 its boiler and cylinders were removed for use in a foundry in Carbondale. Many years later the owners shipped the parts to the Smithsonian Institution in Washington, DC; a full-size replica of the *Lion* is on permanent display at Honesdale. On October 9, 1829 the Delaware & Hudson inclines and levels were opened, but these

RIGHT EARLY AMERICAN "T" RAIL. THE "T" RAIL WAS FIRST LAID ON THE CAMDEN & AMBOY RR IN 1831.

California State Railroad Museum

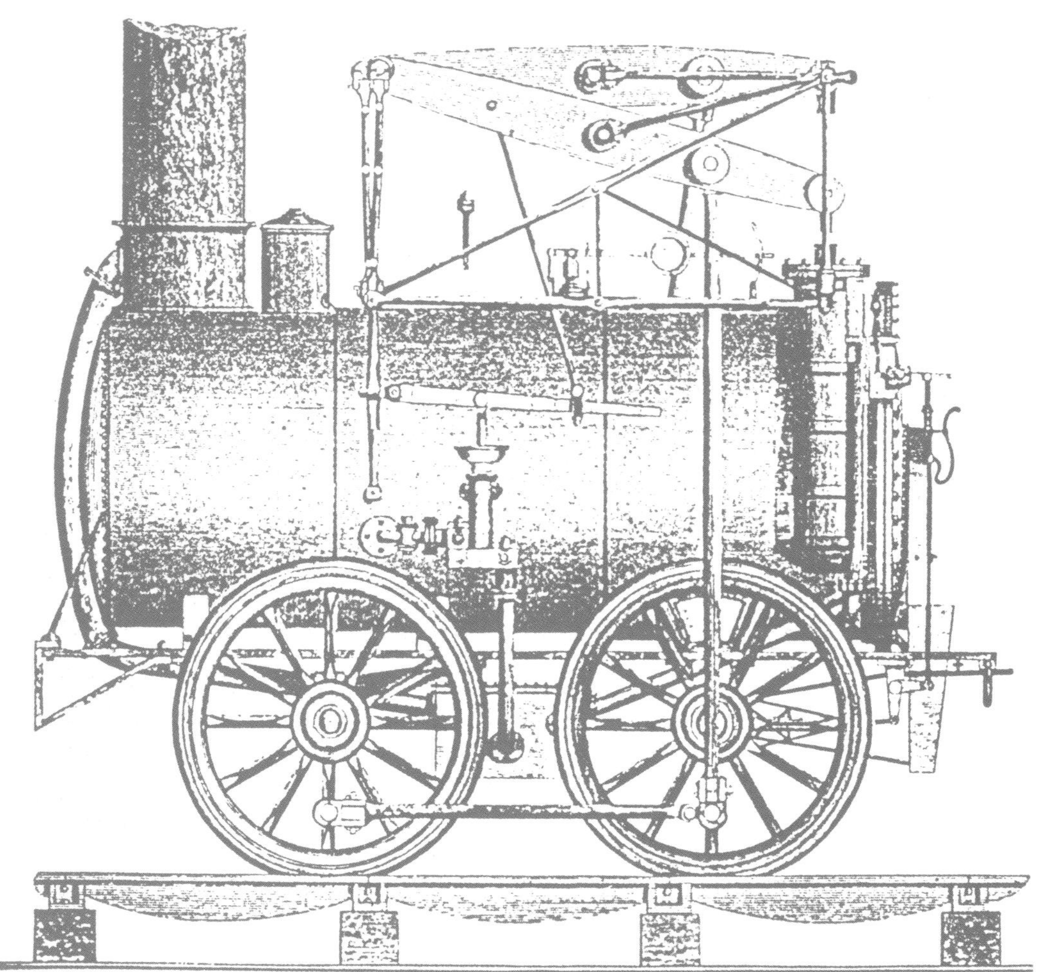

ABOVE STOURBRIDGE LION – A CONTEMPORARY ENGRAVING OF THE FIRST STEAM LOCOMOTIVE IMPORTED FROM ENGLAND IN 1829.

were worked by cable and gravity. January 15, 1831 saw the inauguration of six miles of track out of Charleston, SC, the first railroad in the United States to provide a regular service for passengers and freight hauled by steam. In 1833 the line was extended to Hamburg, just across the Savannah River from Augusta, GA to make a total length of 136 miles, the longest railroad in the world at that time. Its role as a public railroad and common carrier is notable as up to then most lines had been built for specific purposes, such as coal, timber or freight transportation, and were used almost exclusively by their owners.

British locomotives were designed for well-aligned tracks and were found unsuitable for the lightly laid American roads, so the fast-growing nation quickly launched its own locomotive establishments, despite the willingness of British builders to work to United States specifications. Britain had by now established the basic fundamentals of steam locomotive design which were to remain to the end of the steam era, but from the late 19th century onwards most of the major technical advances in steam locomotion were well

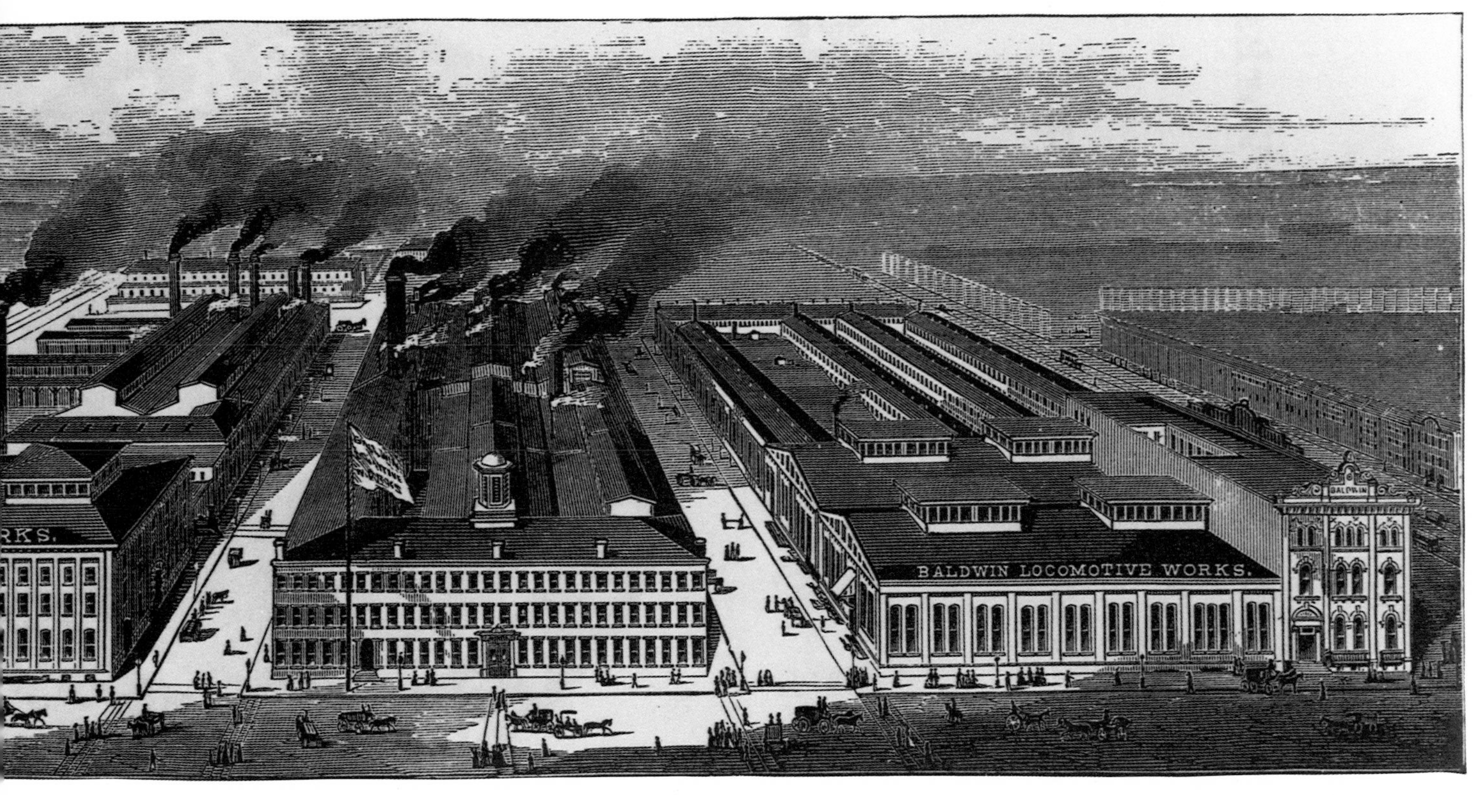

BALDWIN LOCOMOTIVE WORKS.
(Bird's-eye View.)

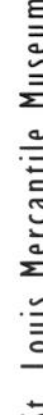

established in the United States decades before they were introduced in Britain.

The years between 1830 and 1841 saw a number of British imports, but at the same time the development of the stateside locomotive industry was aided by a duty on imported iron products and the desire of American railroads to "buy at home". Despite the very poor quality of some of the products of the emerging builders, 1841 saw the last of about 120 imported products, which in any case accounted for only about 25 percent of the locomotives in service in the United States at that time.

With the bulk of the 13 million population in 1830 concentrated in the states to the east of the Mississippi-Missouri rivers, railroad development was concentrated there. The 1830s saw a rapid expansion in railroad building. Such railroads as the Camden & Amboy (built 1830–1), Baltimore & Susquehanna (1828), Boston & Providence, Philadelphia & Reading, Newcastle & Frenchtown (1831), Paterson & Hudson River, Morris & Essex, Mohawk & Hudson, Saratoga & Schnectady, Western of Massachusetts, South Carolina, and others became household names.

ABOVE MATTHIAS BALDWIN OPENED HIS WORKS IN PHILADELPHIA IN 1830. THIS PICTURE GIVES SOME INDICATION OF ITS SIZE BY THE MID-1800S.

BELOW HORATIO ALLEN WAS SENT TO ENGLAND IN 1828 BY THE DELAWARE & HUDSON CO. HE ATTENDED THE RAINHILL TRIALS WITH ROSS WINANS.

• THE BEST FRIEND •

THE NEW TRAINS WERE OFTEN USED IN ARMY MANEUVERS AS SEEN HERE ON THE SOUTH CAROLINA RAILROAD IN THE EARLY 1830S, AND *THE BEST FRIEND* WAS ONE OF THEM.

In addition to the foregoing, the following are key dates in the United States' early history.

1826

• Charter granted for Mohawk & Hudson RR.

1828

• South Carolina Canal & Railroad Company chartered to build from Charleston to Hamburg, SC, on north bank of Savannah River.

• Main Line of Public Works chartered to build railroad from Philadelphia, PA, westward to Columbia on the Susquehanna River. This later became part of the Pennsylvania RR.

1829

• Line from Carbondale to Honesdale, PA, opened October 9.

1830

• First section of Baltimore & Ohio RR opened to Ellicott's Mills, May 24.

• First locomotive built in America delivered from West Point Foundry of New York City for Charleston & Hamburg Railroad (later South Carolina RR). Named *Best Friend of Charleston*, it was destroyed by a boiler explosion on June 17, 1831. (The fireman, irritated by the noise of escaping steam, had held the safety valve down!)

• Matthias Baldwin of Philadelphia established his works, which became one of the most famous builders of steam locomotives in the world. His first locomotive (1832), he called *Old Ironsides*. It was built to the order of the Philadelphia, Germantown & Norristown Railroad, which tried to renege on the last $500 payment.

ABOVE MATTHIAS BALDWIN 1795–1866. INVENTOR AND FOUNDER OF THE FAMOUS BALDWIN LOCOMOTIVE WORKS.

• Iron rails were introduced to replace timber and iron straps.

1831

• B & O opened to Frederick, MD, 60 miles west of Baltimore, December 12.

• *John Bull*, a four-coupled "Planet"-type from Robert Stephenson & Co, England, assembled by Isaac Dripps for Camden & Amboy RR. In its form modified by Dripps (including the earliest cowcatcher) it is now at the Smithsonian Institution, Washington, DC.

• Elizabethtown & Somerville RR incorporated; later formed part of Central RR of New Jersey.

• 17 miles of Mohawk & Hudson RR opened with second American-built locomotive, *De Witt Clinton*, also from West Point Foundry.

1832

• 6ft (1829mm) gauge New York & Erie RR chartered April 1832.

• Portsmouth & Roanoke RR formed – later part of Seaboard Air Line Railroad.

• First "leading truck" incorporated

St. Louis Mercantile Museum

ABOVE THE FIRST TRAIN IN PENNSYLVANIA, NOVEMBER 23 1832, ON THE CAMDEN & AMBOY RR HAULED BY *OLD IRONSIDES* BALDWINS FIRST STEAM LOCOMOTIVE.

in a locomotive by John B. Jervis of West Point Foundry. Locomotive *Experiment*, a 4-2-0 design, was supplied to Mohawk & Hudson RR. Later known as *Brother Jonathan*, it was claimed to have reached a speed of 80 miles per hour.

1833

• New York & Harlem RR opened.

• Paterson & Hudson River RR chartered between Paterson, NJ and Jersey City; also Paterson & Ramapo RR north to Suffern, just across the NY state line.

• South Carolina Canal & Railroad Company at this time had the world's longest line in service.

• Philadelphia & Reading RR chartered.

• Central Railroad & Canal Company of Georgia organized.

• First "cowcatcher" and "pilot" wheels fitted to *John Bull* by Camden & Amboy RR. Later adopted by many railroads, and universally from about 1855. A well-made cowcatcher could throw a buffalo weighing 2000lb some 30 feet.

• Petersburg RR opened between Petersburg, VA and Roanoke River opposite Weldon, NC.

1834

• Philadelphia & Columbia RR opened 81 miles of line in Pennsylvania – the first state-owned track.

• Cayuga & Susquehanna RR completed between Owego and Ithaca, NY; later renamed Lackawanna & Western RR.

• First American-built passenger car, "Victory", to run on two 4-wheel trucks built by Imlay for Philadelphia

RIGHT (ABOVE AND BELOW) TWO STAGES IN THE DEVELOPMENT OF CAMDEN & AMBOY'S *JOHN BULL* WITH THE 2-WHEEL NON-SWIVELING TRUCK AND PILOT ADDED IN ABOUT 1832. THE 4-WHEEL TENDER WAS THE FIRST; THE 8-WHEEL TENDER WAS PROVIDED LATER.

California State Railroad Museum

ABOVE ISAAC DRIPPS (1810–1892) WAS ONE OF THE FIRST AMERICAN RAILWAY MASTER MECHANICS. HE ASSEMBLED THE "JOHN BULL" FOR THE CAMDEN & AMBOY RR IN 1831.

California State Railroad Museum

& Columbia RR. Not quite the world's first: one had been built previously for St. Etienne-Lyon railroad in France.

• Grade-crossing accident on Boston & Worcester RR resulted in demand for locomotives to carry warning bells.

• System of semaphores used to control trains between Newcastle and Frenchtown, PA.

1835

• Senator Chase of Ohio introduced bill to Congress to provide for survey of four possible routes for a coast-to-coast railroad. Much interest, research and speculation, but no positive action.

• Ground broken for New York & Erie RR near Deposit November 7.

• First combined steam railroad and steamboat service from Boston, MA to New York City in 16 hours, later reduced to 14.

• Morris & Essex RR chartered to run from Morristown, NJ to New York.

• Boston & Lowell RR open, June 24.

• Boston & Worcester RR opened July 4.

RIGHT DRAWING OF 1837 PASSENGER CAR TRUCK PROBABLY FIRST USED ON EARLIEST IMLAY CAR *VICTORY* OF THE PHILADELPHIA AND COLUMBIA RR.

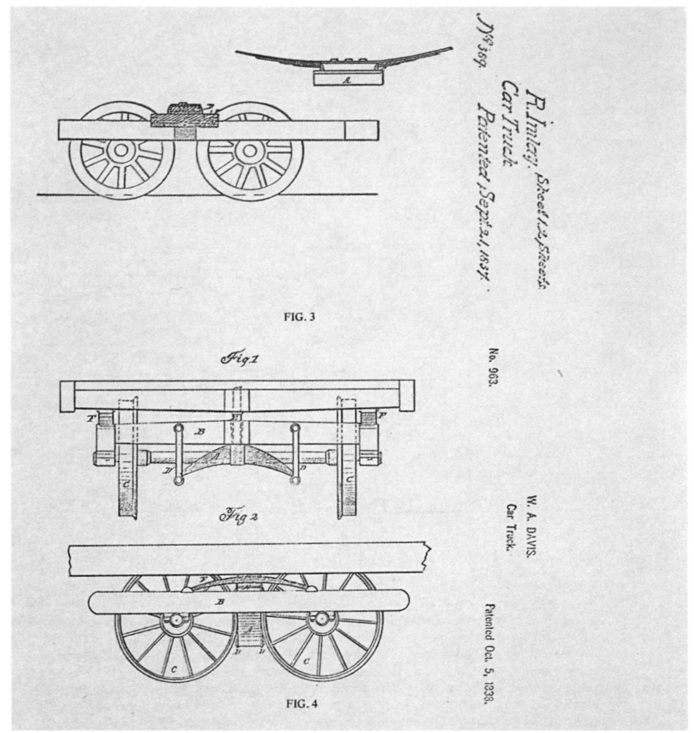

RIGHT BALTIMORE & OHIO DEVELOPED EIGHT-WHEEL DOUBLE-TRUCK PASSENGER CARS BETWEEN 1831 AND 1836. THIS CAR WITH END PLATFORMS AND CENTER-ISLE SEATING WITH FOUR-WHEEL TRUCKS DATES FROM AROUND 1835.

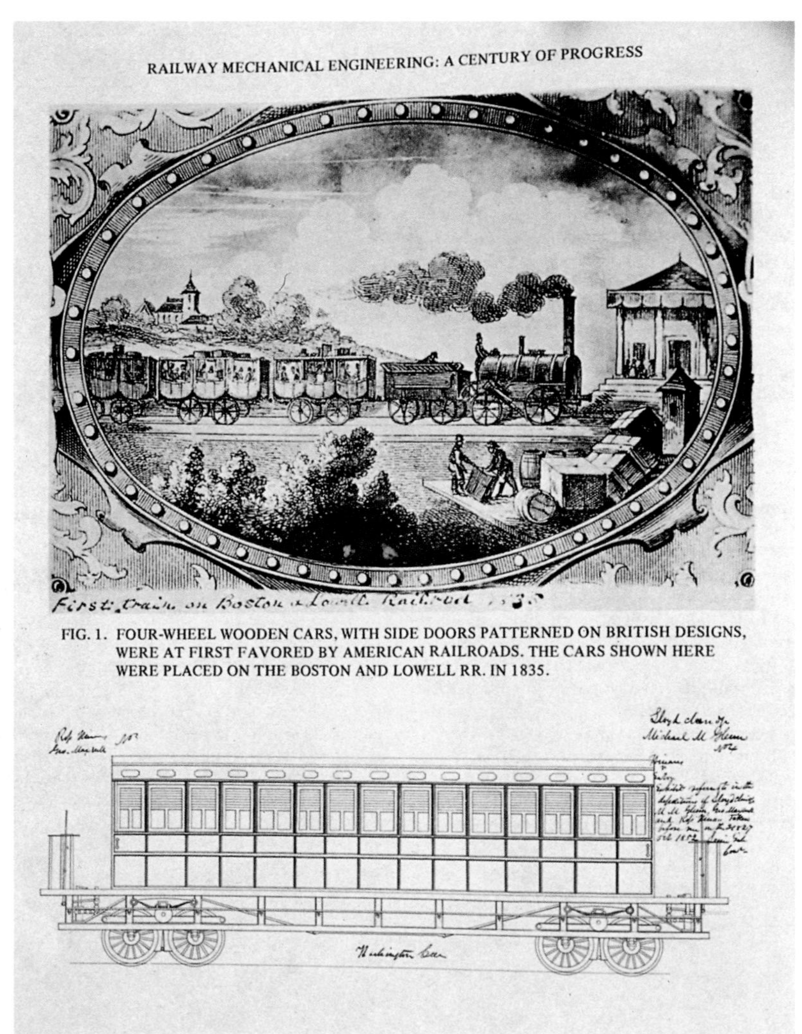

RAILWAY MECHANICAL ENGINEERING: A CENTURY OF PROGRESS

FIG. 1. FOUR-WHEEL WOODEN CARS, WITH SIDE DOORS PATTERNED ON BRITISH DESIGNS, WERE AT FIRST FAVORED BY AMERICAN RAILROADS. THE CARS SHOWN HERE WERE PLACED ON THE BOSTON AND LOWELL RR. IN 1835.

LEFT THE EARLY 'JERVIS TYPE" 4-2-0, *EXPERIMENT*, ALSO KNOWN AS *BROTHER JONATHON*, OF 1832.

BELOW DE WITT CLINTON – SHOWN HERE WITH TRAIN – THE FIRST TO RUN IN THE STATE OF NEW YORK ON THE MOHAWK AND HUDSTON RR.

• Baltimore & Ohio RR reached Washington, DC from Relay, MD.

• Iron bar frames now in general use. They had been introduced into the United States with the delivery of the 0-4-0 *Liverpool*, designed by the British engineer Edward Bury in 1833. Until this time frames had been of reinforced timber.

• State of Massachusetts enacted a law requiring warning bells for locomotives; other states followed.

• Fires destroyed much of New York City and wiped out fortunes of many Erie RR shareholders, delaying construction work.

1836

• Andover & Wilding RR opened August 1836.

• Elizabethport to Elizabeth, NJ opened with horse traction.

• Louisa RR chartered to run from Taylorsville (Doswell) westward to points in Louisa County, VA.

• The first 4-4-0 type locomotive developed by Henry R. Campbell of Philadelphia, Germantown & Norristown RR, built by James Brook of Philadelphia, PA. Campbell was granted a patent on February 5. The eight-wheeler was later to become a classic design, universally known as the "American" type.

• Isaac Drips produced a strange 8-wheel-coupled machine, known as the *Monster*, for Camden & Amboy RR, combining both rod and gear coupling of wheels.

• Cumberland Valley RR introduced "bunk" cars, enabling passengers to lie down, even though journeys were relatively short.

• First reported use in United States of a locomotive steam whistle.

1837

• Great financial and commercial panic began in March and reached its height in May. The crisis brought near-failure to locomotive builder Matthias Baldwin. Owing to leniency

BELOW HENRY R CAMPBELL'S LOCOMOTIVE ENGINE, THE FIRST 4-4-0, CONSTRUCTED IN 1836/7 FOR THE PHILADELPHIA, GERMANTOWN, AND NORRISTOWN RAILROAD.

on part of his creditors and his taking on several partners, Baldwin was able to weather the storm and recovered in six years. His plant in Philadelphia, PA became the largest locomotive factory in the world. Others went under, among them George and Charles Sellers and the Cardington plant which had produced *America* and *Sampson* for Philadelphia & Columbus RR.

• Northern Cross RR chartered to connect Quincy, IL to point on Indiana state line; later renamed Wabash RR.

• B & O opened branch to Washington, DC from Relay (Washington Junction). Line included stone viaduct across Potomac River at Harper's Ferry, WV. Connection with Winchester & Potomac RR constituted first junction of two railroads in United States.

• Anatole Mallet born in France. Builder of the first successful compound locomotive in 1876, he would profoundly influence the design of large American steam locomotives from 1904 onwards.

1838

• By this year there were 345 locomotives in United States.

• Grand Trunk Western RR opened first section of line from Detroit, MI to Chicago, IL.

• Richmond & Petersburg RR connected to Petersburg RR.

• Construction of Erie RR restarted.

1839

• Last locomotives with timber frames built by Baldwin.

• Bells had become commonplace on locomotives. They weighed between 60 and 215lb and could be heard from a quarter of a mile away

•THE MONSTER•

THE FIRST 8-WHEEL (0-8-0) BUILT BY ISAAC DRIPPS FOR THE CAMDEN AND AMBOY RR BETWEEN 1835 AND 1838. GEARS COUPLED THE SECOND AND THIRD AXLES.

ABOVE EXAMPLES OF EARLY AMERICAN TRACK. ON THE LEFT IS AN EXAMPLE OF IRON-FACED TIMBER RAIL, WHILE ON THE RIGHT IS AN EARLY "T"-SECTION CAST-IRON "FISH BELLY" RAIL.

ABOVE A SQUARE CASE HEADLIGHT USED FROM ABOUT 1840. THIS HAS AN OIL LAMP AND PARABOLIC REFLECTOR.

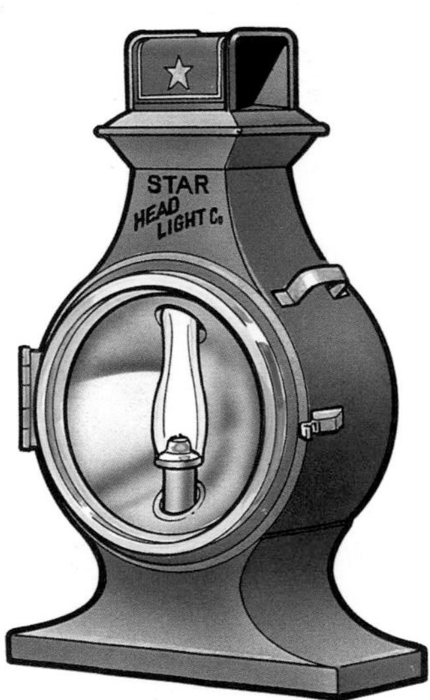

ABOVE THE ROUND CASE HEADLIGHTS CAME LATER AND WERE IN COMMON USE BY 1900.

• Steam replaced horses on Elizabethtown & Somerville RR.

1840

• New York Central & Hudson River RR open from New York to the state capital Albany.

• Wilmington & Raleigh RR opened 161 miles of line to Weldon, NC.

• There were now some 2,800 miles of railroads and 590 locomotives in United States. Greatest mileage (754) was in Pennsylvania.

• Majority of railroads were to what would become the standard gauge of 4ft 8½in; but others varied between 3ft and 5ft, while Erie RR adopted 6ft.

• Passenger cars of two distinct types were introduced. Those charging higher fares were called "Best Cars"; the more common type "Accommodation Cars".

• Locomotive headlights introduced. Night-time operation could be very hazardous over twisting single tracks and keen lookout had to be kept for broken rails, mis-aligned switches, flood-damaged trestles, animals on track, etc. At first a square case fitted ahead of the stack housed an oil lamp. Later a parabolic reflector incorporated with a central wick gave a beam for 1,000 yards.

1841

• Last British locomotive imported – *Gem* of Philadelphia & Reading RR.

• First train ran on New York & Erie RR. Construction costs of low trestle bridges drove company into bankruptcy soon after opening! Construction continued regardless.

1842

• Early locomotives burned coal or anthracite, but wood soon became widely used. Production of live embers and sparks from wood-burners proved a constant hazard and a continuing expense in compensation payments.

• Many different designs of stack of varying efficacy were used. Probably most widely used was design by French & Baird. It became a favorite on southern roads where pine forests and cotton fields made spark-arresting a vital consideration.

• Robert Stephenson's link-motion valve gear first fitted to locomotives in England. While soon adopted in the United States, it was not accepted there so quickly as in Britain, although it was later to become standard in the American eight-wheeler.

• Elizabethtown & Somerville RR reached Somerville, NJ.

1843

• Champlain & Connecticut River RR incorporated to build between Bellows Falls and Burlington, VT as part of route from Boston, MA to Ogdensburg, NY.

• Central of Georgia reached Macon from Savannah in October.

1844

• Samuel Morse experimented with telegraph between Washington, DC and Baltimore, MD on May 24. Telegraph soon became indispensable to operation of American railroads.

1845

• First US "T"-rails rolled in October at Montour Rolling Mills, PA. Previously they had been imported from England.

• Introduced in 1836, by 1842 4-4-0 eight-wheeler had become the most widely used locomotive. There was a number of designers, but the name most firmly associated with outside-cylinder 4-4-0 is that of Thomas Rogers. The eight-wheeler was a flexible locomotive, rode uneven tracks well, was suited to all classes of service including switching, was simple to maintain and repair. Low in first cost and relatively powerful, it was a truly national locomotive.

BELOW WOOD WAS A POPULAR FUEL IN THE EARLY DAYS OF AMERICAN RAILROADS – IT WAS PLENTIFUL AND CHEAP. HOWEVER, DAMAGE WAS OFTEN CAUSED BY LIGHTED EMBERS, AND BONNET STACK SPARK ARRESTORS, OF THE TYPE ILLUSTRATED BECAME NECESSARY TO LIMIT DAMAGE CLAIMS.

California State Railroad Museum

ABOVE WARNING BELLS WERE USED FROM 1835. THIS IS A TYPICAL BRASS BELL WORKED BY A CORD FROM THE DRIVER'S CAB.

ABOVE SOME ROADS USED ORNATE BELLS AS EMBELLISHMENTS AS THIS EXAMPLE ILLUSTRATES.

ABOVE THIS IS A MODERN BELL WORKED BY BOWDEN CABLE. IT IS FOUND ON DIESEL SWITCHERS.

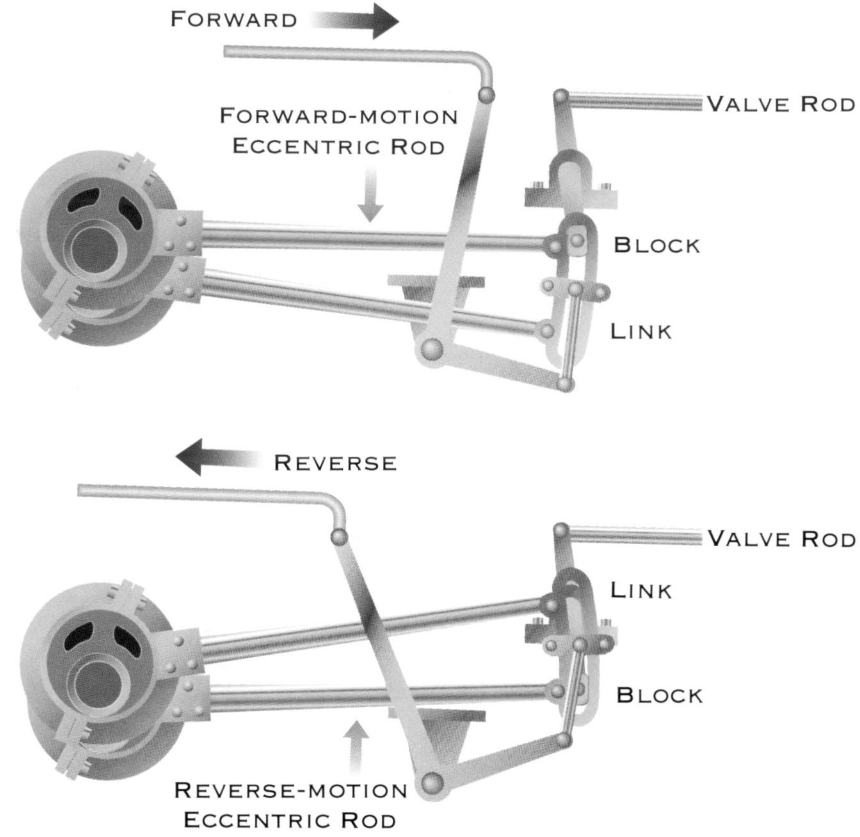

RIGHT THE STEPHENSON LINK MOTION WAS IN GENERAL USE FROM 1850, UNTIL IT WAS SUPERCEDED BY WALSCHAERT'S GEAR IN THE EARLY 1900S.

Inside-cylinder 4-4-0 ("inside-coupled") was never as popular in United States as in Europe.

• Central of Georgia opened 171 miles from Augusta to Atlanta.

• Nashville, Chattanooga & St Louis RR incorporated.

• Old Colony RR opened between Boston and Plymouth, MA and consolidated with Fall River RR. This was the earliest constituent of what became New York, New Haven & Hudson River RR.

1846

• An early example of trade-in was acceptance by Baldwin of his first locomotive *Old Ironsides* as part-payment on a new locomotive.

• Construction of Atlantic & St Lawrence commenced.

1847

• Alton & Sangamon RR chartered to run from Springfield, IL to Alton, 20 miles north of St Louis, MO.

• Atlanta & La Grange (Atlanta & West Point) RR chartered.

• World's first 4-6-0, *Chesapeake*, built by Norris for Philadelphia & Reading RR. The ten-wheeler had small driving wheels and was intended primarily for freight.

• Galena & Chicago Union railroad under construction.

• New Albany & Salem RR organized to build from New Albany, IN, on north bank of Ohio River opposite Louisville, KY to shore of Lake Michigan.

• Rock Island & La Salle RR chartered to build between Rock Island, IL and La Salle, connecting with Illinois & Michigan Canal; later renamed Chicago & Rock Island RR.

• New York & Erie RR reach Port Jervis, NY on Delaware River, 74 miles from Piermont, December 31.

• Milwaukee & Waukesha RR chartered.

1848

• October saw opening of Galena & Chicago Union RR between Chicago and Maywood, IL – forerunner of Chicago & North Western.

1849

• Aurora Branch RR from Aurora, IL to Turner Junction to connect with new Galena & Chicago Union RR, with services to Chicago chartered. Later became Chicago, Burlington & Quincy RR.

• Eugene Bourdon of Paris, France perfected a practical steam-pressure gauge which registered pressure on a dial. The Bourdon gauge was introduced into United States by E.H. Ascent and readily accepted.

•THE CHESAPEAKE•

THE FIRST "10-WHEELER", BUILT BY NORRIS IN 1847 FOR THE PHILADELPHIA-READING RR.

• Evansville & Eastern Illinois RR chartered to build north from Evansville, IN.

• Ligget's Gap RR combined with other lines in eastern Pennsylvania to form corporate structure of future Lackawanna & Western RR.

1850

• Mileage of U.S. railways now exceeded 9,000, New York state leading with 1,361 miles, 121 miles ahead of Pennsylvania.

• Railroads had not yet penetrated west of the Mississippi. Louisa RR reached westward to Charlottesville, VA and became Virginia Central. Louisville & Nashville RR chartered. Milwaukee & Waukesha became Milwaukee & Mississippi RR.

• Mobile & Ohio Railroad launch aided by Congress's Land Grant Bill. Norfolk & Petersburg RR chartered to build line connecting these two Virginia cities; it was the earliest constituent of Norfolk & Western RR.

1851

• New York, Erie & Western RR completed line to Lake Erie, April 22; officially opened in May.

LEFT THERE WAS NO REALLY RELIABLE STEAM PRESSURE DEVICE UNTIL EUGEN BOURDON INVENTED HIS PRACTICAL STEAM PRESSURE GAUGE IN 1847.

• THE NEW JERSEY •

THIS ROGERS 4-4-0 WAS THE FIRST MODERN LOCOMOTIVE AND HUNDREDS WERE BUILT TO THIS GENERAL PATTERN ALMOST TO THE END OF THE 19TH CENTURY.

• Alton & Sangamon RR opened Springfield, IL to Alton, 20 miles north of St Louis, MO.

• Montgomery & West Point RR opened 88 miles of standard gauge in Georgia to add to 32 miles of road constructed earlier.

• Virginia Central built own line from Taylorsville to Richmond. New Albany & Salem RR opened to Salem, IN.

• Illinois Central RR chartered to build from Cairo, IL at confluence of Ohio and Mississippi rivers, to Galena, with a branch from Centralia to Chicago. Construction aided by the first ever Land Grant Act.

• Milwaukee & Mississippi RR reached Waukesha, WI, 20 miles.

• Nashville, Chattanooga & St Louis RR opened first nine miles. Ground broken for 5ft 6in gauge Pacific RR at St Louis, MO, July 4.

• First rail tunnel in United States started – Hoosac Tunnel in the Berkshires.

1852

• Through road from Philadelphia to Pittsburgh, PA, December 1852. Construction of first rail suspension bridge over Niagara River, NY commenced.

• "Most modern 4-4-0" introduced in United States. This was the *New Jersey* and epitomized the type built in increasing numbers over next three decades as classic "American" eight-wheeler. Chief characteristics: two outside cylinders; spread (long) wheel-base leading truck;

Stephenson link-motion and wagon-top boiler.

• Chicago & Aurora RR (former Aurora Branch RR) authorized to build to Mendota, IL.

• First train between Chicago & Joliet, IL (Rock Island RR) October 10, hauled by 4-4-0 *Rocket*.

• New York & Erie leased Paterson & Hudson River RR and Paterson & Ramapo, and built connection at Suffern, NY.

• Mobile & Ohio opened from Mobile to Citronelle, AL, 30 miles.

• New York City-Albany through-rail route established.

• First four miles of Pacific RR opened, with first train to operate west of Mississippi River.

1853

• B & O reached Ohio River at Wheeling, WV, 379 miles from Baltimore, on January 1, almost 25 years from commencement.

• Pennsylvania RR reached Ohio River at Pittsburgh, PA.

• New York Central & Hudson River RR open throughout to Buffalo, NY on August 1.

• Niagara Falls (NY) suspension bridge opened March 8.

• Evansville & Eastern Illinois RR opened from Evansville to Vincennes, In.

• Delaware, Lackwanna & Western RR established.

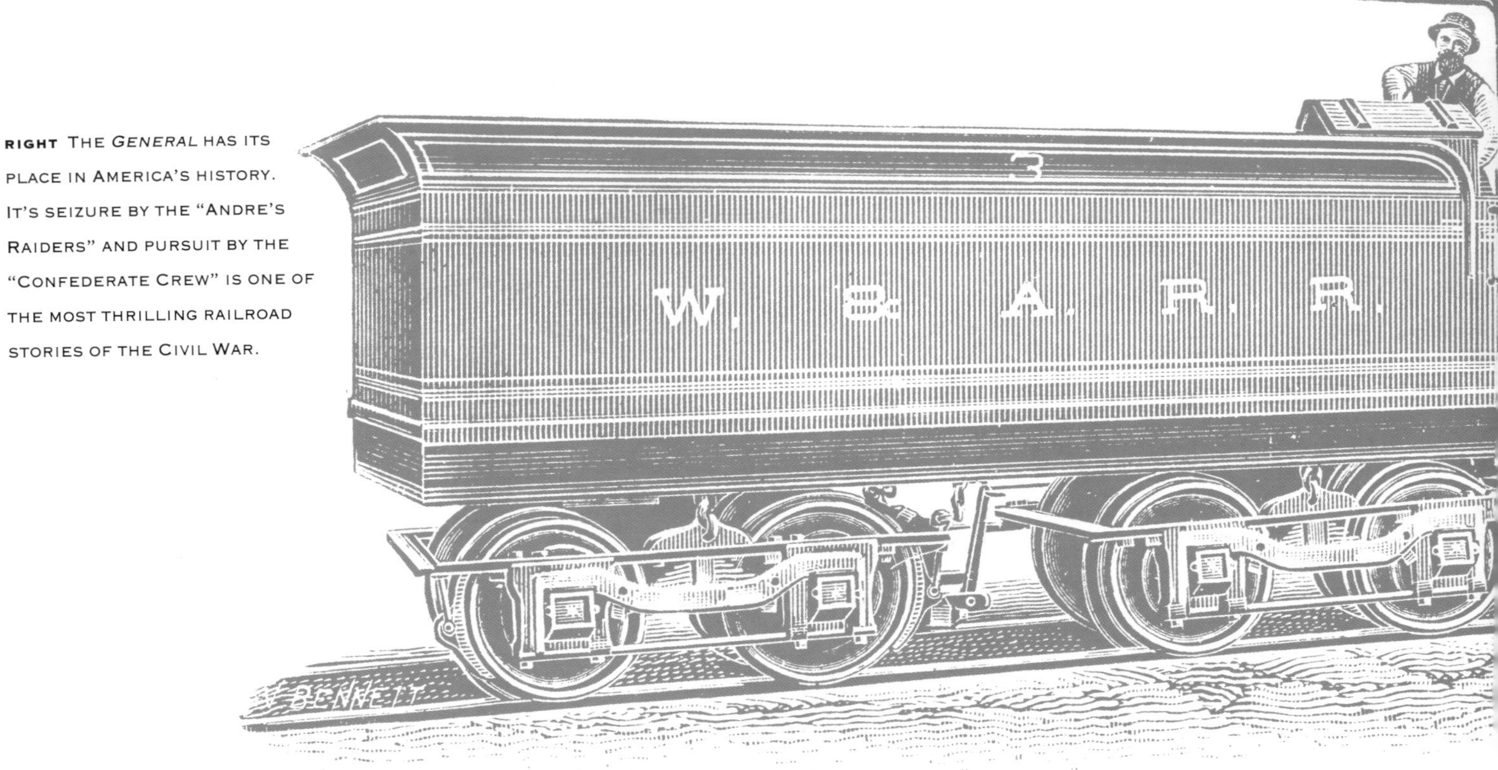

RIGHT THE *GENERAL* HAS ITS PLACE IN AMERICA'S HISTORY. IT'S SEIZURE BY THE "ANDRE'S RAIDERS" AND PURSUIT BY THE "CONFEDERATE CREW" IS ONE OF THE MOST THRILLING RAILROAD STORIES OF THE CIVIL WAR.

• Nashville, Chattanooga & St Louis opened to Bridgeport, AL.

• Atlantic & St Lawrence completed between Portland, ME and Montreal, Canada. Leased by Grand Trunk Railway of Canada.

• Thirteen railroads between Albany and Buffalo consolidated as New York Central.

1854

• Rails reached Mississippi at Rock Island, IL.

• Evansville & Eastern Illinois RR opened to Terre Haute, IN.

• Chicago & Rock Island line opened to Rock Island, February 22.

• Chattanooga, TN reached by Nashville, Chattanooga & St Louis RR, with connection to Atlanta, GA provided by Western & Atlantic RR.

• Atlanta & La Grange RR opened with 5ft gauge.

1855

• First railroad tunnel in the US, the Hoosac, through the Berkshires, MA, opened to traffic.

• Typical eight-wheeler by now had following characteristics:- 4-4-0 with 15 × 20in outside cylinders; 60in wheels; 100lb steam pressure; weight 20 tons; tractive effort 6,375lb. Type represented by the *General*, a product of Rogers Locomotive Works, Paterson, NJ, preserved and exhibited in Smithsonian Institution, Washington DC; this is slightly larger, with 15 × 22in outside cylinders; 60in wheels; 140lb steam pressure; weight 22½ tons; tractive effort 9,820lb.

• First United States coal-burning locomotive, *Daniel Webster*, completed trials on Illinois Central RR. By 1855 there were about 6,000 locomotives in United States and conversion from wood to coal.

• Wilmington & Raleigh RR renamed Wilmington & Weldon RR.

• B & O opened from Grafton to Ohio River at Parkersburg, WV.

• Chicago & Aurora became Chicago, Burlington & Quincy RR.

• Railroad opened between Galesburg and eastern bank of Mississippi opposite Burlington in western Illinois.

• Delaware & Cobb's Gap RR completed (part of DL&WRR). Made end-on connection with Central of New Jersey at Hampton, NJ.

1856

• String of railroads including Chicago, Burlington & Quincy linked Chicago with Quincy, IL via Galesburg.

• Chicago & Rock Island connected with Mississippi and Missouri by bridge, opened at Davenport, IA on April 21. Damaged on May 6

A.S.M.E

LEFT The interior of a typical American passenger car of the 1850s as shown in an engraving from the *Illustrated London News* of April 10, 1852.

BELOW AN EARLY PULLMAN SLEEPING CAR WITH OPEN END PLATFORMS, HAND BRAKES AND LINK AND PIN COUPLERS.

California State Railroad Museum

(deliberately?) by steamboat *Effie Afton*; rebuilt and re-opened on September 8. Start of 10-year "war" between railroad and steamboat interests during which no new bridges were built.

1857

• Financial crisis caused closure of many small lines and railroad construction companies, many of whom had unwisely extended credit to potential purchasers. Example: Seth Wilmarth was under contract to build a large number of locomotives for Erie RR, who promised payment in cash. Financial flurry caused railroad to renege and payment was offered in stocks instead. Wilmarth's creditors demanded cash. He was forced to suspend production. Typical was Breeze, Kneeland & Company of New Jersey, which was forced to close by "the iniquitous conduct of certain western railroad managers who were buying engines on credit while they knew their companies were hopelessly insolvent."

• Rails extended from Charleston, SC to Memphis, TN, although gauges varied from 2ft to 6ft.

• First vestibuled train ran in Connecticut.

• Milwaukee & Mississippi RR reached Prairie du Chien.

• Atlanta & La Grange RR re-named Atlanta & West Point.

1858

• Levi Bissell patented swivelling two-wheel leading truck. From this time, smaller wheeled 2-6-0 began to supersede 4-4-0 for freight work.

1859

• George Mortimer Pullman converted two passenger cars of Chicago, Alton & St Louis RR to sleepers.

• First major road to abandon wood for coal burning was Reading RR.

• New York & Erie entered receivership. Re-organized as Erie Railroad with Jay Gould as President.

• John Brown's raid on Harper's Ferry, WV, October 17.

1860

• 30,635 miles of railroad completed in the United States; major states were Ohio with 2,946 miles, Illinois with 2,799 and Pennsylvania with 2,598. During 1860s there was great expansion of railroad-building in the South.

• 1000th locomotive built by Norris. By now, about 9,000 locomotives were in service in the United States.

• Modern practice of "re-manufacture" was already established.

• The steam injector was introduced to replace unreliable boiler feed pumps. Invented by the French balloonist Henry Giffard, the injector was introduced to the United States by William Sellers of Philadelphia.

• Morris & Essex RR extended from Morristown, NJ to New York.

• Louisville & Nashville RR opened

RIGHT TYPICAL WOODEN PASSENGER CARS OF THE 1840S, LATER MODIFIED WITH AIR BRAKES AND AUTOMATIC COUPLINGS AS SEEN HERE.

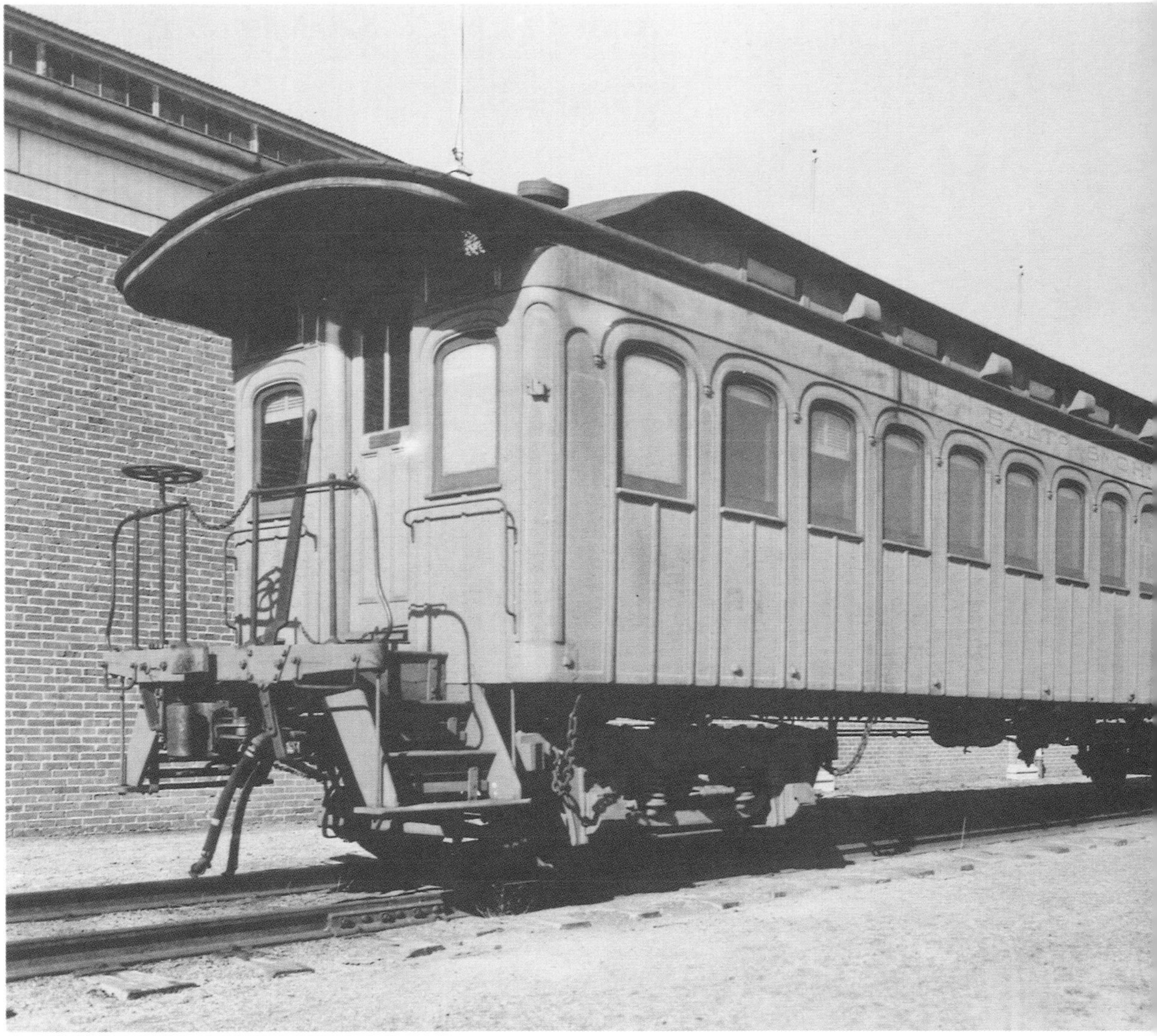

ABOVE GEORGE MORTIMER PULLMAN, 1831–97, FOUNDER OF THE PULLMAN PALACE CAR COMPANY IN 1867. HE BUILT *PIONEER* IN 1864.

B & O Railroad Museum

between Louisville, KY and Lebanon, TE in March; completed westward into Nashville, TE in May with new bridge over the Cumberland River and another over the Green River at Munfordville, KY.

1861

• In February, Abraham Lincoln traveled by rail to his first inaugural with stops at principal cities.

• Outbreak of Civil War, which would far outshadow any financial "panic" in its effect on rolling-stock prices. Example: the price of a standard eight-wheeler rose 280 percent in little over three years. Many railroads benefitted considerably from inflated wartime traffic. Demands of United States military railroads enabled some roads to unload obsolete locomotives at a handsome profit. Other roads, particularly in the Confederacy, were either halted, abandoned, or blown up.

• Mobile & Ohio RR completed to port of Cairo, IL, April 22.

• Alton & Sangamon RR extended and purchased by St Louis, Alton & Chicago, RR.

• Virginia Central RR's westward expansion halted by Civil War, even though it would have been valuable to Confederacy.

1862

• July 1 saw signing of the Enabling Act by President Abraham Lincoln, creating the Union Pacific Railroad Company and authorising it to "lay out, construct, furnish and maintain and enjoy a continuous railroad and telegraph line, with appurtenances, from a point on the 100th meridian of longitude west from Greenwich between the south margin of the valley of the Republican river and the north margin of the valley of the Platte in the Territory of Nebraska to the western boundary of Nevada Territory."

• System of hand signaling in use on Hudson River RR.

• St Paul & Pacific RR ran its first train between St Paul & Anthony (now Minneapolis), MN.

• Maine Central RR incorporated. All four roads between Portland ME, Waterville and Bangor, broad gauge lines converted to standard gauge.

• Nashville, Chattanooga & St Louis roadway badly damaged by floods.

A Railway Coast to Coast

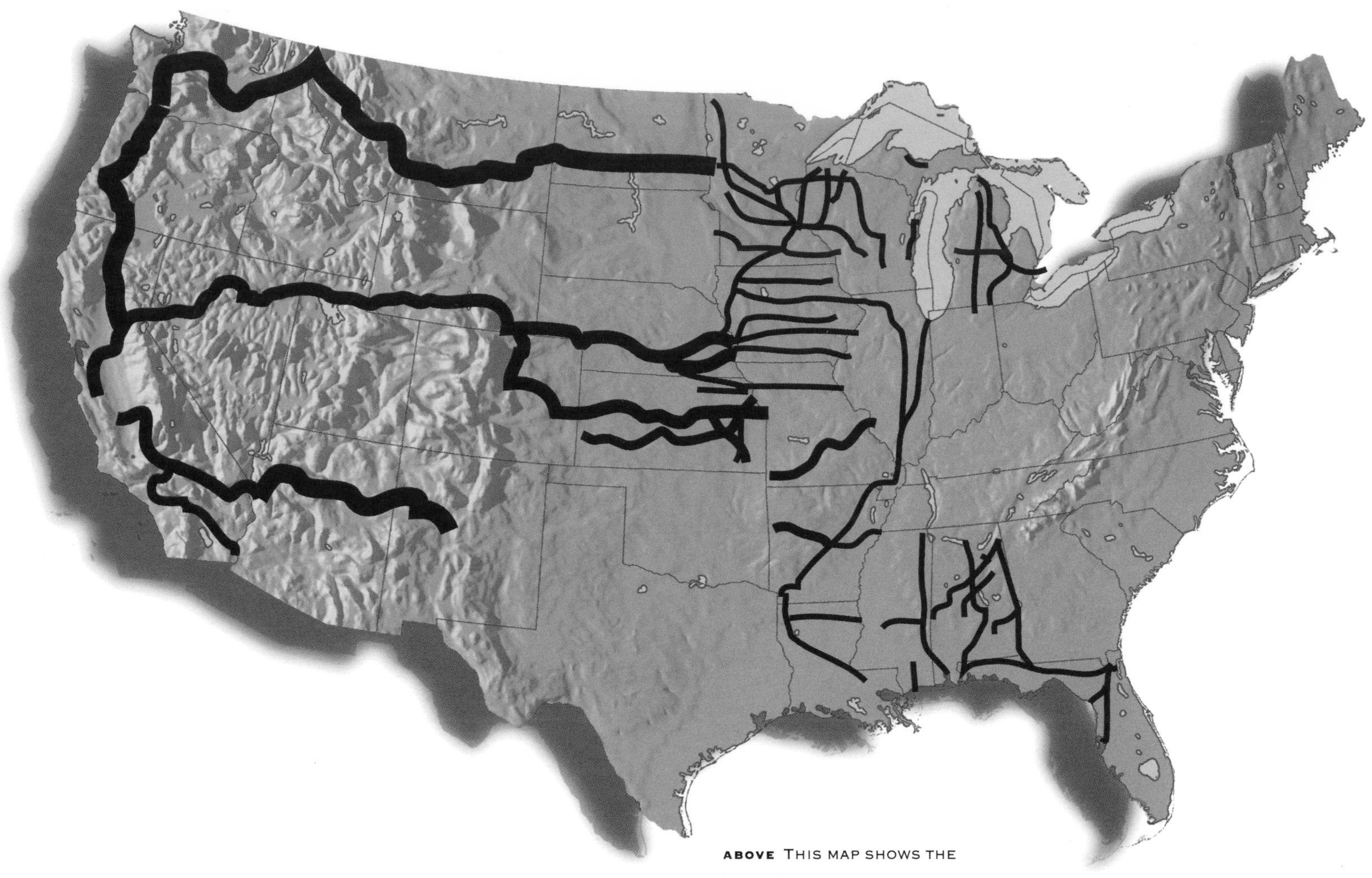

ABOVE THIS MAP SHOWS THE LAND GRANTS TO RAILROADS IN THE OPENING OF THE WEST.

The beginning of the Civil War in 1861, probably more than any other factor, showed the vulnerability of the nearly isolated West Coast and the need for direct communication between east and west. It also pointed up the communication problems presented by the largely standard (4ft 8½in) gauge lines of the North and the mainly 5ft gauge and fragmented lines of the South. It was national defence which led to the introduction of the Enabling Act in Congress which was passed in the House of Representatives in May and was approved by the Senate in June 1862. The Pacific Railroad Act was signed by President Lincoln on July 1, 1862.

The Pacific Railway Act empowered the Central Pacific Railroad Company to build a line from California eastward and a new company, the Union Pacific Railroad Company, to provide a connection between a point on the western boundary of the State of Iowa and the 100th meridian (the exact point to be determined by the President) "... to the western boundary of the State of Nevada, there to meet and connect with the line of the Central Pacific Railroad Company of California." This was all to be completed by July 1, 1874. It also provided for land grants and bond issues to help finance the railway, which was to receive a strip of land 130 yards wide along its whole length. In addition it was granted 3000 acres of land "to be freely selected by the railway authorities within ten miles of the tracks for every mile of line." There was still difficulty in raising money, so in July 1864 Lincoln doubled the land grants.

Although the President had signed the formal Enabling Act, there were disagreements and disputes from the start. The engineers wanted the new line to connect with the existing standard gauge line east from Bellevue, MO, and started construction there, spending $100,000 before the President forced a stop. Lincoln specified Council Bluffs, IA, across the Missouri opposite Omaha, NE, as the UP railhead, and he was not prepared to change his decision.

California already had a 5ft gauge line east from San Francisco to Sacramento, and Lincoln supported its

CP Limited

LEFT CONSTRUCTION OF THE TRANSCONTINENTAL LINES WAS A FORMIDABLE TASK. HERE A TRACK GANG IS LAYING TIES ON A STRETCH OF TRACK THROUGH PINE FOREST.

demand for 5ft gauge on the new line. But Congress prescribed standard gauge through an Act which declared that "the gauge of the Pacific Railroad and its branches throughout the whole extent, from the Pacific coast to the Missouri River, shall be, and hereby is, established at four feet eight and one half inches". This also established officially the standard gauge as the gauge for railroads throughout the United States, as it is today.

The first sod was cut at Sacramento, CA on January 8, 1863. The start from Council Bluffs was made on December 2, 1863 but because the Civil War was raging the first rails were not laid until July 1865. The task of providing raw materials was formidable. These included 6,250 ties and 50,000 tons of rails, which had to be carried over hundreds of miles by ox cart or by boat up the Missouri River.

As construction progressed, 30 rails at a time were conveyed to the end of the line by open rail wagons hauled by two horses; the final move to the end of the line was by a team of 10 men, five at each side of the wagon, who unloaded each length of rail and.placed it in position. An average length of two miles a day was constructed by these means. Construction westward to

ABOVE THERE WERE MANY HAZARDS CROSSING THE PLAINS. HERE A CONSTRUCTION GANG DEFEND ITSELF FROM AN ATTACK BY MARAUDING INDIANS.

California State Railroad Museum

LEFT AN IMPRESSIVE AND TYPICAL CURVED WOODEN TRESTLE IN THE HIGH SIERRAS AT SECRETTOWN, NEVADA ON THE CENTRAL PACIFIC RR IN THE 1870S.

BELOW A 10-WHEELER WOODBURNER AND TRAIN, TYPICAL OF THE 1870S, CLIMBING THROUGH THE SIERRA NEVADAS.

the Sierra Nevada was by Irish navvies, and eastward from California by Chinese coolies.

On the plains there were frequent attacks by Indians, who made railroading a hazardous operation. The Indians saw the railroad as a threat. It opened up new territory and was responsible for the virtual extinction of the buffalo (on which the whole economy of many Indian nations depended), destroyed the Indian's hunting grounds and led ultimately to their confinement in reservations.

The construction gangs took everything they needed with them, and trains of special dormitory cars accompanied the construction teams. Every few miles a new "end-of-track" construction town grew up complete with saloons, gambling houses and brothels operated by unscrupulous hangers-on, who saw a way of making easy money. Known as "Hell-on-Wheels", the traveling community would often revolt. On one occasion an army detachment from Fort Russell, WY had to be called in to restore order. The whole population was run out of the shanty town and permitted to return only when a measure of law and order had been re-established.

By 1867 the UP line over the Rockies was being constructed and reached its maximum altitude of 8,247 feet at Sherman Hill, between Cheyenne and Laramie, WY. However this was not all. The Central Pacific company was building its road along watercourses up the western slopes of the Sierra Nevada, performing incredible feats of engineering with Chinese labor and

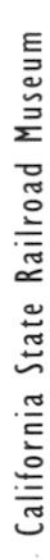

California State Railroad Museum

the crudest of tools – notably gunpowder. Instead of stopping at the Nevada state line the Central Pacific pressed on across the flat plains of Nevada and into Utah, making for the Great Salt Lake.

Both companies pushed forward as fast as possible, eager to obtain grants for land. They met in early 1869 in western Utah but neither company would acknowledge the existence of the other. They continued to build parallel lines in opposite directions. It was on April 9 that a deputation representing both sides met in Washington DC and agreed that the meeting point of the two roads would be at Promontory Summit, a few miles north of Great Salt Lake. (By now, the two competing roads had a 225-mile overlap!) The meeting point was swiftly approved by Congress.

The inauguration ceremony on May 10, 1869 at Promontory Summit in Utah included the driving of two spikes of silver and two of gold into a specially polished California laurel tie by Governor Sandford of the State of California, President of Central Pacific, and Dr Thomas C. Durant, President of Union Pacific. Two trains had been brought up face to face, the Central Pacific's train with *Jupiter*, a wood-burner, and Union Pacific's No 119 from Omaha, a coal-burner, both eight-wheelers. Both locomotives were detached from their cars and moved forward until their cowcatchers touched, at which point bottles of champagne were broken in celebration. The ceremony was recorded by the photographer A. J. Russell.

The locomotives were then re-coupled to their respective cars and moved in turn over the ceremonial tie. The ceremonial spikes and tie were then replaced by conventional materials, after souvenir hunters had torn the ceremonial tie to pieces. Six more ties and two rails had to be replaced over the next six months!

The Union Pacific had built 1,086 miles from Omaha, and Central Pacific 689 miles from Sacramento in five years under the Congress deadline. The "first total cost" was officially returned as $115,214,587 and 79 cents – a good price for opening up the West!

In just under three decades from the opening of the first ever American railroad, the rails extended from the Atlantic to the Pacific. Passengers and freight could now go from New York City to San Francisco, although such through traffic was at first chiefly freight. The railway now linked New York with Philadelphia, Pittsburgh, Chicago, Omaha, Cheyenne, Ogden, Salt Lake City, Sacramento and San Francisco.

Track construction was, by European standards, rudimentary with rough-hewn timber ties laid either with minimal ballast or even directly on the earth or rock. Steel flat-bottomed rails were laid directly on the ties and secured for the most part by a spike driven into the tie on each side of the rail. Tracks were normally unfenced and undefended against cattle and other wild animals, as well as marauding Indians and the lawless. It made the use of powerful headlights and cowcatchers (not to mention armed guards at times) essential.

The electric telegraph was an essential feature of these early railroads: it was specified in the Enabling Act that the coast-to-coast operation was to be a Continuous railroad and telegraph line. The telegraph was used as a crude signalling system, and the location of a train between depots had to be known before another train was despatched. The telegraph was also a valuable asset to the many lonely townships all along a route for contact with the outside world.

California State Railroad Museum

RIGHT This picture depicts the scene at the joining ceremony when the Golden Spike was driven to complete the first Transcontinental line, bringing the Union Pacific RR and Central Pacific RR together at Promontory, Utah on May 10, 1869.

•THE CONSOLIDATION•

THE FIRST TRUE 2-8-0 WAS DESIGNED IN 1865 BY ALEXANDER MITCHELL. IT'S NAME WAS DERIVED FROM THE MERGER OF THE LEHIGH VALLEY RR WITH THE LEHIGH MAHONEY.

Meanwhile, there are a few more entries for the "diary" to take us up to the end of the first 40 years.

1864

• Steel-making revolutionized by the Bessemer process, cutting price of steel rails by half. Iron rails were gradually replaced and steel rails adopted on new projects.

• Design perfected for the three-point suspension of the Hudson-Bissell swiveling two-wheel leading truck for locomotives.

1865

• First true 2-6-0 was introduced with the Hudson-Bissell swiveling two-wheel truck.

• George Mortimer Pullman produced first real sleeping car, the *Pioneer*, with folding upper berths and extensible seat cushions for the lower berths.

• Candle lighting in passenger cars replaced by kerosene lamps.

• "Block" signaling system introduced on New Brunswick, New Jersey and Philadelphia RR, March 27.

• On April 2, Confederate government evacuated by the Richmond & Danville RR from Richmond to Danville, VA.

• Chicago, Burlington & Quincy had virtual railroad monopoly in western Illinois and southern half of Iowa.

• Milwaukee & St Paul (Milwaukee Road) formed by amalgamation of Milwaukee & Prairie du Chien and La Crosse & Milwaukee Road.

• Montgomery RR shut down following attack by Union forces a few days after General Lee's surrender.

• Virginia Central RR restored and running again.

• Nashville, Chattanooga & St Louis RR restoration by U.S. Government's military railroad completed and returned to owners.

• Pacific Railroad reached Kansas City, MO, 279 miles.

1866

• Class-name "Mogul" probably applied for first time to a 2-6-0, fitted

RIGHT THIS EARLY 2–6–0 "MOGUL" OF THE VIRGINIA & TRUCKEE RR WAS ONE OF THE EARLY APPLICATIONS OF THE 2-WHEEL "BISSEL" SWIVELING LEADING TRUCK, PATENTED IN 1858.

Railroad Museum of Pennsylvania

BELOW MOUNT WASHINGTON IN NEW HAMPSHIRE WAS THE FIRST COG WHEEL RAILROAD IN THE WORLD. THIS VERTICAL BOILER LOCOMOTIVE *PEPPERSASS* WAS ITS FIRST.

California State Railroad Museum

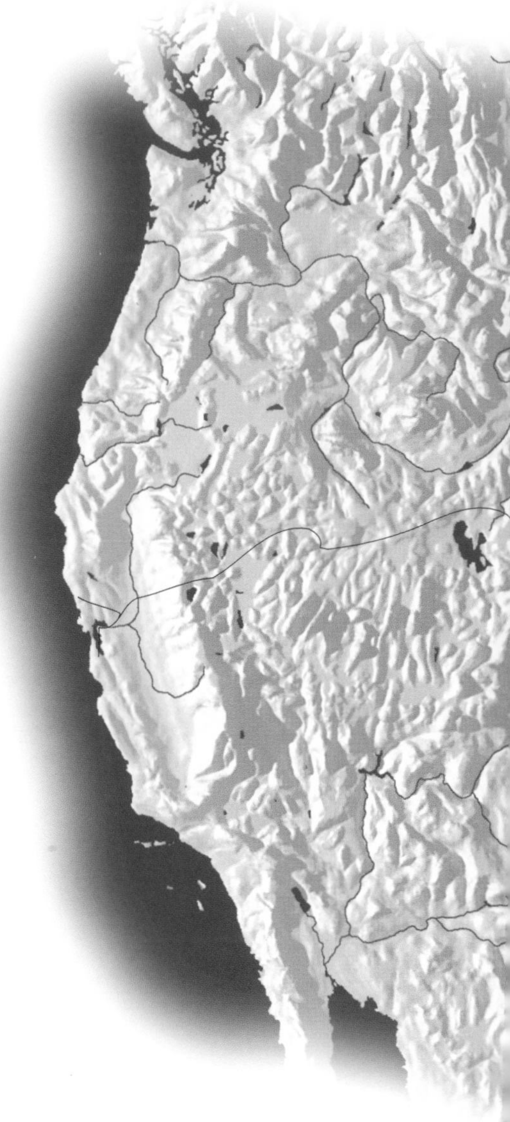

ABOVE A MAP SHOWING THE DEVELOPMENT OF THE U.S. RAILROADS IN THE 1860S AND 1870S. THE CONSTRUCTION IN THE EASTERN STATES AND THE ONE TRANSCONTINENTAL SHOW UP CLEARLY.

with a two-wheeled Bissell truck, built by Taunton Locomotive Works, MA, for the Central RR of New Jersey.

• First 2-8-0, named *Consolidation*, built by Baldwin for pusher service. It gave its name to the type.

• Pennsylvania RR commenced building their own locomotives in their Juniata, PA shops.

• First "rack" railroads demonstrated by Sylvester Marsh in the United States and by Nicholas Riggenbach in Switzerland.

• B & O leased Central Ohio line from Bellaire, OH, through Newark to Columbus.

• New York & Oswego Midland RR incorporated to build a line from Oswego, NY on shore of Lake Ontario, to New Jersey state line, and thence to terminal on the Hudson River.

• Montgomery Railroad reconstruction began with gauge conversion from standard to 5ft!

1867

• Formation of Master Car Builders' Association, a voluntary association of U.S. and Canadian railcar engineers and managers that aimed to secure standardization of freight car, brakes, coupling devices, etc.

• First compound-expansion locomotive built in the United States for the Erie Railroad. It was a rebuild of No. 122 by Shepherd Iron Works of Buffalo, NY.

• George Mortimer Pullman founded the Pullman Palace Car Company. Pullman owned all the sleeping cards on the Chicago & Alton, Burlington & Quincy, Michigan Central, Great Western of Canada and New York Central railroads. He built the first "hotel car", a forerunner of the dining car, for Great Western of Canada.

• Illinois Central reached Dubuque, IA (Sioux City, 1870).

• Cornelius Vanderbilt gained control of New York Central RR.

1868

• Col. Holliday turned first shovelful of earth in Kansas City, KS in construction of Santa Fe RR.

• Lehigh & New England RR inaugurated. Built to haul cement, slate and anthracite from Hauto, PA to Campbell Hall, NY.

• First dining car, named *Delmonico's*, had its initial trip on the Chicago & Alton RR.

• Virginia Central and Covington &

Ohio RRs consolidated as Chesapeake & Ohio RR.

1869

• First experiments with compressed-air brakes (non-automatic) by inventor George Westinghouse.

• Opening on July 3 of Sylvester Marsh's Mount Washington Cog Railway in New Hampshire. First cog-railway in world by six months.

• B & O penetrated westward by leasing line from Newark to Sandusky, OH on Lake Erie.

• Central of Georgia leased South Western RR, gaining access from Macon westward to Columbus and then southward into Alabama at Eufaula.

• Evansville, Terre Haute & Chicago RR chartered.

• Lackawanna RR leased Morris & Essex to avoid using Central of New Jersey tracks.

• New York, Ontario & Western RR opened from Oswego, on Lake Ontario, southward to Norwich, NY.

• NYC RR and Hudson River RR consolidated by Cornelius Vanderbilt as NYC & HR Railroad.

• Construction of Grand Central Station (Depot) commenced at corner of 42nd Street and Fourth Avenue, New York City.

• Pacific Railroad conversion to standard gauge completed, July 18.

Chapter Two

The Railroad Monopoly

By the year 1870 the railroads were firmly established as the overwhelmingly dominant means of medium- and long-distance transport for passengers and freight. From the the commercial point of view the die was cast and things did not change much until well into the 20th century. Wherever the rails advanced, the other carriers and coach firms retreated, although the river steamboats challenged the railroads on the big rivers; they could hold their own on bulk carriage but not on speed.

The rivalry between companies for the domination of territory continued and although the physical battles between rival concerns of the previous three decades abated they were replaced by more subtle, and often equally vicious, commercial battles dominated by the railroad barons. Many smaller railroads were consolidated into larger units, and this process was most pronounced in the New England states where many small roads had grown up in the earlier years.

The first rail tunnel had been built through the Berkshires in place of a canal tunnel that had been proposed some 50 years earlier. The proposed canal route became a railroad to connect Boston, MA with the Great Lakes at Oswego or Buffalo, NY. Although begun in 1851 by the state of Massachusetts, the tunnel was not completed until 1875. A battle between six competing roads for control resulted in a legislative committee proposal to consolidate all of them, which the roads all but turned down!

The Fitchburg RR wanted to control the 4.7 mile long tunnel, but the state would permit this only if the Fitchburg had its own route to the Hudson River. In the 1880s the Fitchburg acquired three other roads, including the Boston, Hoosac Tunnel & Western and three branches. Ultimately the Fitchburg became a part of the Boston & Maine RR.

W.A.B.C.O.

The rail gauge, as already noted, was standardized at 4ft 8½in, and this enabled former isolated systems to be joined and rolling-stock standards to be established, although the process took quite a long time. It was not until 1886 that railroads in the South, almost all built to 5ft gauge, were converted to standard gauge.

The rapid growth of the United States into an industrial nation was crucially aided by the railroads, and by the late 1880s vast industrial empires were being built. Famous names like Daniel Drew, Cyrus Field, Jay Gould, Cornelius Vanderbilt and Edward H. Harriman were synonymous with railroading. They and others assembled railroad systems, bought connecting lines, and built empires, buying parallel lines to control competition. Often they would just buy up railroads for the sake of it! These titans of industry often collected for the railroads more than their fair share of publicity. Railroads were larger than most other contemporary

Above Portrait of George Westinghouse – inventor of the Compressed Air Power Brake.

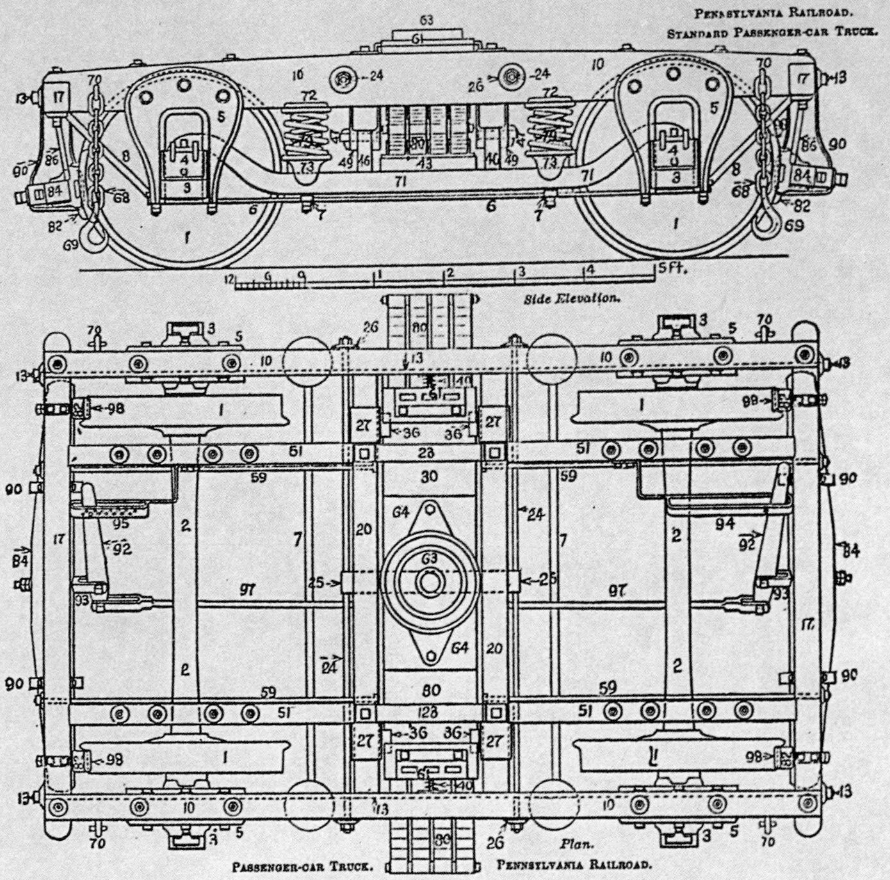

PENNSYLVANIA RAILROAD.
STANDARD PASSENGER-CAR TRUCK.

Side Elevation.

Plan.

PASSENGER-CAR TRUCK. PENNSYLVANIA RAILROAD.

FIG. 4 EQUALIZED, SWING HANGER PASSENGER CAR TRUCK

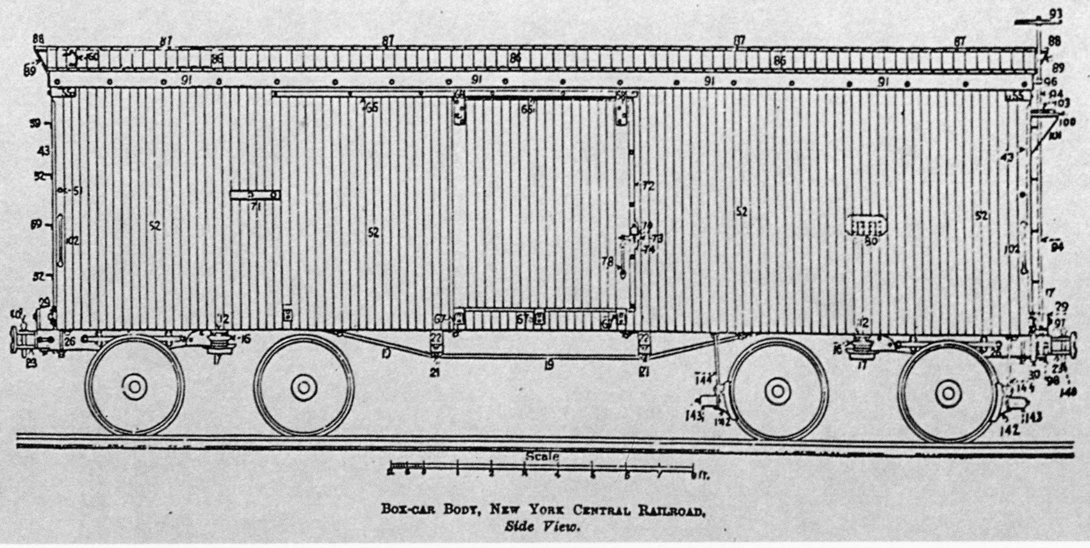

BOX-CAR BODY, NEW YORK CENTRAL RAILROAD,
Side View.

A.S.M.E

ABOVE THE TYPICAL AMERICAN BOX CAR OF THE 1870S WAS OF TIMBER CONSTRUCTION, ABOUT 35 FEET LONG, RAN ON TWO 4-WHEEL DIAMOND-FRAME TRUCKS, HAD TWO SCREW-DOWN HAND BRAKES, AND WAS PROBABLY JUST BEING FITTED WITH AN EARLY FORM OF AUTOMATIC COUPLING.

POOR RIDING OF THE PASSENGER CARS ON INDIFFERENT TRACKS WAS A LIMIT ON HIGHER SPEEDS. RIDING WAS GREATLY IMPROVED BY THE INTRODUCTION OF EQUALIZED TRUCKS AND AN EXAMPLE OF THE PENNSYLVANIA RR STANDARD TRUCK IS ILLUSTRATED HERE.

100 YEARS OF PROGRESS IN RAILWAY MECHANICAL ENGINEERING–ELECTRIC LOCOMOTIVE DEVELOPMENT

FIG. 1-2 EDISON'S LOCOMOTIVE OF 1880

FIG. 1-3 "THE JUDGE" BY FIELD & EDISON, 1883

A.S.M.E

LEFT THOMAS EDDISON PRODUCED THIS STRANGE-LOOKING ELECTRIC LOCOMOTIVE IN 1880 TO DEMONSTRATE THE PRACTICALITY OF ELECTRIC TRACTION.

BELOW THIS SMALL FOUR-WHEEL ELECTRIC LOCOMOTIVE WAS BUILT IN 1893 AND EXHIBITED AT THE COLUMBIAN EXPOSITION IN CHICAGO. BY THIS TIME A NUMBER OF ELECTRIC STREET CAR LINES WERE ALREADY ATTRACTING ATTENTION.

FIG. 1-4 COLUMBIAN EXPOSITION LOCOMOTIVE

A.S.M.E

RIGHT ANOTHER STRANGE-LOOKING DEVICE WAS THIS BALDWIN-WESTINGHOUSE ELECTRIC LOCOMOTIVE. THIS WAS THE BEGINNING OF A COLLABORATION BETWEEN THE TWO COMPANIES WHICH LASTED TO THE SECOND HALF OF THE TWENTIETH CENTURY.

enterprises and, as today, industrial empires and tycoons preoccupied newspapers and magazines.

Regulation, however, was just round the corner. In the Mid West and West, for example, farmers were more dependent on railroads than in the East to move their products to market; also railroads were fewer. The farmers complained that rates were unfair, with favored shippers receiving rebates. Rates were often higher where one railroad had a monopoly.

As early as 1871 the state of Illinois passed legislation regulating freight rates and, in 1873, passenger fares. Minnesota did the same in 1874. By 1880 pressure for regulation had reached national level and resulted in the Interstate Commerce Act of February 1887, effective April 5, 1887.

The Interstate Commerce Commission (ICC), whose first president was Judge Thomas M. Cooley, was set up by the Act to regulate all railroads engaged in interstate commerce, even if they were located entirely within one state. Today the Act also applies to motor carriers, water carriers (river boats, barges, ferries, etc) owned or controlled by railroads, and freight forwarders operating in interstate commerce. The Act stated that rates charged by the railroads had to be "just and

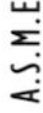

ABOVE THE EIGHT-WHEELER, OR *AMERICAN* (4–4–0), HELD SWAY FOR A LONG TIME BUT INCREASING FREIGHT TRAIN LOADS SOON REQUIRED A LARGER BOILER AND AN ADDITIONAL PAIR OF WHEELS. THE TEN-WHEELER ALSO HAD A SHORT PERIOD OF POPULARITY.

reasonable," but the members of the commission could not agree as to what was meant by "reasonable."

In exchange for land grants, the government stipulated that the railroads had to provide reduced-rate transportation for government property, mails and employees. This provision continued well into the 20th century, by which time the government had received more than 10 times the value of the land it had granted!

Railroads were forbidden to give preference, advantage, special rates or rebates to any person, company, location or type of traffic. They were not allowed to charge more for a short haul than for a long haul, Pooling (that is, sharing of revenue or freight) was forbidden, and railroads were required to publish their rates and give advanced warning of any change. In general this was accepted until in 1897 the Supreme Court ruled that the ICC had no power to fix rates; and this took most of the bite out of the clause requiring that short haul should cost no more than long haul.

In time other acts modified the terms of reference and the ICC became more powerful, with widespread responsibilities, with the effect that the railroads found themselves more and more inhibited commercially.

While major existing railroads consolidated on the 4ft 8½in gauge, there developed strong support for narrow-gauge lines, particularly the 3ft gauge. The Denver & Rio Grande RR is probably the best example. The D & RG was incorporated in 1870 and, with the mountainous terrain of Colorado and New Mexico to contend with, chose the narrow gauge because it was less costly to build than standard gauge. Locomotives and cars were smaller and cheaper, tracks could follow the contours and curves of mountainous terrain more easily, and the smaller rolling stock required smaller cuts and tunnels.

The original intention was to build from Denver, CO south to Pueblo, west along the Arkansas River and over the Poncha Pass into the San Louis Valley, then south following the Rio Grande to El Paso, TX. In 1877 there was the silver rush at Leaville, CO, and this resulted in skirmishes with the Santa Fe over the occupancy of Raton Pass and the Royal Gorge on the Arkansas River. The D & RG gave way and changed its ultimate goal to Salt Lake City.

In 10 years the Denver & Rio Grande had built lines between Denver and Pueblo, Leadville, Walsenburg, Alamosa and Antonito to Chama, NM. A year later there was a line from Chama to Durango and another from Salida to Gunnison. Within 30 years many of the narrow-gauge lines were converted to either mixed gauge or standard gauge, although narrow gauge was to remain on some routes well into the 20th century.

The 30 years from 1870 saw big advances in technology. In the 1880s steam heat and electric light began to replace stoves and oil or gas lamps – a

BELOW STEAM WAS USED AT FIRST ON THE NEW YORK ELEVATED RR. HERE IS A NEW YORK CITY ELEVATED TRAIN HAULED BY A FORNEY 0–4–4 TANK LOCOMOTIVE SOME TIME PRIOR TO ELECTRIFICATION IN 1890.

A.S.M.E

•THE FORNEY TANK•

MATTHIAS FORNEY DEVELOPED THIS 0-4-4 LOCOMOTIVE PRIMARILY FOR SHORT LINES IN NEW ENGLAND. MORE IMPORTANTLY, IT WAS USED IN SOME NUMBERS BY THE NEW YORK ELEVATED RAILWAYS.

welcome move since the timber car construction was particularly vulnerable to fires, sometimes fatal, caused by overheated stoves or spilled oil. Automatic air brakes and automatic couplers were developed and adopted and there was a gradual change from locomotives burning wood in favor of coal or anthracite, both of which were plentiful.

Automatic block signaling and electric locomotives appeared in the last 10 years of the century. Last, but not least, the standard eight-wheeler steam locomotive gave way to the rapid development of larger and more sophisticated types as train weights and speeds increased with the gradual introduction of much better and stronger tracks.

In 1888 the first practical electric streetcar appeared. From this evolved the electric interurban railroad (today's equivalent is light rapid-transit). Rolling stock was smaller than standard and rails ran partly in the street, partly on private right of way. The emphasis was on local service, traffic which the main-line railroads found difficult and expensive. Some railroads encouraged neighboring electric roads, but in the main they were either ignored or treated with open hostility.

Geographical development led to mechanical improvement and more sophisticated operating methods. Locomotives and rolling stock grew in physical size and train weights increased. Track beds were improved and tracks re-laid to stand up to the heavier rolling stock and higher speeds which commercial pressures demanded. Many of the earlier railroads had been built to convey coal, iron ore and other minerals to meet the demands of growing industrial production, and much of this traffic was lost to the canal companies who had themselves had the foresight to invest in their own railroads, particularly in the east and south.

Speed brought problems of safety and train control. From 1851 train despatching from a central point had been instituted, and all railroads set about installing telegraph lines. As traffic grew, trains were despatched on a time-interval system. Where there were double tracks this system worked well enough. But after a disastrous accident between New York City and Philadelphia in 1863, when two trains met head-on – and there had been many such incidents – Ashbel Welch, President of the New Jersey Canal & Railroad Companies, instituted a system of block working.

On the line between New Brunswick, NJ and Philadelphia, PA Ashbel Welch installed a system of signals. Each signal consisted of a red banner which

BELOW ELECTRIC STREETCARS AND SUBURBAN RAILWAYS DEVELOPED RAPIDLY FROM AROUND 1900. THIS EXAMPLE WAS BUILT IN 1900 FOR THE CLEVELAND AND EASTERN RR.

St. Louis Mercantile Museum

ABOVE SIGNALING "TOWERS" SOON BECAME A FAMILIAR SIGHT AND THIS PENNSYLVANIA RAILROAD TOWER IS TYPICAL OF THE 1920S.

was dropped into view by a signalman through a hole in a box the moment a train had passed. The track ahead was thus closed (blocked) until a message was received over the telegraph from the next station that the train had passed. The block was then cleared and the red banner was removed. The system was formally adopted by the road on March 27, 1865.

There were a number of places where tracks of rival companies crossed on the level, at grade. One such point was in the prairie outside Chicago, IL, known as Grand Crossing, where the Illinois Central tracks crossed the rival Southern Michigan. This was a notorious place where trains of one road raced to get to the crossing before trains of their rival, and in 1853 a serious collision left a wrecked locomotive, several wrecked cars, sixteen passengers dead and many more injured. This caused the authorities to issue an edict that no train might enter a crossing with another road at grade until after it had stopped and the crossing was seen to be clear. This rule was made state law in

BELOW GEORGE WESTINGHOUSE DEVELOPED HIS STRAIGHT AIR BRAKE AND THIS HAD ITS FIRST PRACTICAL DEMONSTRATION ON THE PANHANDLE RR – LATER PENNSYLVANIA – IN 1869 WITH THIS 4–4–0 LOCOMOTIVE AND PASSENGER CAR.

W.A.B.C.O.

Massachusetts in 1854 and most states followed suit; the law was soon extended to apply to most busy junctions.

This grade crossing rule led ultimately to the adoption of an invention of 1856 by the English engineer, John Saxby, which eliminated this nuisance and led to the development of the modern signaling system. In Saxby's invention signals and switches were operated by levers from a central tower, with the levers interlocked to eliminate incorrect movements. This system was first installed in the United States in 1870. The control of train movements came into the hand of one man instead of having several men operating switches, with the ever-present problem of communication. Trains could now run safely through such crossings and junctions without the need to "stop, look and listen."

The trial installation worked so well that the first permanent installation was made at East Newark, NJ in February 1875 on what had become the Pennsylvania RR. It was refined in the light of experience, and soon trains were detected by means of electrical track circuits, invented by Dr Andrews of New Jersey in 1871. Essentially, an electric current was fed into sections of the rails so that the passage of a train over the sections caused an electrical relay to operate and either work a signal or release a lock to enable the signalman to operate a switch or signal. It was vital that the system should be fail-safe, and the presence of a train "shorted" the relay coil so that the relay was de-energized and its contacts completed an electrical lock. At the same time, a light was illuminated on a diagram to show the controller that the particular section of track was occupied.

In the early 1880s compressed air was experimentally integrated with electric circuit controls to operate switches and signals in complex switch interlocking arrangements. This meant that switches several miles away from any given control tower could then be reliably operated in the correct sequence in order to establish a "safe route." By 1890 this all-American system was well established.

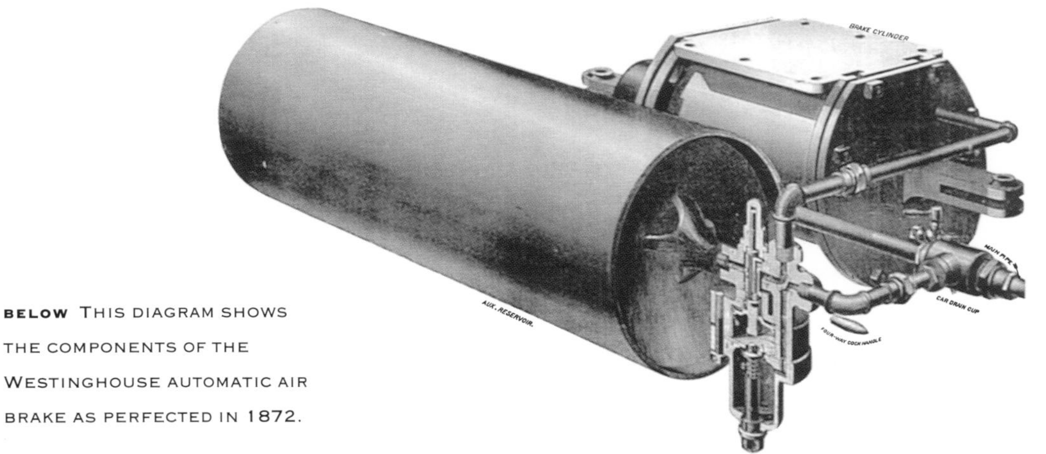

LEFT THE THREE MAJOR COMPONENTS OF THE WESTINGHOUSE AUTOMATIC AIR BRAKE FOR A PASSENGER OR FREIGHT CAR.

W.A.B.C.O.

BELOW THIS DIAGRAM SHOWS THE COMPONENTS OF THE WESTINGHOUSE AUTOMATIC AIR BRAKE AS PERFECTED IN 1872.

BRAKE CYLINDER
CONDUCTOR'S VALVE
BRAKE CYLINDER
TO BOILER
EXHAUST
ENGINEER'S BRAKE VALVE
AUXILIARY RESERVOIR
AUXILIARY RESERVOIR
TRIPLE VALVE
TRIPLE VALVE
MAIN RESERVOIR
STOP COCK
STOP COCK
STOP COCK
COUPLING
CAR DRAIN COCK
COUPLING
DRIP COCK
AIR INLET
PASSENGER CAR
TENDER
AIR PUMP
ENGINE

THE "WESTINGHOUSE" PLAIN AUTOMATIC AIR BRAKE 1872.

W.A.B.C.O.

It took quite a long time for railroad chiefs to accept what many of them saw as obstructive: the costs of better signalling diverted funds from building new lines or money from investors' pockets; and it was not until after 1885 that safe signalling enabled the "full stop" at grade crossings and junctions to be finally abolished.

Productivity was improved by the passage of more trains through busy junctions, and time schedules were shortened. Gradually signal systems and rules were standardized. It was largely the action of the railroads, through the General Time Convention of 1874 – the body responsible for the introduction of a standard time and four time zones throughout the United States and Canada, which was finally adopted by railroads in 1883 – that rules were formulated for harmonization of signalling, cars, train movements and safety appliances. The rules were still only recommendations, rather than mandatory requirement – although non-observance was often not regarded favorably. The convention became the American Railroad Association in 1891.

The desire to increase train speeds meant that the means of stopping them safely had to be improved. From the earliest times locomotives had been fitted with hand brakes. These had been superseded first by "screw-down," then by steam brakes. Gradually passenger and freight cars were also fitted with hand screw-down brakes and brakemen rode the trains to operate them when required. Still, train speeds had to be low enough to be able to stop in all conditions.

To stop a train at a particular point, however, was quite an art and needed good judgment. Each train carried an engine crew and a train crew of conductors and brakemen. When a train had to be stopped at a station, or for some other reason, the driver first blew the steam whistle to alert the brakemen. The brakemen were then expected to proceed along the tops of freight cars, regardless of weather, jumping from car to car to apply the brakes and hope they had been given enough time to stop at the required point.

By the 1850s and 1860s a few applications of the

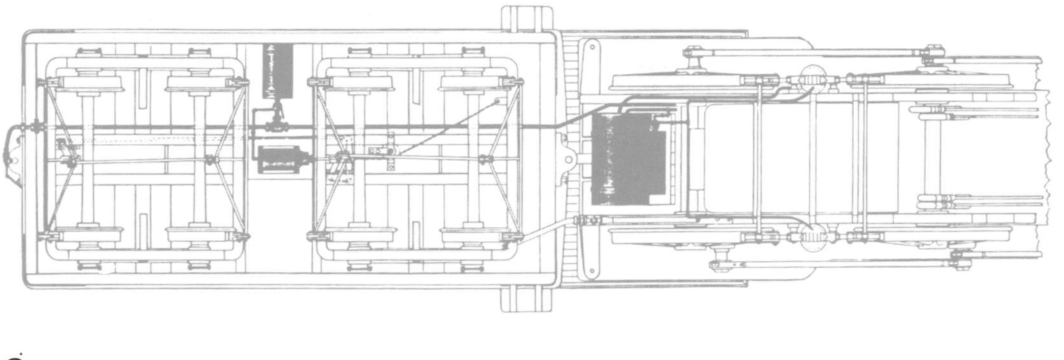

RIGHT A DRAWING OF AN *EIGHT WHEELER* WITH THE COMPONENTS OF THE WESTINGHOUSE AUTOMATIC AIR BRAKE.

W.A.B.C.O.

European-style vacuum brake had been made on railroads on the eastern seaboard. The vacuum brake, dependent on atmospheric pressure, quickly lost effectiveness with increased altitude and so had severe limitations in North America.

The Civil War brought about a considerable interchange of rolling stock, particularly of freight cars, where track gauges allowed, and it was soon apparent that a degree of vehicle standardization was needed. This brought about the founding of the Master Car Builders' Association in 1867. Its purpose was to facilitate the interchange of cars among railroads, and in 1876 it established rules for the prompt interchange of cars and of repairs to damaged and defective cars, with billing and payment for the repairs. The association then went on to establish standards for other car parts which, for example, helped to reduce the enormous variety of axles and journal boxes at the time to only five different types.

Another problem tackled by the Master Car Builders' Association was one which had arisen from the growth of the many unconnected railroads – namely that of the confusion of parts names. In 1871 a publication called *The Railroad Gazette* was produced which served as a dictionary, defining by words and pictures everything from "adjustable globe-lamp" to "yoke."

To return to the subject of brakes, we have already mentioned the invention and application in 1869 by George Westinghouse of the world's first continuous air brake. This was demonstrated between Pittsburgh and Steubenville, OH on the Panhandle RR (the so-called Panhandle of West Virginia), later part of the Pennsylvania system. It was a straight air brake: compressed air, generated by a steam-driven compressor and stored in a reservoir on the locomotive, was fed by a valve operated by the driver into a pipe which ran the length of the train. Cylinders on each vehicle pressed "shoes" onto the wheel tyres. At the end of each car, a flexible pipe took the air to the next car.

The trial installation, early in its life, prevented a

BELOW A PASSENGER CAR OF THE 1970S SHOWS THE LAYOUT OF THE AUTOMATIC AIR BRAKE EQUIPMENT. THE CAR IS ALSO SHOWN WITH AUTOMATIC COUPLERS.

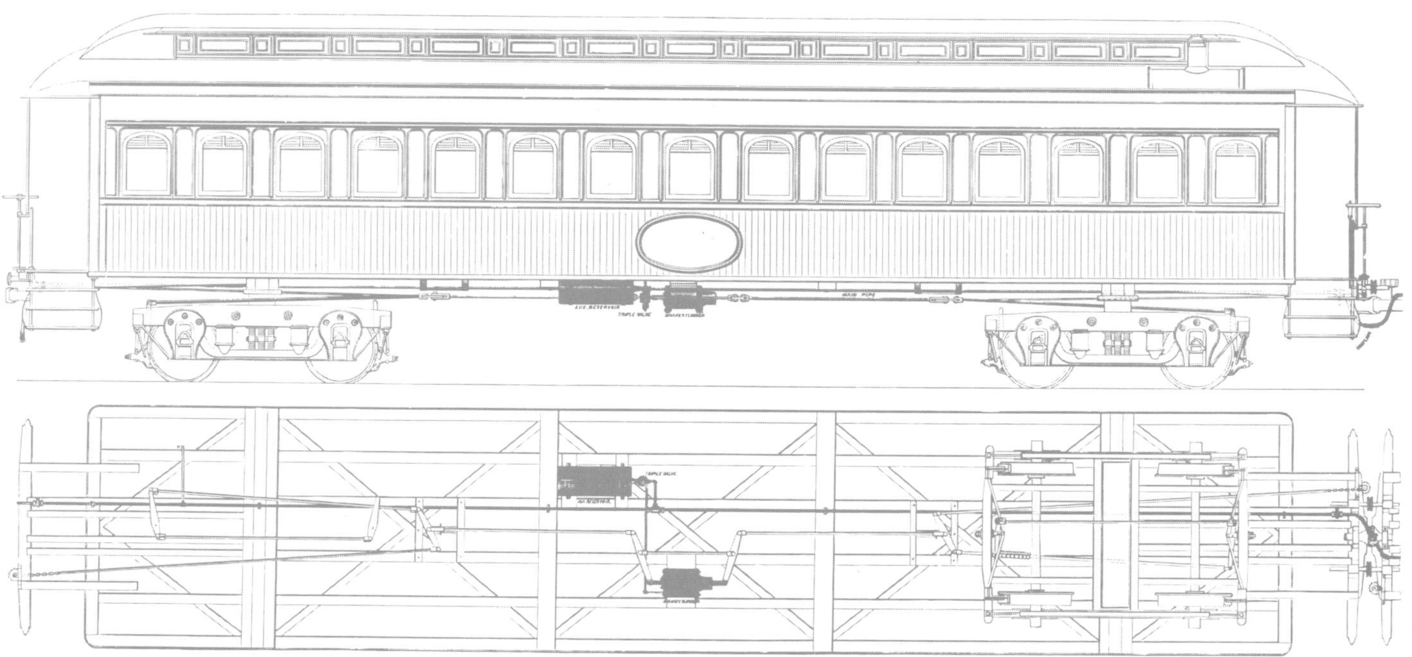

W.A.B.C.O.

serious accident when a farm wagon stalled on a grade crossing and the horses could not move it. The driver first yanked on the steam whistle cord to call up the brakemen, and then the air brake was applied. The train was brought to a safe stop and no lives were lost.

The "straight" air brake had three undesirable features. If one of the flexible pipes developed a leak, the air went to waste and all braking effect was lost. If cars became uncoupled on up-grades – and at that time this was no rare occurrence – only hand brakes could save them from rolling backwards. Also, with long trains it took a considerable time for the air pressure to build up on the most rearward cars.

Two of these problems were solved in 1871 when Westinghouse invented the automatic brake with a fail-safe system. In this system, the air pipe was charged at a specific pressure all the time, and each car carried a small auxiliary air tank and a special triple valve. This valve was operated by a change in pressure in the main pipe. Any reduction of pressure in the pipe applied the brakes, while recharging the pipe to normal pressure released the brakes.

With normal running conditions all the auxiliary air tanks, air pipes and flexible hoses are charged at the same pressure and form a continuous system; the triple valves shut off the air to the brake cylinders. To stop the train the driver (engineer) operates the control valve in his cab and reduces the air pressure in the train pipe. This causes the triple valve on each car to operate and allow air to flow from the auxiliary tanks to the brake cylinders and so slow down or stop the train. The brakes are released by recharging the train pipe to normal pressure. This allows the triple valve to void the air from the brake cylinders, at the same time equalizing the auxiliary tank pressure with the train pipe.

The system has been refined over the years but one feature which was important then and has remained so is the ability to "fail safe." Anything which results in a reduction of the air pressure in the train pipe will cause the brakes to be applied. For example, rupturing of a flexible pipe, such as might be caused by a coupling breakage, will activate the brakes on all cars, bringing both the separated sections of the train to a stand. The brakes can then be released only manually on each car of the broken-away section of the train or by replacing the faulty flexible hose.

It was a serious accident on an Eastern Railroad, forerunner of the Boston & Maine, which brought about the fitting of continuous brakes. An express out of Boston, MA on a foggy night in August 1871 crashed. Twenty-nine passengers were killed and 57 were injured when the train ploughed into the back of another which had

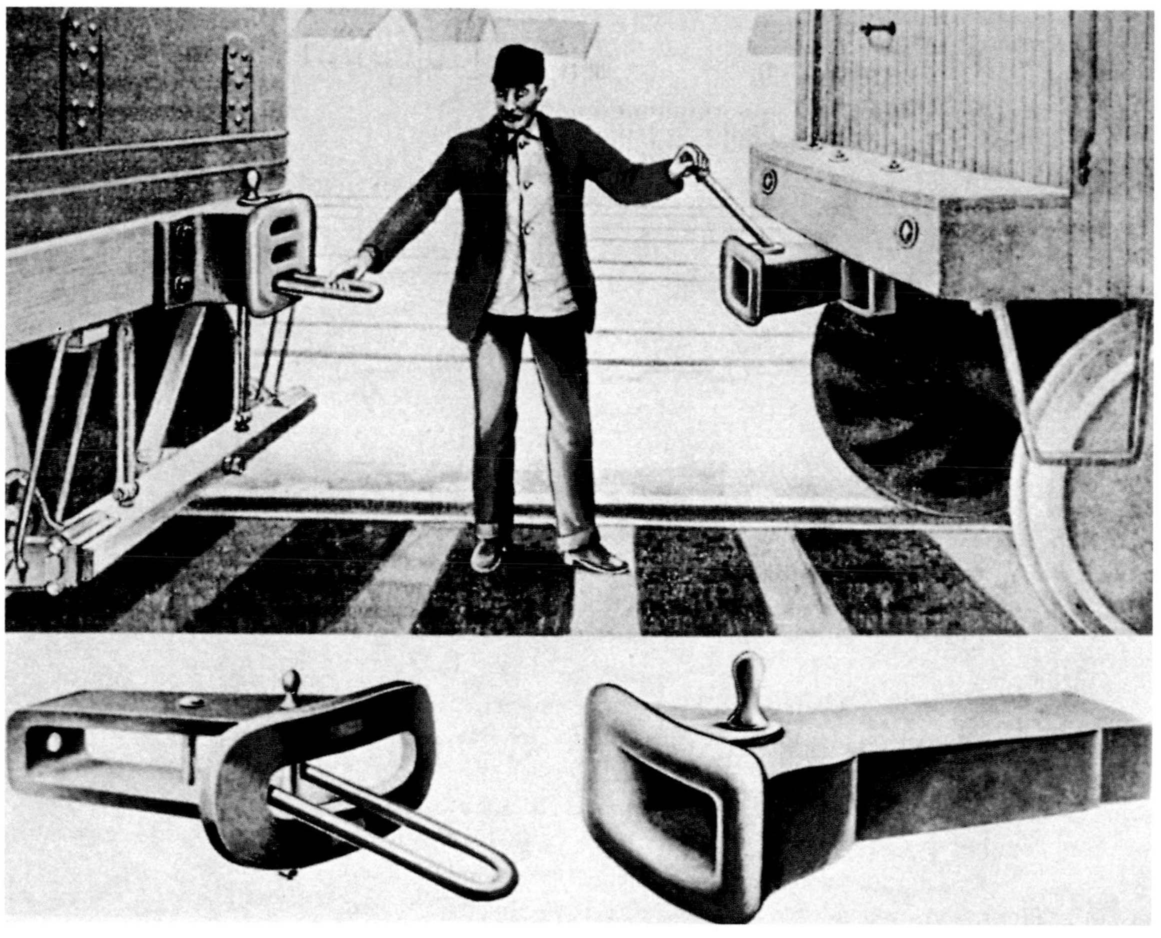

A.S.M.E

stopped at Revere. The public and press denounced the directors of the Eastern Railroad as murderers! The railroad reacted and the fitting of continuous brakes to passenger trains began.

It took another 20 years or more before continuous brakes were fitted to all freight cars. Many roads were reluctant to spend the money on fitting all freight cars, and mixed braked/non-braked trains were the result, with the "fitted" vehicles marshaled at the head. Regulations compelled car owners at least to fit through-brake pipes if not air brakes, so that "mixed" trains could be run. Even so such trains presented an operating hazard, particularly on mountainous lines with long trains. Braking was accompanied by much bunching and surging as trains slowed down, and breakaways were not unknown.

George Westinghouse established a small works in Pittsburgh, PA in 1870 with a work force of 105. By 1872 the Westinghouse automatic brake was in full production. Even so, with the link and pin couplers then in vogue, train separations were a quite common occurrence and the new brake took this into account. Passenger-train separations were considerably reduced and by the late 1870s most passenger rolling stock was equipped with some form of air brake.

By the early 1880s developments were in hand to

ABOVE AN EXAMPLE OF LINK AND PIN COUPLERS USED BEFORE AUTOMATIC COUPLINGS WERE MADE OBLIGATORY IN 1887. THE LOWER ILLUSTRATION IS OF THE MILLER HOOK WHICH HAD ALREADY BEEN ADOPTED BY SOME RAILROADS FOR PASSENGER CARS.

RIGHT TYPICAL LINK AND PIN COUPLER USED ON PASSENGER AND FREIGHT CARS UNTIL THE 1890S.

California State Railroad Museum

enhance the braking of freight trains and a new device was being fitted to freight vehicles: the brake cylinder pressure-retaining valve. This valve allowed safe operation on long grades and permitted the brake system to be recharged from time to time without having to release and re-apply the brakes.

A British invention of 1856 had far reaching effects in revolutionizing the process of rail manufacture. The introduction to steel-making of Henry Bessemer's converter resulted in the quantity production of stronger, more durable and less expensive steel rails. The widespread use of steel rails led to the development of bigger and heavier cars, longer trains and more powerful locomotives. At the same time, with the interchange of rolling stock, the need was recognized by the middle 1880s for an acceptable standard continuous-power brake system. From tests organized by the Master Car Builders' Association, a quick-action automatic air brake system was developed in 1888 and adopted in 1889 as the American standard.

The Westinghouse system was modified to allow air to be voided to the atmosphere, not only at the driver's control valve but at every triple valve in a train. Trials conducted in 1886 at Burlington, IA by the Master Car Builders' Association with three different types of brakes applied to strings of 50 box cars weighing a total of 1000 tons showed that the lag of 20 seconds or more in braking effect between the front and rear of the train gave unsatisfactory emergency stopping distances. The modified Westinghouse system improved this so much that there was now only one and a half to two seconds delay between the front and rear of the train. This was known as the quick-acting (QA) triple valve.

These tests also demonstrated the need for sweeping changes to car drawbars and couplings. Until that time the standard coupling had been the combined drawbar, link and pin coupling. As car and train weights increased this type of coupling proved too weak, was dangerous to operate and introduced a considerable amount of free slack in a long train. By the 1870s passenger cars were already using some form of semi-automatic coupling – the Miller Hook was heralded as the greatest life-saving invention of the age – but even so American draft gear was not designed generally to absorb energy as was the case in Europe, where cushioned screw couplings and spring-loaded side buffers were the norm.

In 1868 Major Eli Janney invented (and in 1873

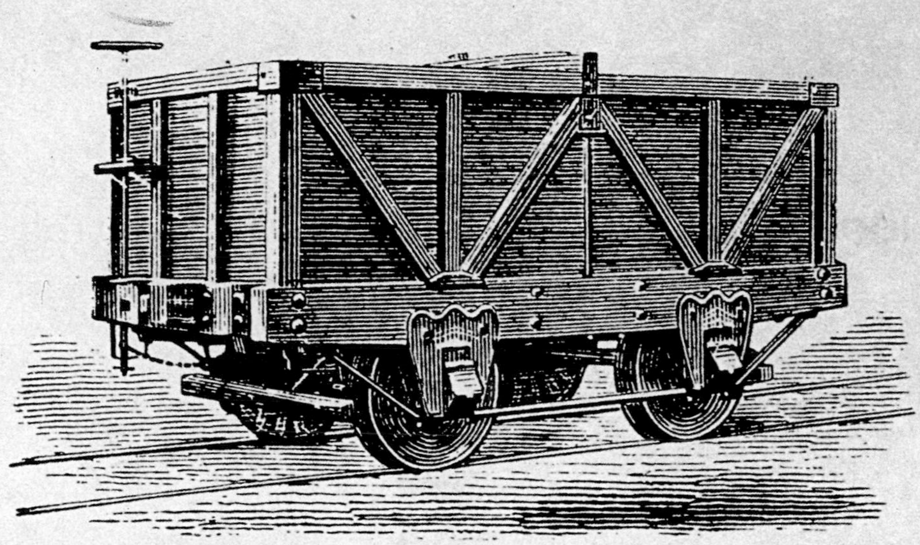

FOUR-WHEELED HOPPER-BOTTOM COAL CAR.

FIG. 2

ABOVE EARLY FREIGHT CARS WERE BUILT ENTIRELY OF TIMBER AND SOON PROGRESSED FROM 4-WHEEL TO 8-WHEEL, 2-TRUCK CARS. THE 2-TRUCK CAR SHOWN HERE WAS USED TO CARRY COKE. IT HAS ONLY HAND BRAKES AND LINK AND PIN COUPLINGS.

patented) an automatic knuckle-coupler which operated in the vertical plane. In the next decade many other coupler designs of the same general type emerged. By 1889, there were around 80,000 freight cars in the United States and 39 different varieties of coupler, the majority of which would not intercouple! It is thought this was the single greatest factor responsible for the formation of the Master Car Builders' Association. They adopted automatic couplers in 1887. Due to their efforts the number of designs was reduced to 16 and subsequently to twelve, all able to intercouple.

The first truly automatic coupler was the Tower coupler, invented in 1892. It would couple and lock on impact (as indeed would many other designs), but it could also be unlocked and the knuckle thrown fully open by means of a lever at the side of the car.

Many railroads were slow to adopt automatic couplers and other safety devices until the Safety Appliances Act was passed by Congress in 1893. This made it mandatory after January 1, 1898 that all cars used in interstate commerce must be equipped with couplers capable of coupling automatically by impact and uncoupled without the need of trainmen. Coupler development was stimulated as the result.

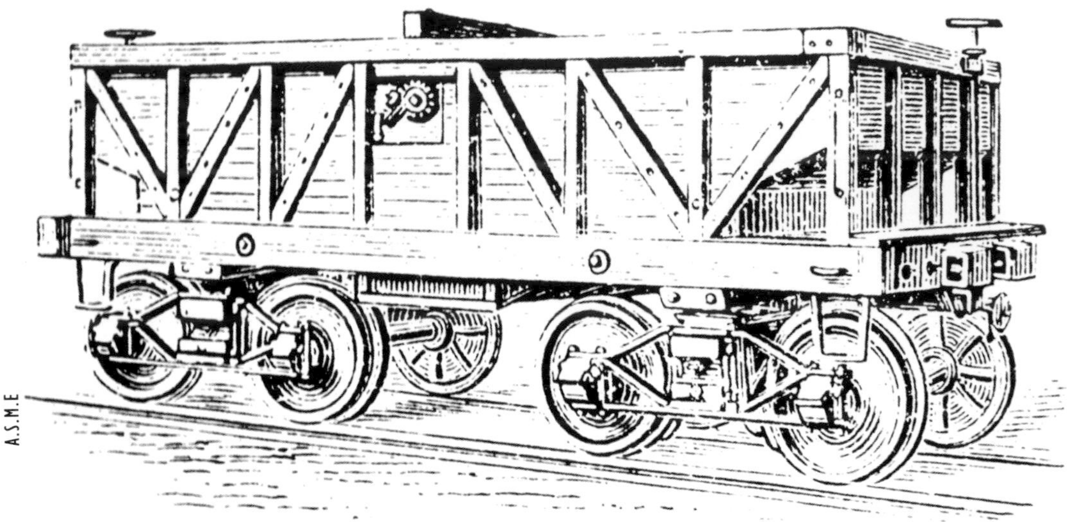

A.S.M.E

LEFT HOPPER BOTTOM COAL CARS WERE AN EARLY INNOVATION. A NUMBER OF THE ROADS IN THE EASTERN STATES WERE PRIMARILY COAL HAULERS AND THE HOPPER BOTTOM WAS AN AID TO UNLOADING AT PORTS AND WHARVES.

In the same period the strength of freight cars was improved. Early freight cars had been made entirely of timber. As early as 1829 the Delaware & Hudson Railroad had introduced an anthracite coal movement in New York state with timber open-top hopper cars each running on two four-wheel trucks. This general type of car, updated, still appeared in the *Carbuilder's Dictionary* in 1878 with a carrying capacity of 40–50,000lb.

Box cars of timber construction averaged about 28 feet in length and had a capacity of about 30,000lb. By 1888 the length had grown to about 35 feet, with a capacity of 50,000lb and a tare weight of 24,800lb, giving an axle load, fully laden of a little over 9 tons. About this time timber frames gave way to wrought iron.

Tank cars had been established for the carriage of water or oil from early times; the first purpose-built one went into service in Pennsylvania in 1865. The tank was formed from riveted steel plates and was strapped on to a timber underframe with timber cross-members. It typically had an empty weight of 28,000lb and a capacity of 3,700 gallons.

Development of the passenger car was also proceeding apace and the period 1865–80 was one of transition from cars which were small, uncomfortable boxes to deluxe vehicles costing 10 to 15 times as much. These luxury cars aimed to encourage people to make long-distance journeys in comfort. Passage between adjoining cars when the train was in motion had been extremely hazardous in earlier cars, as the platforms were narrow and fully open to the elements, and there were no buffers or tread plates between the end sills of the cars. Some early cars were fitted with various types of semi-automatic couplers, such as the Miller hook, but there were no continuous brakes.

Car bodies were of timber and were constructed like

California State Railroad Museum

ABOVE BOX CARS WERE PROVIDED FOR GENERAL MERCHANDISE AND TWO OF THE EARLY TYPES ARE ILLUSTRATED HERE. THE TOP ONE IS AN EARLY GRAIN CAR, THE SECOND A CAR FOR GENERAL FREIGHT. BOTH HAVE AUTOMATIC COUPLINGS AND AIR BRAKES.

A.S.M.E

California State Railroad Museum

ABOVE FLAT CARS WERE USED FROM THE EARLIEST TIMES TO CONVEY CARRIAGES, MACHINERY, AND OTHER LOADS NOT SUITABLE FOR BOX CARS. THE CAR ILLUSTRATED COULD BE FITTED WITH VERTICAL STAKES IN THE SIDE POCKETS TO PROTECT LOADS.

LEFT THE CARRIAGE OF LIQUIDS HAD BEEN AN EARLY REQUIREMENT AND SELF-CONTAINED TANK CARS WERE INTRODUCED IN THE 1850S FOR WATER AND OIL.

RIGHT THE BOX CAR WAS DEVELOPED QUICKLY TO CARRY PERISHABLE LOADS. THIS HAS BOGIES WITH INDIVIDUAL SPRINGS, AUTO-COUPLERS, AND AIRBRAKES.

California State Railroad Museum

PENNSYLVANIA RAILROAD.
P. R. R.
LOCOMOTIVE AND TENDER, PENNSYLVANIA RAILROAD.
93
PENNSYLVANIA R.R. BAGGAGE
BAGGAGE CAR, PENNSYLVANIA RAILROAD.
20
PENNSYLVANIA RAIL ROAD. U.S. MAIL.
U. S. POSTAL CAR, PENNSYLVANIA RAILROAD.
PENNSYLVANIA.
920
PASSENGER CAR, PENNSYLVANIA RAILROAD.
PULLMAN PARLOR CAR
OCEAN
LAUDERBACH CO
PARLOR CAR, PENNSYLVANIA RAILROAD.
PULLMAN DRAWING ROOM SLEEPING CAR
OHIO
LAUDERBACH CO
SLEEPING CAR, PENNSYLVANIA RAILROAD.
V

St. Louis Mercantile Museum

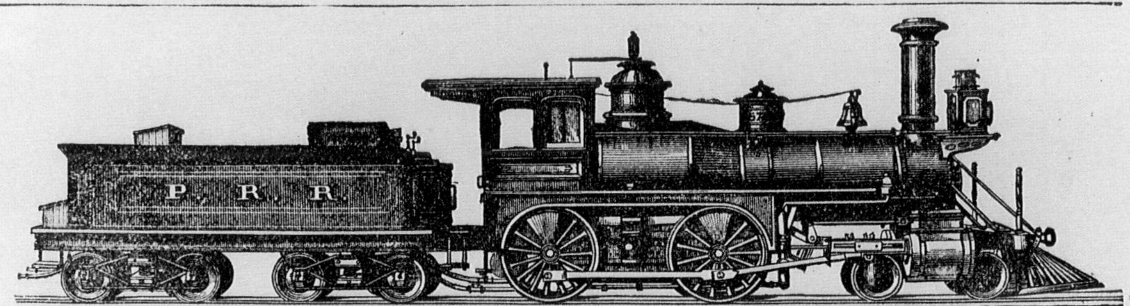

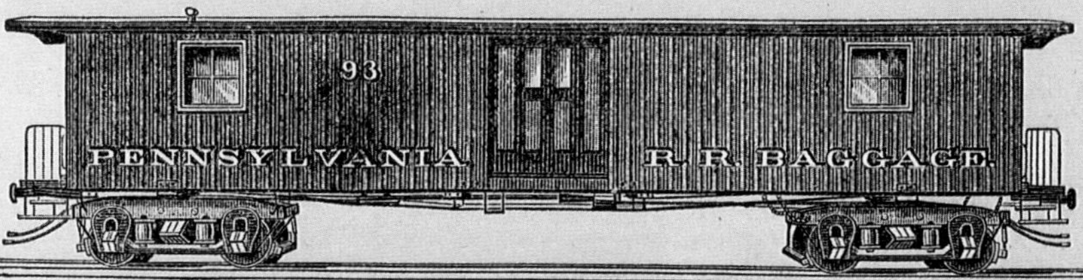

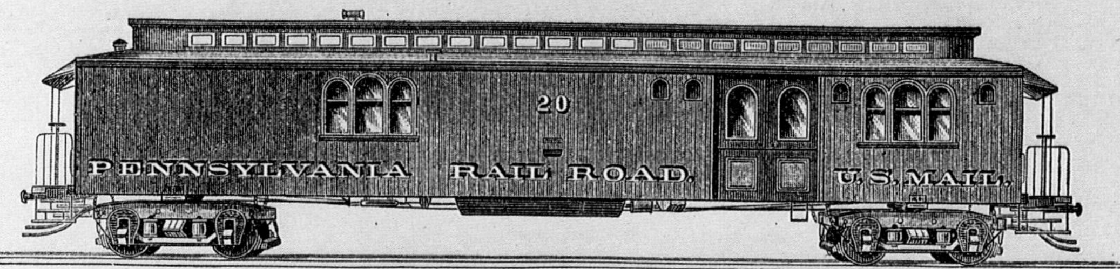

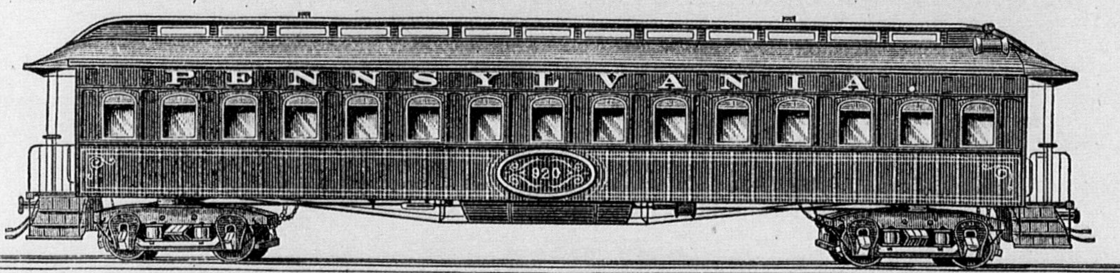

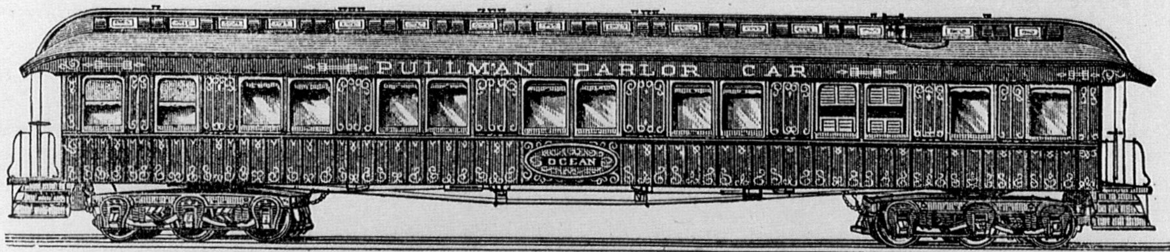

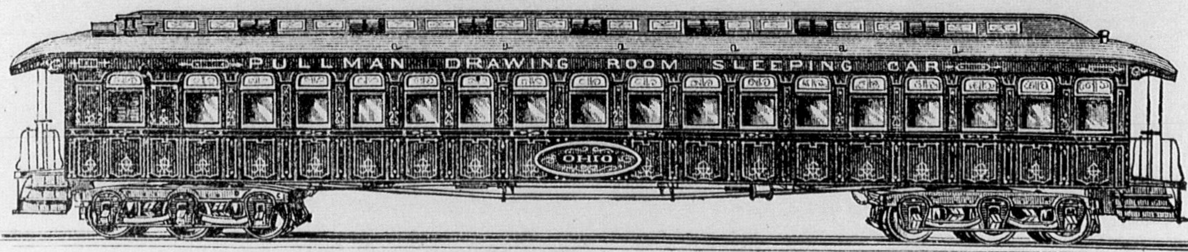

California State Railroad Museum

LEFT LOCOMOTIVE AND PASSENGER ROLLING STOCK OF THE 1880S. THIS DRAWING OF PENNSYLVANIA RR EQUIPMENT IS FAIRLY TYPICAL OF MANY RAILROADS OF THE PERIOD.

a simple bridge truss, with wrought-iron diagonal tension rods in the side framing. Support and control of vertical deflection was by wrought-iron truss rods under the floor. Brakes were primarily manual and in the 1860s some cars were equipped with elementary non-automatic vacuum brakes introduced from England. Westinghouse straight air brakes were introduced on some cars in the early 1870s. Speeds were relatively low and did not normally exceed 35–40 mph.

Passenger cars carried their own coal- or wood-burning stoves, although the luxury cars were equipped with circulating hot-air or hot-water systems from Spear & Baker heaters. As early as 1856 a heating and ventilating system was developed that brought in fresh air from the top of the car. Forced in as the train moved, the air was passed through a plenum chamber, where it received heat from a hot-air stove, the warm air being distributed into the car through ducts in the ceiling. Cold air was removed through suction heads and went back to the stove for reheating. Steam heating from the locomotive was first introduced in 1883 on New York's Manhattan Railroad. Steam was passed through pipes running around each car.

Timber-truss construction continued to be used to the

ABOVE A CLERESTORY CAR BUILT FOR THE CENTRAL PACIFIC RR OF CALIFORNIA BY WILSON OF SPRINGFIELD, MASSACHUSETTS, IN 1869. THIS WAS THE FIRST CAR TO ARRIVE BY RAIL AND WAS FORMED IN LELAND STANFORD'S PRIVATE TRAIN.

A.S.M.E

ABOVE A JACKSON & SHARP TIMBER BODY CAR OF 1895. THIS CAR HAS AUTOMATIC COUPLERS, AIR BRAKES ENCLOSED END VESTIBULES, HOT WATER HEATING, AND GAS LIGHTING. LENGTH HAD ALSO INCREASED.

RIGHT INTERIOR OF AMERICAN CAR OF THE LATE 19TH CENTURY.

A.S.M.E

A.S.M.E

ABOVE UNTIL 1887, VESTIBULE CONNECTIONS HAD BEEN OPEN AT THE BOTTOM. THIS PICTURE SHOWS ONE OF THE FIRST EARLY NARROW ALL-ENCLOSED VESTIBULE CONNECTIONS BETWEEN TWO 12-WHEEL PULLMANS.

end of the 19th century, although it was developed so that the car side, rather than the underframe, was used to support the car weight. Elaborate timber trusses or arch constructions were developed for use between the side sill and the belt rail, although truss rods continued to be used under the cars.

By the early 1890s the automatic locking knuckle coupler with friction draft gear was developed to the point where knuckle contours could be standardized. Henceforward cars could be interchanged between different roads, so that it was not longer necessary to change trains between one system and another.

In 1887 the enclosed-end vestibule was invented by a Mr Sessions, permitting passengers for the first time to walk safely through a moving train and thereby encourage the use of dining, lounge, and other special-purpose cars. At first the vestibule was only between step wells, but by 1893 it was enlarged to cover the full width. From the first,. in conjunction with automatic couplers, the construction used a metal face plate with canvas curtain to aid moving between adjacent cars.

Although George M. Pullman did not invent the sleeping car, he developed its design and construction to the point where it became a national institution. Pullman was a cabinetmaker from Brocton, NY, and after successfully remodeling (with Benjamin Field) two Chicago, Alton & St Louis cars in 1859, he decided to go into the sleeping-car business.

In 1863 he set up his first works in Detroit, MI and built a luxury car he named *Pioneer*, which was larger and more luxurious than other cars of the era. Legend has it that *Pioneer* was in the train that carried Abraham Lincoln's body home to Springfield, IL in April 1865. The Pullman Palace Car Company was chartered in 1867 and the first build was 48 cars. The company grew, acquiring cars from other operators which it leased out to railroads, and moved to a larger plant nearer Chicago, IL.

Pullman entered into arrangements with railroads whereby he would provide the cars and staff and the railroads would haul, light and heat them. The railroad charged the regular coach fare for each passenger journey, and a supplement was charged plus a charge for a single berth or seat occupancy, which went to Pullman. Pullman was not the only sleeping car operator – there were some 40 others in the second half of the 19th century – but ultimately all the others failed or were absorbed into his empire.

The Pullman Company was renowned for its standardization of both cars and service. Staff were trained from manuals which stipulated everything from the positioning of the pillows and the correct way to fold towels to the proper way in which to serve beer. The usual staff per car was one African-American porter and one Filipino lounge attendant.

By the time Pullman died in 1897 the company had a virtual monopoly of sleeping-car services in the United States and ran dining- and parlor-car services as well. Its railroad car plant was the largest in the world and it was a pioneer in the building of steel cars. It later expanded into the production of freight cars by acquiring other car builders.

The period following the end of the Civil War saw expansion of the rail tracks westwards and the uniform adoption of standard gauge. The few non-standard-gauge lines of the eastern states and the 5ft gauge lines of the South were converted to standard gauge by 1886; but there remained many miles of narrower gauge, mainly 3ft, chosen because of economy or for reasons of the local terrain: their trains could negotiate sharper curves than those of standard or broad gauge. We shall return to these later.

Although the American Civil War properly belongs to the previous chapter it is appropriate to dwell on it here because it demonstrated the strategic and tactical importance of railroads. Railroads in the South had been built primarily to give inland cities and rural communities ready access to the coast. As a result there were many individual companies plying parallel routes, rather than any kind of integrated network. Through services and joint stations were few and far between – and this had to be corrected quickly during the war.

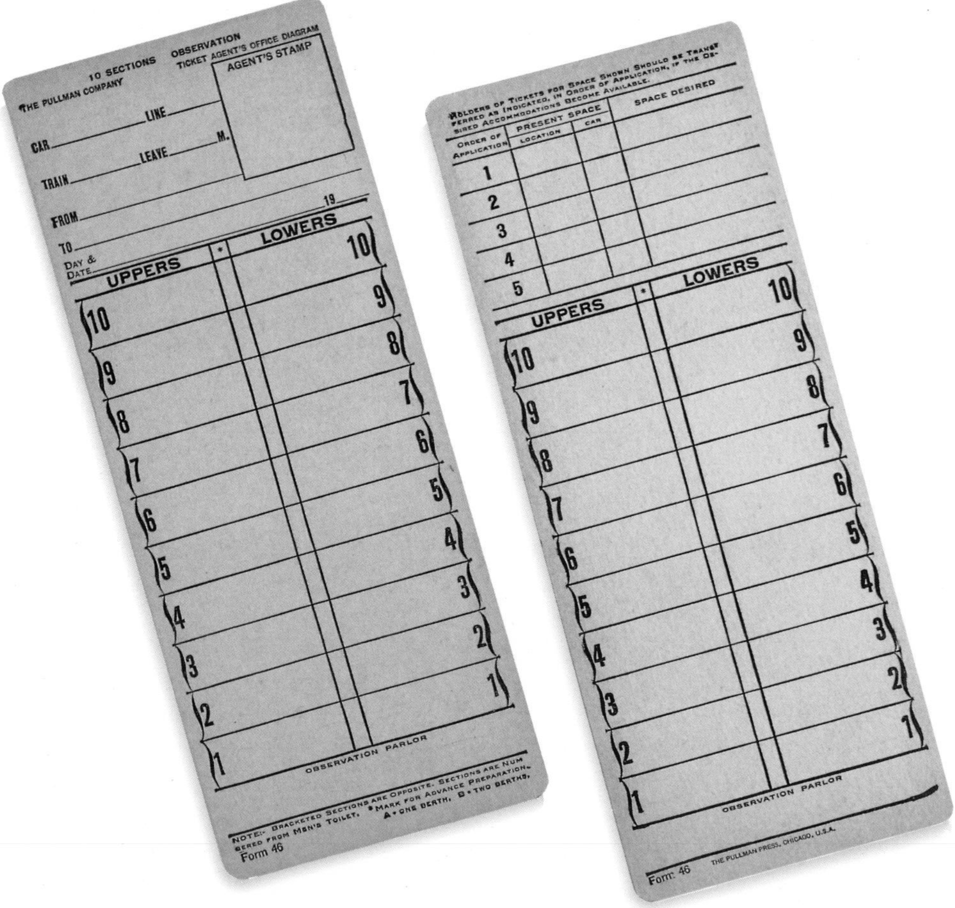
THE PULLMAN COMPANY
10 SECTIONS OBSERVATION
TICKET AGENT'S OFFICE DIAGRAM
AGENT'S STAMP
LINE
CAR
LEAVE M.
TRAIN
19
FROM
TO
DAY & DATE
UPPERS
LOWERS
10 9 8 7 6 5 4 3 2 1
OBSERVATION PARLOR
NOTE: BRACKETED SECTIONS ARE OPPOSITE. SECTIONS ARE NUMBERED FROM MEN'S TOILET. *MARK FOR ADVANCE PREPARATION. A=ONE BERTH, B=TWO BERTHS.
Form 46

HOLDERS OF TICKETS FOR SPACE SHOWN SHOULD BE TRANSFERRED AS INDICATED, IN ORDER OF APPLICATION, IF THE DESIRED ACCOMMODATIONS BECOME AVAILABLE.
ORDER OF APPLICATION | PRESENT SPACE: LOCATION, CAR | SPACE DESIRED
1
2
3
4
5
UPPERS
LOWERS
10 9 8 7 6 5 4 3 2 1
OBSERVATION PARLOR
Form 46
THE PULLMAN PRESS, CHICAGO, U.S.A.

RIGHT TICKET AGENT'S BOOKING FORMS FOR PULLMAN SLEEPING CAR BERTH RESERVATIONS. THESE FORMS GAVE THE PULLMAN CAR ATTENDANT THE INFORMATIION NEEDED FOR THE DAY OF TRAVEL.

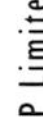

ABOVE THE CANADIAN TRANSCONTINENTAL LINE WAS OPENED IN STAGES AND HERE THE FIRST TRAIN TO ARRIVE AT PORT MOODY, BC, IS INSPECTED BY INTERESTED SPECTATORS.

Serious damage was inflicted and both sides in the conflict seized equipment so that troop movements were hampered. Chattanooga, TN was fought over for more than a year because it was the center of crossing lines. The Nashville & Chattanooga RR was destroyed by floods in 1862 before either warring army could tear it up. It was rebuilt and destroyed again before the Civil War was over.

The Confederates twice raided the Baltimore & Ohio at Martinsburg, WV. "Stonewall" Jackson's troops raided the B & O shop and engine house in 1861; they destroyed 42 locomotives and removed another 14 partially dismantled units, using horses to drag locomotives and cars along dirt roads to the Confederate-controlled Virginia Central Railroad at Staunton, VA for use in the South. The B & O was vulnerable because it had been built to the 5ft gauge.

Other railroads were destroyed to prevent their use – this, on the Union side, was General William T. Sherman's specialty; but he also exploited the railroads in his campaigns, especially his famous march to the sea. The great locomotive chase that resulted from Captain James J. Andrews and his Union raiders' capture of the Confederates' Western & Atlantic 4-4-0 *General* at Big Shanty, GA, began about 25 miles northwest of Atlanta on April 12, 1862. Confederate forces gave chase in 4-4-0 *Texas* and finally caught up when the *General* ran out of steam about 20 miles short

CP Limited

CP Limited

ABOVE SNOW WAS A NATURAL HAZARD AND A TRACK GANG IS EXTENDING A TIMBER RETAINING WALL IN ROGERS PASS, BRITISH COLUMBIA, FOLLOWING AN AVALANCHE AND ROCK FALL IN 1884.

of safety at Chattanooga, TN. Railroads were big movers of troops and the evacuation of the entire Confederate government staff from Richmond to Danville, VA on April 2, 1865, less than a week before General Robert E. Lee's surrender at Appomattox, VA was mentioned in Chapter 1.

Construction of other lines was abandoned owing to shortage of money, even though some, like the Covington & Ohio RR might have been valuable to the Confederacy. Other lines, either destroyed or abandoned, were rehabilitated by the U.S. Military Railroad, the most famous being the Nashville & Chattanooga RR, which was completely rebuilt in 1865–6 and returned to its former owners.

A look at a United States railroad map of 1870 would show a single transcontinental line and a burgeoning network of lines in the East. A 1890 map would show four main transcontinental lines plus other connecting lines and a very dense network of lines in the East and around the Great Lakes, with minor networks in Colorado and Utah.

With the original transcontinental route from Omaha, NE to Sacramento, CA completed, thoughts were

RIGHT ARRIVAL OF THE FIRST TRANSCONTINENTAL AT VANCOUVER, BC IN MAY 1887 WAS GREETED BY A LARGE CROWD. THE 4–4–0 LOCOMOTIVE IS SUITABLY DECORATED.

RIGHT A "RED LETTER DAY" FOR CANADA, SAYS THE POSTER ANNOUNCING THE OPENING OF THE RAILWAY TO THE PACIFIC OCEAN ON JUNE 28, 1886. NOTE THE DEPARTURE TIMES ARE GIVEN ALSO BY 24-HOUR CLOCK.

CP Limited

directed to the development of other routes on the basis of those proposed between 1853 and 1855. Several rail routes to the Pacific were constructed during the 1880s. The Santa Fe and Southern Pacific met at Deming, in southwestern New Mexico, in 1881 and three more routes were completed in 1883. Santa Fe now had its own route across northern New Mexico and Arizona, while Southern Pacific completed its line from New Orleans, LA to Los Angeles CA. At the same time the Northern Pacific opened its line through the Rockies from Duluth, MN to the Pacific at Portland, OR.

Competition was such that the Union Pacific also set its sights on the northwest and in 1884 it opened a route from Ogden, UT through Idaho to Portland. In Canada, also, the first trans-Canada route was opened by the Canadian Pacific in 1885.

The Dominion of Canada was created on July 1, 1867, but British Columbia did not join the other states until 1871. Canada's first railroad (mentioned briefly in Chapter 1), the Champlain & St Lawrence, opened in 1836 between the St Lawrence River and St John's, Quebec, at the head of open-water navigation on the Richelieu River which flows from Lake Champlain.

By the time British Columbia joined the Dominion in 1871 it had been promised a railroad by the Canadian government to link with the rest of the country and, other lines not being interested, the Canadian Pacific Railroad was incorporated in 1881 to build a western extension from Callander, Ontario to the Pacific at what is now the BC capital, Vancouver.

The builders of the trans-Canada railroad had to cross 1,300 miles of wilderness, 1,000 miles of prairie and 500 miles of difficult Rockies terrain. While construction of the line along the shores of Lake Superior was difficult enough, nationalistic sentiment prevented a detour through United States territory. Construction of the route over the Rockies was a formidable challenge, involving gradients of 1 in 22 (4.5 percent). The line was opened on November 7, 1885. The grades were later eased by the boring of two spiral tunnels.

Coincidentally with the line to the west, construction was also proceeding eastward to Ottawa and Montreal.

RIGHT A CANADIAN PACIFIC PASSENGER TRAIN ENTERS ONE OF THE MANY TUNNELS ON THE CANADIAN TRANSCONTINENTAL AT MYRA CANYON, BRITISH COLUMBIA.

CP Limited

By 1890 the eastern lines extended from Windsor, Ontario through Montreal, over the national frontier into Maine and onward to Saint John, New Brunswick.

The other major railroad system is the Canadian National which was formed by the merging of five major components – Intercolonial, National Transcontinental, Canadian Northern, Grand Trunk Pacific, and Grand Trunk Railroad.

Intercolonial began operations between Halifax, New Brunswick and Rivière du Loup, Quebec province, in 1876, taking in the operation of Grand Trunk's line from Rivière du Loup to the west of Levis, across the St Lawrence from the city of Quebec, in 1879. National Transcontinental was a product of the Canadian administration that took office in 1896 and its subsequent history is discussed in the next chapter. The Canadian Northern began in the 1890s when William Mackenzie and Donald Mann merged a series of other projects. Again, the events are discussed in the next chapter, as are those of the Grand Trunk Pacific.

The Grand Trunk Railroad was incorporated in 1852 and included the former Champlain & St Lawrence Railroad. By 1856 it was operating between Levis and Windsor, Ontario. Three years later it opened the

California State Railroad Museum

ABOVE EARLY PENNSYLVANIA 2–8–0 *CONSOLIDATION* – CLASS "R" OF 1895. THE 2–8–0 WHEEL ARRANGEMENT BECAME THE MOST POPULAR FOR FREIGHT IN THE UNITED STATES AND OVER 21,000 WERE BUILT FOR DOMESTIC USE.

Victoria Bridge across the St Lawrence at Montreal. The cost was so high that the GTR had to ask the Government to bear most of the cost.

When Canada became a Dominion in 1867 it was proposed to extend the Grand Trunk west to the Pacific and east to New Brunswick and Nova Scotia at public expense. Public opinion was against the proposal and in the end GTR built south to Chicago, IL, which it reached in 1880. It used the tracks of several short lines it purchased, and the Michigan lines were then connected to the rest, first by ferry and in 1890 by the St Clair Tunnel. By 1890 GTR owned a majority interest in the Boston & Maine RR and went on to expand in the first few years of the 20th century.

Mention should also be made here of Mexico. Mexico's railroads are now government-owned. The nation's first railroad to be built, and the last to be nationalized, the Ferrocarril Mexicano (FCM), was constructed between 1864 and 1873 by British interests to connect Veracruz, on the Gulf of Mexico, and Mexico City. Connection with United States railroads was discouraged by the Mexican government for a while, and as a counterpoise to FCM's monopoly, concessions or subsidies were granted to railroads prepared to construct other lines between the Gulf and the interior.

But Mexico could not afford to ignore the United States, and ultimately both the lines connecting the frontier with Mexico City were built with the aid of concessions. The principal line from El Paso, TX across the Rio Grande through Ciudad Juarez, was built by Santa Fe interests as the Mexican Central and completed in 1884. Another line from Laredo, in eastern Texas, was commenced in 1881 and built to the 3ft gauge as the Mexican National by General William Jackson Palmer, builder of the Denver & Rio Grande RR. It reached Mexico City in 1888. It later had branches in the north from Monterrey to Matamoros on the Gulf of Mexico, and, farther south, from Acámbaro to Uruapan.

Another line, the United Railroads of Yucatán (UdeY) was opened in 1881 and developed a system of narrow- and standard-gauge lines linking much of the state of Yucatán, in southeast Mexico, with its capital Mérida and with a line into the neighboring state of Campeche.

In the United States, to keep pace with the expansion of the railroads and the ever-increasing traffic, motive power had to develop also. Financial panics and the Civil War had between them reduced the number of locomotive constructors considerably; but those who

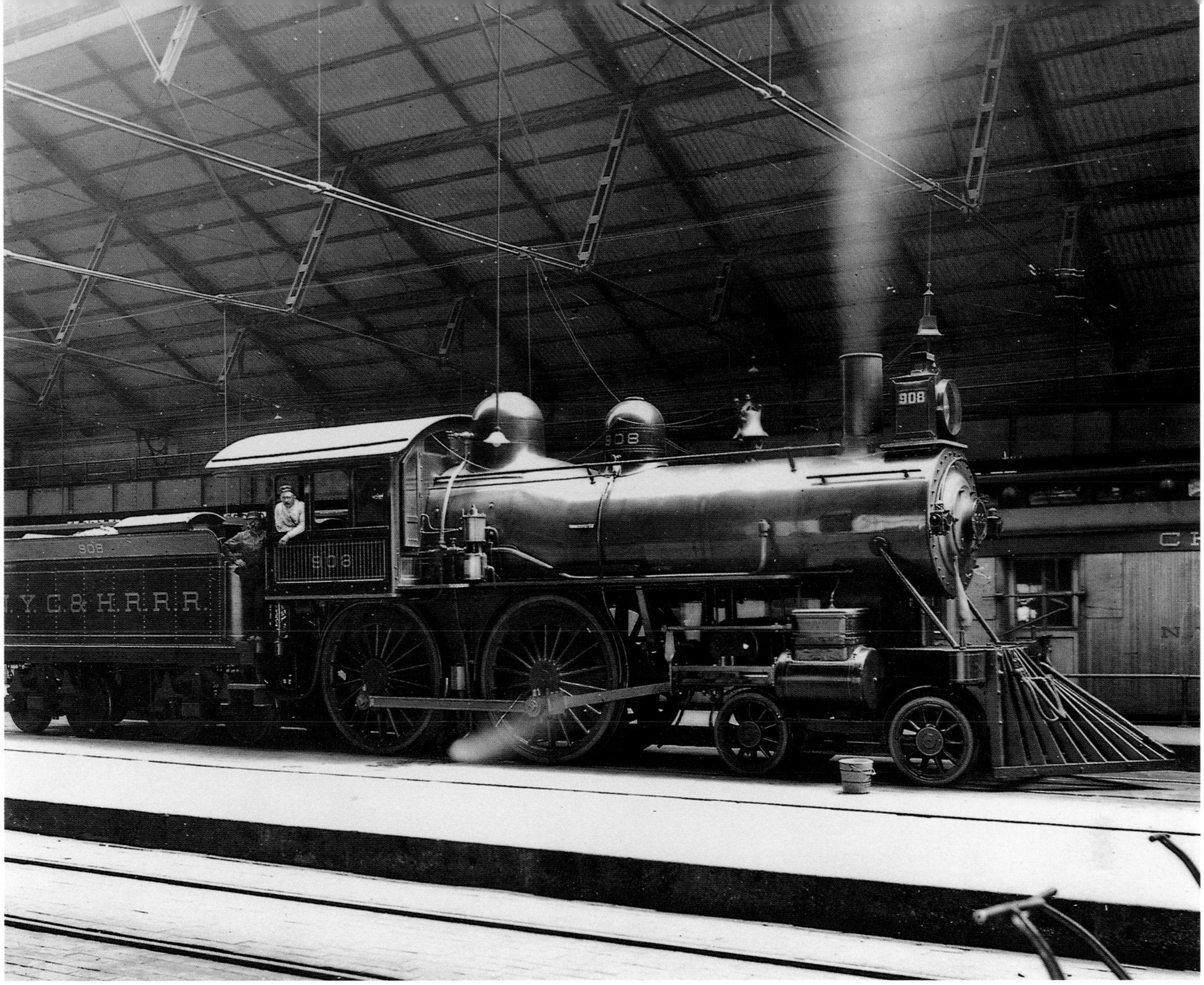

ABOVE SOME LINES HUNG ON TO THE 4–4–0 FOR PASSENGER WORK LONGER THAN OTHERS. THE NEW YORK CENTRAL RR WAS ONE BUT THEIR 1895 MODEL WAS A MORE "MODERN" LOOKING MACHINE IN KEEPING WITH THE PERIOD.

had weathered the storms were in a strong position. Some railroads, like the Pennsylvania and the Reading, were building their own locomotives and had developed design teams to produce locomotives specifically suited to their needs. There was still a number of independent builders, the two best known being Baldwin and the American Locomotive Company (ALCO). Other well-known names were: Long & Norris of Philadelphia, PA, Norris Brothers of Schenectady, NY, Sellers Brothers of Cincinnati, OH, and Eastwick & Harrison of Philadelphia, PA (and later of Aleksandrovsk, Russia).

The fundamentals of American steam locomotive design had been well established by 1870 and differed in some important respects from current European practice. Simplicity and ease of maintenance were two important principles which have always characterized American practice with, as far as possible, the use of outside cylinders. Multi-cylinder designs were never popular if they involved inside as well as outside cylinders.

In the 1860s and 1870s many strange beasts were produced in order to satisfy the operators' needs for more powerful locomotives, but in the end convention won the day. The eight-wheeler, or "American" type, was the standard passenger locomotive and was used on freight haulage until loads and gradients made the provision of more specialized types necessary. "Helpers" to assist trains over the steep gradients of the Alleghenies were built with more driving axles and, often, no carriers. Typical was James Millholland's 0-12-0 *Pennsylvania* built in 1863 in the Reading's own shops. It was intended for pusher service for coal trains on the summit between the Delaware and Schuykill rivers in eastern Pennsylvania, but it had to be rebuilt in 1870 as an 0-10-0 for better curving ability, and was then provided with a tender.

Interest was soon shown in coupled eight- and ten-wheelers of more conventional design, although the inferior tracks of the time often handicapped locomotives with long wheelbases. Alexander Mitchell, the master mechanic of the Lehigh Valley RR, drew up a design for a 2-8-0 freight locomotive. In 1865 Baldwin built it from Mitchell's drawings with some reluctance, predicting it would be a "colossal failure." Instead, the machine demonstrated its prowess by hauling a train of 100 empty coal cars weighing 340 tons up a 1 in 67 (1.5 percent) gradient near Delano, PA. To commemorate the railroad's merger with a number of feeder lines

BELOW A. J. STEVENS 4–8–0 OF THE CENTRAL PACIFIC RR NO. 229, BUILT IN SACRAMENTO SHOPS IN 1882. THESE LOCOMOTIVES WORKED TRAINS OVER THE HIGH SIERRAS AND WERE THE FIRST IN AMERICA TO HAVE POWER REVERSE.

California State Railroad Museum

which included the Beaver Meadow Railroad, the Lehigh Valley christened the locomotive *Consolidation*, which henceforward gave its name to the 2-8-0 configuration. More than 30,000 "Consolidation" workhorses were constructed in American shops for many railroads over the following 45 years.

Encouraged by his success, Mitchell in 1867 designed a 2-10-0, of which two were built by James Norris's engine works at Lancaster, PA. But the *Ant* and the *Bee*, as they were named, were handicapped by poor tracks and derailed so frequently that they were converted to 2-8-2s. Much later, in 1897, Baldwin christened some 2-8-2s for Japan's Nippon Railroad "Mikado", and this was the name by which the type was known until World War Two.

On the other side of the continent, big was also deemed to be beautiful. The Central Pacific Railroad in 1882 built a 4–8–0 locomotive, *Mastodon*, designed by their mechanical superintendent A. J. Stevens, at their Sacramento, CA shops, to cope with the steep grades of the Sierra Nevada. It was capable of hoisting a 240-ton train up a 25-mile grade with a vertical rise of 3,900 feet (an average gradient of 1 in 34, or 3 percent. Twenty more were built by Danforth-Cooke.

Encouraged by their success, in 1883 Stevens designed a 4-10-0, *El Gobernador*, which weighed 73 tons without a tender – by far the largest American locomotive at that time. But the Central Pacific's trestles had to be strengthened to accommodate it and it stood idle for a year. It turned out to be an unreliable machine and often broke down in the High Sierras.

Another type of locomotive which enjoyed popularity was the "camelback". In 1877 John E. Wootten, of the Philadelphia & Reading RR, improved the stability of a waste-anthracite-burning locomotive with its characteristically wide firebox by placing the grate above the rear drivers on a new design of 4-6-0. The cab was placed above the firebox and the fireman stoked the grate from an unprotected platform on the tender. A machine of this type was sent to Europe, but owing to restricted tunnel clearances in France and Italy the cab had to be moved forward and lowered. Thus

California State Railroad Museum

was born the camelback or "Mother Hubbard". The wide firebox became known universally as the Wootten firebox and was used worldwide.

Various designs of camelback were built, but a second, rudimentary cab had to be provided, usually mounted off the end of the firebox, to protect the fireman. The design lasted well into the 20th century and was used on some very large locomotives.

With reliable brake systems it was possible to run at higher speeds and by the late 1880s the thoughts of engineers turned to maximum speeds as high as 100 miles per hour. In order to keep piston speeds at reasonable levels, designers increased the diameters of the driving wheels. Locomotives, with these taller drivers were known as "high wheelers"; most were 4-4-0s, and a few were 4-4-2s, but all were more sophisticated than the standard "American" type. Typical high wheelers were those turned out to the designs of William Buchanan of the New York Central & Hudson River Railroad.

The most famous of New York Central's high

ABOVE ALCO 4–4–0 NO. 999 IS REPUTED TO BE THE FIRST STEAM LOCOMOTIVE TO HAVE EXCEEDED 100 MPH – ALLEGEDLY 112.5 MPH – ON THE NEW YORK CENTRAL'S *EMPIRE STATE EXPRESS*.

J.W. Swanberg Collection

ABOVE A NATURAL DEVELOPMENT OF THE 4-4-0 WAS THE 4-4-2 OR *ATLANTIC*. THIS CHICAGO, BURLINGTON & QUINCY *ATLANTIC* IS A COMPOUND ON THE VAUCLAIN SYSTEM.

wheelers was No. 999, which hauled the crack *Empire State Express.* On May 10, 1893 No. 999, with a light train, covered a measured mile of slightly downhill track west of Batavia, NY in 31.2 seconds – a speed of 112.5 mph. This was claimed as a record but was later the subject of much controversy. Nonetheless, No. 999's 80-inch drivers and 24-inch piston travel undoubtedly gave it the potential for very high speeds.

A pair of Baldwin 4-4-2 camelbacks built for the Atlantic City Railroad in 1896 regularly ran the 55.3 miles between Atlantic City and Camden, NJ at an average start-to-stop speed of 70 mph and could develop 1,450 horsepower at that speed.

The advance of technology was nowhere more widely evident than in motive power. Towards the end of the 19th century the steam locomotive was climbing rapidly out of the form from which it had first developed. It was growing in size following the introduction of continuous train brakes and stronger couplings, which enabled much longer and heavier trains to be operated. This in turn led to the need for more powerful "pusher" locomotives on the long, steep grades of, in the East, the Alleghenies and, in the West, the Sierra Nevada, the Rockies and their outliers.

In freight and pusher service, the greater the number of driving wheels the better was the traction; and, as speeds were of necessity low, small wheels gave high pulling power. On the other hand, passenger-train speeds were becoming ever higher and loads much less, so that large driving wheels were the order of the day. Some high wheelers had drivers as tall as 86 inches. But it was the details which were improved – to reduce maintenance, increase power output, reduce fuel consumption, and so on. The external appearance of locomotives was changing, too, with the advent of larger-diameter boilers.

American locomotives could be built big because the physical dimensions of the early railroads were not inhibited by tunnels and bridges to anything like the extent they were in Europe, and in Britain in particular. There is little doubt that Russian railroads were strongly influenced by American engineers and built locomotives of much the same dimensions, and their choice of the 5ft gauge was probably no coincidence.

Be that as it may, by the end of the 19th century locomotives in the United States were rapidly increasing in size and power. Ten driving axles became popular for freight locomotives, particularly pushers: while, for passenger trains, the ten-wheeler locomotive replaced the eight-wheeler. The 4-4-2, or "Atlantic", was popular as the addition of the trailing axle permitted a wide firebox of the Wootten type and a correspondingly larger boiler. By the turn of the century the salient characteristics of the American steam locomotive were established and used to the full.

As locomotives grew bigger, so the consumption of fuel and water increased. There had always been a plentiful supply of fuel, first wood and later coal. The United States had huge reserves of coal and little thought was given to possible alternative locomotive fuels in the 19th century. The first regular use of oil as a fuel for locomotives seems to have been in Russia in 1882, when Thomas Urquhart, superintendent of the Grazi Czaritzin Railroad, developed a system and by 1885, 143 oil-burning engines had been fitted.

American engineers kept an eye on developments in Europe and those features which were considered to be suitable for American conditions were tried or adapted and developed for their particular needs. For example,

BELOW THESE 1895 ELECTRIC LOCOMOTIVES WERE USED IN PAIRS TO HAUL TRAINS OVER THREE MILES THROUGH THE TUNNELS UNDER BALTIMORE WHICH INCLUDED THE WAVERLEY AND CAMDEN STATIONS. CURRENT AT 600 V DC WAS DRAWN FROM AN OVERHEAD RAIL AS WELL AS COLLECTOR SHOES FROM A "THIRD" RAIL.

B & O Railroad Museum

California State Railroad Museum

valves for the distribution of steam in the cylinders had always presented problems with lubrication and wear. Piston valves were introduced successfully on the North Eastern Railway in England in 1887 and were used in the United States by 1898.

The growing size of locomotives meant more coal and water had to be carried if more frequent or longer water-replenishment and refuelling stops were not to cancel out any gains in speed made possible by increases in power. In Europe fuel economy for other reasons had led to experimenting with compound expansion, in which steam was fed to one or more cylinders at boiler pressure, and then exhausted to another cylinder or cylinders for further expansion. Theoretically, steam exhausted from one cylinder at about half boiler pressure could exert the same force on another piston of twice the surface area.

In 1889, 33-year old Samuel M. Vauclain was General Manager of the Baldwin Locomotive Works – his father had been one of those who built the *Old Ironside*. He invented the "tandem compound" system which used high- and low-pressure cylinders mounted one behind the other. By 1893 he had refined the system sufficiently for the Atchison, Topeka & Santa Fe RR to take delivery of the first of an order for 86 successful 2-10-2s.

Other types of compounding were developed, probably the most successful being that of Alfred de Glehn in France, first used in 1886. His system employed four cylinders, two outside the frames at high pressure and the two low-pressure cylinders between the frames. Two similar systems were developed in the United States, one by Vauclain and another by Francis J. Pitkin of the American Locomotive Company. They both claimed savings of up to 20 percent in fuel.

ABOVE BRIDGE WITH AUTOMATIC SIGNALS NEAR 16TH STREET STATION, OAKLAND, CALIFORNIA ON THE CENTRAL PACIFIC RR C.1903, SHOWING THE FIRST TRAIN TO PASS.

RIGHT A MAP OF AMERICAN RAILROADS IN THE 1890S. COMPARISON WITH THE MAP ON PAGES 40/41 SHOWS THE RAPID EXPANSION THAT HAD TAKEN PLACE IN JUST 30 YEARS.

Meanwhile, other engineers were showing interest in the possible use of electric traction, particularly on mountain lines with long tunnels and on other lines with tunnels within city limits, where smoke from steam locomotives could prove a health and safety hazard.

One of the best-known of the early interurban lines was the Chicago, North Shore & Milwaukee RR. Beginning in 1891 as the Waukegan & North Shore Rapid Transit Co., a trolley line for the city of Waukegan, 36 miles north of Chicago, IL, it was extended south to Lake Bluff and became the CNS & M Electric RR when it was extended farther to Chicago.

1895 saw the first haulage by electric locomotives of main line trains on standard gauge. The Baltimore & Ohio RR tunneled under the city of Baltimore and the sections between the Waverley and Camden stations – a distance of about 3½ miles – were electrified by the Westinghouse Electric Company in 1895 to eliminate the smoke nuisance created by steam locomotives. At first a conventional train including a coke-burning locomotive with steam shut off and the valve gear in mid-gear, was hauled by pairs of Bo+Bo electric motors through the tunnel sections.

This was the forerunner of the Baltimore Belt System. The electrification was at 600V dc on the overhead system. Because of the high current demand, instead of a contact wire, an overhead rail supported from insulators was provided and current was collected by a pantograph arm with a shoe which ran along the rail. The locomotives were of the "steeple-cab" type with four gearless traction motors. This pick-up system was later replaced by a third rail.

This properly brings us to the end of the 19th century. Railroads were firmly established and travel by train could now be accomplished in reasonable comfort from the Atlantic to the Pacific in under six days!

CHAPTER THREE

CONSOLIDATION

The first three decades of the 20th century saw consolidation rather than expansion, although some new railroads were built. Railroads were being extended, merged, taken over, leased and otherwise changed by control or sale. The industrialized northeast had a dense network of large and small roads which had multiplied faster than anywhere else, although roads in some other regions were catching up rapidly. The railroads were the most important single factor in the development of modern America.

As large railroad corporations grew and became more powerful it suited them either to acquire smaller roads or to squeeze them out of business. Many had serious financial problems and were glad to be rescued by more prosperous concerns.

In 1901 The Baltimore & Ohio, the oldest U.S. railroad, had a large slice of its stock acquired by Pennsylvania RR and Leonor F. Loree was installed as president. He immediately commenced a large program of route improvement which included reducing grades and curves and doubling many miles of track. He also secured a large interest in the Reading RR, which in turn brought in the Central Railroad of New Jersey, already under Reading control. The Central passed fully into control by the Pennsylvania after a few years.

In 1910 Daniel Willard became President of the B & O. In the same year B & O acquired the Chicago Terminal Transfer Railroad, which was retitled the Baltimore & Ohio Chicago Transfer Railroad. Further acquisitions extended the B & O's area of operation from New York City in the east to Chicago in the north, and St Louis, MO in the west. By 1929 B & O operated 5,658 miles of railroad and owned 2,364 locomotives.

CP Limited

As traffic grew it became necessary to review many of the routes. The west and east had been connected by the completion of the transcontinental lines. Financial problems had affected the fortunes of both the Southern and Union Pacific and it became necessary to improve the transcontinental tracks to take heavier trains. Railroads had grown not only in stature and mileage operated: traffic potential was also giving rise to physical growth. Early tracks and trains had been small and relatively light, but by the turn of the century the sheer volume of traffic meant that permanent way and bridges (particularly trestles) needed strengthening, many curves needed straightening and gradients easing. In other words, new alignments, cut-offs and even abandonment of some parts of routes were necessary.

A prime example is the original transcontinental route completed in 1869. It was soon found that little revenue was generated by through traffic from the east. Local traffic produced much of the revenue, which was in itself modest as development of the country was slow

ABOVE SIR WILLIAM VAN HORNE WAS THE DRIVING FORCE BEHIND THE TRANS-CANADA RAILWAY AND BECAME PRESIDENT OF CANADIAN PACIFIC IN 1888.

St. Louis Mercantile Museum

LEFT IN THE EARLY 1900S THERE WERE MANY ROUTE IMPROVEMENTS. THE REINFORCED CONCRETE TUNKHANNOCK VIADUCT, 2375 FEET LONG AND 240 FEET HIGH IS AT NICHOLSON, PA ON THE DELAWARE, LACKAWANNA & WESTERN RR.

BELOW THE LUCIN CUT-OFF OVER PART OF THE GREAT SALT LAKE BETWEEN OGDEN, UTAH, AND LUCIN WAS BUILT BY THE SOUTHERN PACIFIC RR. A TRESTLE WAS CONSTRUCTED AND THEN INFILLED AS SHOWN IN THIS PICTURE.

California State Railroad Museum

Union Pacific Railroad

ABOVE 50 YEARS AFTER THE COMPLETION OF THE LUCIN CUT-OFF, STREAMLINER *CITY OF SAN FRANCISCO* OF THE CNW AND UNION PACIFIC RR LEAVES THE LUCIN CUT-OFF OVER THE GREAT SALT LAKE. THE TRAIN IS COMPOSED OF HEAVYWEIGHT CARS FITTED WITH THE LATEST AIRBRAKE EQUIPMENT.

at first. The railroad starved and passed into the hands of the receivers. Then Edward H. Harriman took the transcontinental in hand and used extraordinary energy to make it pay.

Thirty years after it was completed the Union Pacific and Southern Pacific had to pay a huge price for the speed and cheapness of the original work. As early as 1869 a federal commission had criticized the location and route of the Central Pacific in the Sierra Nevada thus:

> "The curvature was excessive and needlessly sharp. Throughout a large portion the ascents and descents had been multiplied needlessly. Grades of 70 to 80 feet per mile (1.3 percent to 1.5 percent) had been introduced where one of 53 feet per mile (1.0 percent) would have sufficed, and grades of 53 feet per mile where one half that rate of ascent was required. In the Humboldt Valley, between Lake Humboldt and Humboldt Wells, the difference in elevation of a little over 1,100 feet had been overcome by ascents and descents amounting to 6,232 feet in a distance of 290 miles."

In fairness, it should be remembered that the track in question was completed seven years ahead of the original estimate and at the time of construction facilities were very crude compared with 30 years later. History also maintains that "A good deal of improvement was purposely left to the future, when traffic developments should justify the expense."

By 1900 these "developments" had made the task of reconstruction and improvement essential and they had to be put in hand. This involved tearing up and replacing much of the old track, abandoning some

RIGHT TIMBER TRESTLES WERE REPLACED BY STEEL STRUCTURES. THIS ONE IS THE LONG RAVERE VIADUCT OVER BLUE CANYON, CALIFORNIA PHOTOGRAPHED IN 1912/4 WHEN A SECOND TRACK HAD BEEN ADDED.

California State Railroad Museum

sections altogether to construct new, additional tunneling to ease gradients and curvature, and replacement of wooden trestles by steel bridges.

The original line between Summit, in west Omaha, and Lane covered 21 miles for a "bee-line" of 12 miles. The Omaha Cut-off which replaced it, runs in a straight line over rugged, rolling and partly unstable ground. To keep it as level as possible construction involved excavating 2.8 million cubic yards and filling about 4.0 million cubic yards of embankment. At one point the embankment is 65 feet high, just over a mile (5,600 feet) long and required some 1.5 million cubic yards of soil. Another fill, across Little Papillon, took the track 89 feet above the floor of the valley and was 3,100 feet long.

Perhaps the best known rerouting project is the Salt Lake, or Lucin, cut-off across the Great Salt Lake, UT, completed in 1904. This saved 43.5 miles over the original line round the northern end of the lake which was heavily graded with many curves. Unfortunately for history it removed the track from the original point connecting east and west at Promontory Summit, about 30 miles west of Brigham City, where there is now a commemorative museum. The actual meeting place is designated the Golden Spike National Historical Site. The original line was abandoned and the rails lifted only in 1942.

California State Railroad Museum

ABOVE Steam Rotary Snow Plow clearing snow in the High Sierras on the Central Pacific RR. These were and still are vital in keeping the mountain lines open.

From Sacramento, CA eastward the line had to climb the western flank of the Sierra Nevada and from Roseville the climb was 7,000 feet in 140 miles to Donner Pass, about 30 miles west of the Nevada state line. Bridges were strengthened and track realigned to ease gradients and curvature. The ruling gradient was eased to 1 in 42 (2.4 percent), although there were still some sections as steep as 1 in 38 (2.63 percent). Protection of the track from the avalanches needed a total of 40 miles of snow sheds and 39 tunnels. Track was relaid to take the heavier rolling stock which Edward Harriman's revitalization program necessitated.

The transcontinental changed the nature of the country through which it passed and helped open up the West. In less than 30 years Omaha became the third largest packing station for meat products in the country; Fremont, 30 miles northwest of Omaha, grew from nothing into a thriving city; the prairie became a great agricultural region as well as an exporter of livestock and minerals; Lexington, on the Platte River, grew on the site where South Cheyenne Indians had in 1867 burned a freight train; Laramie, WY became a mining center with railroad workshops; and, some 200 miles to the west, Green River, WY became the junction for the northward route, via Idaho, to Portland, OR and Seattle and Spokane, WA.

In the east, the competition for passengers between the major cities was intense, nowhere more so than between New York City and Chicago. Publicity-conscious railroads introduced named luxury trains, and the ideal of "Chicago in 24 Hours" from New York City was soon bettered. The New York Central had its *Empire State Express* and the Pennsylvania had the *Pennsylvania Limited.* The Vanderbilts controlled the New York Central and the President of the Pennsylvania was

Union Pacific Railroad

ABOVE SNOW, THE ENEMY OF TRANSPORT, BEING CLEARED QUICKLY AND EFFECTIVELY BY A STEAM SNOW-PLOW ON THE UNION PACIFIC YELLOWSTONE BRANCH IN MARCH, 1961.

Alexander J. Cassatt. To say there was considerable rivalry between them is an understatement, but fortunately they confined their hostility to undercutting each other on rates and rival services.

The New York Central & Hudson River and its ally, the Lake Shore & Michigan Southern, operated the Water Level Route, so called because it ran for the most part in sight of water (notably the Hudson River) and was therefore relatively easily graded. Its route mileage between the two cities was 961. The rival "mountain" route of the Pennsylvania Railroad negotiated 1 in 50 (2 percent) grades and climbed to 2,193 feet across the Alleghenies, but it had a shorter route mileage of 912 (and, moreover, called at Philadelphia, PA on the way). An overall average speed of 40 mph does not seem much by today's standards but was very creditable in the last few years of the 19th century. Stops en route were necessary as locomotives had to be changed, water replenished and attention given to train-service requirements.

In New York City the two railroads had separate stations: the New York Central had its Grand Central Terminal (remodeled and enlarged in 1900) in Manhattan, but the Pennsylvania's terminal was across the Hudson at Exchange Place, Jersey City. They shared the same terminal in Chicago, in La Salle Street. The rivalry became intense when, in 1902, the New York Central introduced a new luxury train and called it *The Twentieth Century Limited* which cut the time between the two cities to 20 hours – an average of 48 mph.

The inaugural train on June 15, 1902 consisted of only five timber-bodied cars – two sleepers, a diner, a buffet car and an end-platform observation car. It was hauled by a high-wheeler of the same type as the speed-record holder, No. 999 (which resides today in

Railroad Museum of Pennsylvania

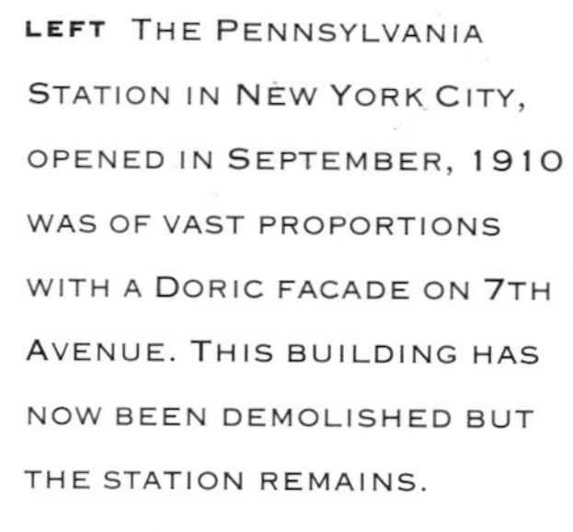

St. Louis Mercantile Museum

LEFT THE PENNSYLVANIA STATION IN NEW YORK CITY, OPENED IN SEPTEMBER, 1910 WAS OF VAST PROPORTIONS WITH A DORIC FACADE ON 7TH AVENUE. THIS BUILDING HAS NOW BEEN DEMOLISHED BUT THE STATION REMAINS.

ABOVE THE VAST PENNSYLVANIA STATION IN NEW YORK CITY, OPENED IN SEPTEMBER, 1910, HANDLED A HALF-MILLION PASSENGERS A DAY AND THIS IS A TYPICAL RUSH-HOUR SCENE.

the Chicago Museum of Science and Industry). On the day *The Twentieth Century Limited* was inaugurated it was challenged by the Pennsylvania, which inaugurated the *Pennsylvania Special*, running its 912 miles also in 20 hours – an average of 45.6 mph.

While both trains left New York City from different stations in different directions, sharing the same station in Chicago caused the most rivalry. As they both departed from La Salle Street at the same time (12.40 pm) for the journey to New York on parallel tracks, there was usually a race for the first few miles to Gary, IN.

So successful were these trains that patronage grew quickly and by 1903 two trains for each road were often necessary. Special rolling stock was built and in 1903 steel cars were introduced – and up-graded at regular intervals as one railroad stole a march on the other. Trains became longer and heavier, so larger steam locomotives were soon required, and more will be said about this later in the chapter.

The New York Central terminal in Manhattan was approached by tunnel. Some 700 daily trains in and out of Grand Central produced considerable smoke nuisance and by the early 1900s it had given rise to serious concern. This was compounded in 1902 by a serious accident in the approach tunnel when a train overran a stop signal obscured by smoke and 15 people were killed. In 1903 the New York legislature passed a law prohibiting the use of "smoking locomotives" south of the Harlem River (effectively south of 125th Street) after July 1, 1908. The railroad had to act or it would be barred from its prestigious and conveniently located Manhattan terminal. It chose electrification.

The B & O had earlier used electric locomotives in its tunnels under the city of Baltimore. The New Haven RR had electrified some of its Connecticut branch lines on the third rail system at 600V dc, and this was the system chosen for the lines into Grand Central.

A total of 35 electric locomotives were built by the American Locomotive Company (ALCO) and General Electric and delivered in 1906, and electric haulage was introduced in 1907, the change-over point being Wakefield. In 1913 electrification was extended to Harmon, some 33 miles from New York City on the east side of the Hudson River, where steam locomotives were exchanged for electric and vice versa, and where a large locomotive depot was built. The New Haven RR, which shared Grand Central Terminal, had a change-over point, also on the east side of the river, a couple of miles away at Croton. Electric multiple-unit cars were introduced on local services.

Pennsylvania's terminal being in Jersey City meant that travelers to New York City had to complete their journey by ferry. In 1900 the "Pennsy" acquired the Long Island RR, and, after a study of possibilities for bridges and tunnels, it began construction in 1904 of Pennsylvania Station on Manhattan Island. Sited between Seventh and Eighth Avenues and 31st and 33rd Streets, it was in a good position. A twin tunnel was constructed under the Hudson and four single tunnels under the East River which, together with a double-track main line across the Hackensack Meadows, connected the new terminal to its road east of Newark, NJ. All these lines were electrified, again on the 600V dc third rail system. The new Pennsylvania Station was opened in 1910 and electric haulage in and out of the terminal commenced, steam locomotives being changed for electric and vice versa at a station called Manhattan Transfer, where it was also possible to make cross-platform interchange with the Hudson subways.

On November 24, 1912 the *Pennsylvania Special* was renamed *Broadway Limited*. The name was coined not to honor the entertainment industry but in recognition of the fact that much of the route between New York and Chicago was quadruple track – a subtlety probably lost on most travelers! Both roads had to introduce steel

BELOW NEW YORK CENTRAL 600 V DC THIRD RAIL 2Do2 ELECTRIC LOCOMOTIVE OF 1906 AT THE HARMON CHANGE-OVER POINT DEPOT IN 1966. NOTE THE SMALL PANTOGRAPHS FOR BRIDGING GAPS IN THE CONDUCTOR RAIL SYSTEM.

J.W. Swanberg Collection

In 1900 the situation on the nation's railroads was as follows:

Miles of single track	192,556
Miles of auxiliary track	14,074
Miles of sidings	52,154
Total	258,784
Locomotives	37,663
Passenger cars	34,713
Freight cars	1,365,531

("Auxiliary tracks" refers to lengths of double line, passing loops, etc, and indicates the increased volume of traffic over some routes.)

BELOW A LARGE *MOGUL* HAULS A LONG COAL TRAIN ON THE PENNSYLVANIA RR.

Railroad Museum of Pennsylvania

rolling stock as all timber cars were banned from using the tunnels.

For the railroads generally the mere fact that competition was so great had a side effect. The struggle for traffic forced down rates to a point where none but the strongest roads could earn a profit. Although there were agreements to maintain rates, these were just pieces of paper and there was practically no limit to the rebates extorted by the shippers and their agents under threat of diverting traffic to other carriers. There was discrimination and undue preference in the most insidious and corrupting form. While many large industries prospered by these practices, the railways suffered proportionately.

In the 10 years to 1900 the number of freight cars had increased by 64.5 percent and locomotives by only 29.5 percent, indicating better utilization as well as increased locomotive haulage capacity. Passenger cars too had increased but by a smaller figure than freight cars, 41.2 percent. The figures indicate the intensive development which had been characteristic of American railroads over the decade. The demand for increased transport along established lines encouraged the laying of double tracks. There was considerable investment in improving facilities, easing gradients, and realigning routes, which was made possible largely by reducing or withholding dividends to stockholders.

Earnings from both passenger traffic and freight were low and attempts by the carriers to increase these rates to compensate for mounting expenses in 1900 brought forth more protests to the ICC and to Congress. The so-called Elkins Amendment to the Commerce Act strengthened its provisions, forbidding special rates, rebates, or other devices granting undue preference to any individual or species of traffic. In addition, the publication of tariffs was made obligatory and any practice on the part of carriers to transport any article at a lower rate than that named in the tariffs was prohibited under severe penalty.

While Senator Elkins gave his name to the legislation, it was in fact a joint effort on the part of railway

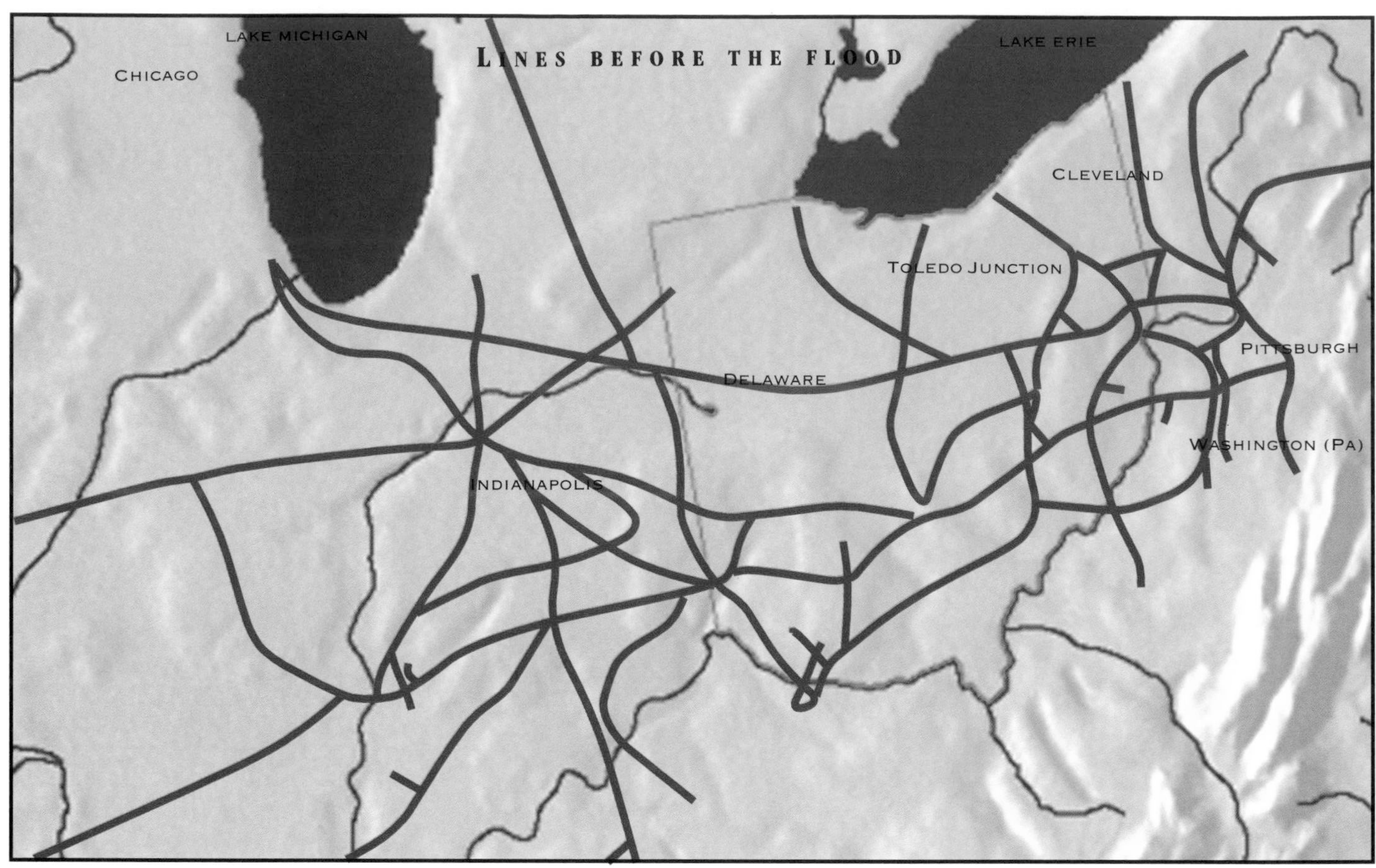

executives under the leadership of President Cassatt of the Pennsylvania Railroad to root out the demoralizing and destructive practices of unscrupulous corporations, which threatened to disgrace the entire transportation system and led it into financial disaster.

In 1906 the ICC finally got what it wanted. On June 20 Congress approved the Hepburn Bill which gave it authority to prescribe rates in place of those which, after complaint and hearing, it pronounced unjust, unreasonable or discriminating. Even so, in 1907, although the railroad managers had accepted the act in good faith, little progress had been made in implementing its provisions, and suits were filed questioning the right of Congress to delegate to any tribunal the authority to establish an interstate rate.

It was not until 1910 that the position was finally clarified, and the Commission received almost absolute authority over the rate-making phase of railroad management. Not only was it authorized to suspend rate increases until the circumstances had been investigated but the act imposed the burden of proof on carriers to justify any proposed rate advances. The immediate effect of this was to put the brakes on expansion and construction. The mileage in the six years following the passing of the act showed a drop of 34 percent compared to the six years before. Receipts from freight dropped by $30 million a year.

The effects of stringent regulation were not the only things to affect the railroads. For the fifth time in eight decades they were again caught in the middle of financial panic in the fall of 1907. In the very heyday of their usefulness the railroads found themselves in a situation which lost them $300 million, or over 11 percent of earnings in one calender year. Prompt and drastic retrenchment was essential which reduced the payroll by nearly 18 percent in 1908. The recovery of the national economy and the railroads from this panic was not complete until 1910.

Space has been devoted to this particular period because the effects of this stringent regulation on railroads had a lasting effect on their fortunes. Although the first three decades of the century saw many changes in the railroads of the U.S., the regulations, together with natural disasters, a world war and somewhat bridled government resulted in many financial failures, mergers, buyouts, etc.

Natural disasters are nothing new to many citizens of the United States of America. From their inception American railroads have had to face storms in all seasons and floods in the spring from the melting of accumulations of winter snow. Many lines followed water courses with tracks often only a few feet above normal high water levels, and others endured washouts and destruction by torrential rain in hills and mountains. Lines west of the Mississippi follow or cross many rivers which turn into rushing torrents from time to time,

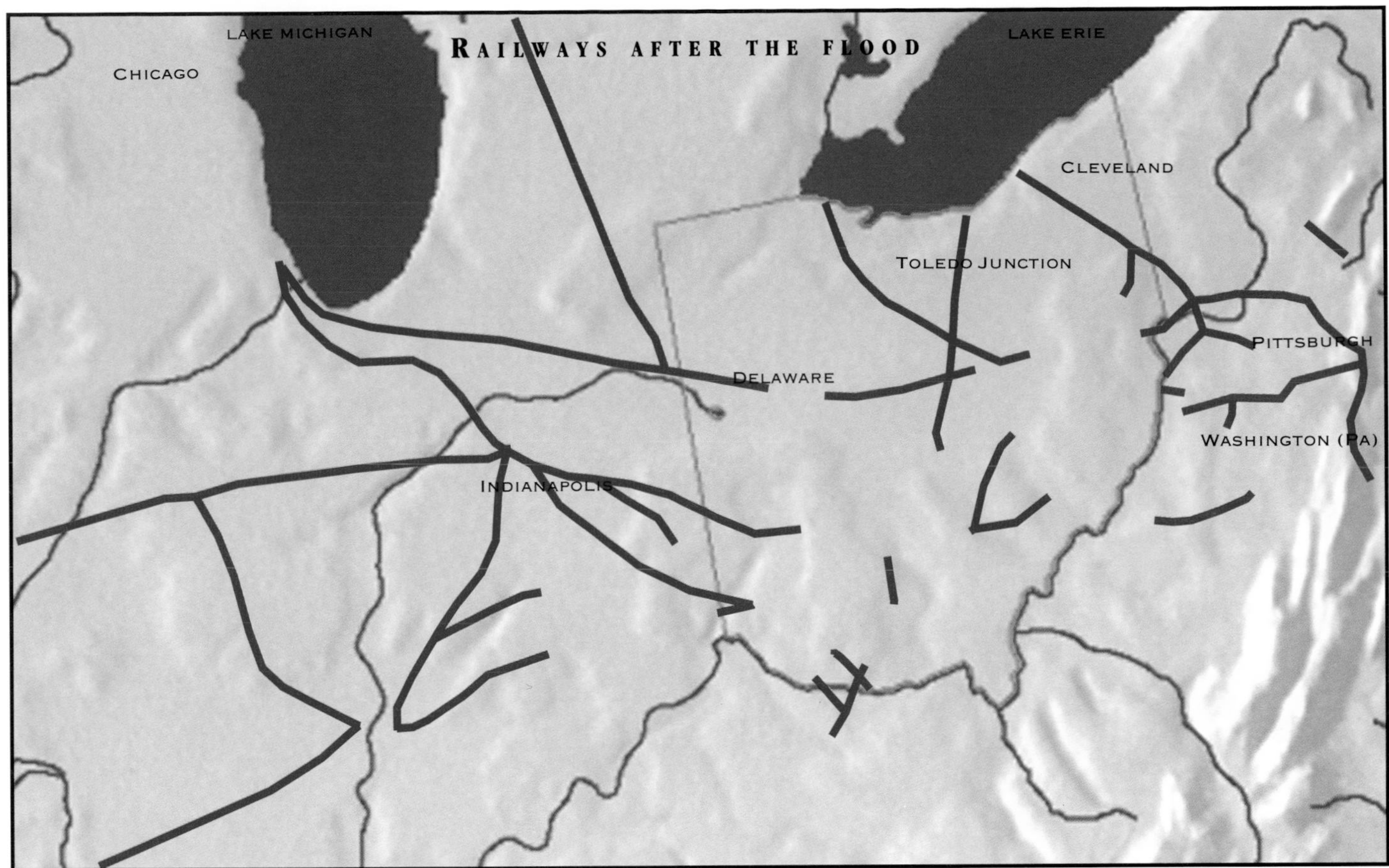

irrespective of season. The Mississippi itself has been responsible for much railroad destruction.

The San Francisco earthquake of 1906 devastated the city. The railroads suffered also but not so seriously, and they played a significant role in the rescue work. On the first day of the disaster railroads brought in food from Los Angeles by special fast freight, and moved 1,073 car loads of refugees into the countryside. Between April 18 and May 23 Union Pacific and Southern Pacific together brought in 1,603 car loads of supplies and carried out 224,069 refugees, absorbing costs which amounted to over $1 million.

Slason Thompson wrote: "The bears of the stock exchange in New York did not fail to take note of the calamity. The psychological tremor that struck San Francisco was felt across the continent and shook more than $1 billion of market value out of railroad securities. Between April 17 and May 20 the shares of the leading companies sold off all the way from 6 to 48 points. Industrial stocks showed their sympathetic sensitiveness to anything affecting the railways by even greater losses." *Short History of American Railways*, 1925.

As willing rescuers, railroads have played their part in first aid to the injured in every state in the Union and have mostly been taken for granted. Another illustration is the way Southern Pacific saved the Imperial Valley after the floods of 1905.

Briefly, Imperial Valley today is the name by which a

LEFT AND ABOVE MAPS SHOWING THE LINES IN THE STATE OF OHIO (LEFT) IN 1913, AND (RIGHT) AFTER THE FLOODS OF MARCH 1913.

rich section of southern California is known, famed for its glorious climate and golden harvests, both agricultural and mineral. It is a depression in the earth's surface about 100 miles long and 35 miles wide, once covered by water to a depth of 300 feet at its deepest part. It originally formed part of the Gulf of California, but in time the Colorado River built up a barrier of silt and left the upper stretch a great salt lake. Slowly the water evaporated and an arid basin called the Salton Sink was left. There is geological evidence that from time to time in past ages the Colorado River broke through the barrier and the process which formed the Sink was repeated over and over again.

In 1902 a canal was dug from the Colorado River at Pilot Knob, opposite Yuma, AZ. The Sink was renamed the Imperial Valley and 400 miles of ditches were dug to irrigate 100,000 acres of land. The railway, a branch of the Southern Pacific, came in 1904 bringing with it more than 10,000 settlers, and numerous townships were established. The capacity of the canals and ditches was quadrupled and by the beginning of 1905, 120,000 acres of reclaimed land were under cultivation. The soil was so rich that it would produce almost anything. The

FIG. 2-3 DETROIT RIVER TUNNEL LOCOMOTIVE

A.S.M.E

ABOVE TO HAUL TRAINS THROUGH THE NEW YORK CENTRAL RR'S DETROIT RIVER TUNNEL, OPENED IN 1910, GENERAL ELECTRIC BUILT SIX OF THESE 600 V THIRD RAIL DC BO-BO ELECTRIC LOCOMOTIVES.

air of the valley was so dry men could work in a shade temperature of 120°F without exhaustion.

Nobody seems to have realized that the bottom of the valley was far below the level of the Pacific Ocean. In 1904 silt from the Colorado River clogged up the canal and the California Development Company cut a new intake from the river but failed to provide head-gate control. In February 1905 it flooded, but not seriously. A second flood followed shortly afterwards, and in March the volume of water, increased by the rapid melting of snow, enlarged the size of the intake. The breach increased in size so rapidly that no amount of plugging by piles, brushwood, and sandbags was of any use. Water flowed into the valley through a breach 100 feet wide at the rate of 90,000 cubic feet a second: a new Salton Sea was forming.

The full story of the rescue operation mounted by the Southern Pacific is long but suffice it to say the railroad poured in a great deal of money and resources to a successful final conclusion as remarkable in its way as its operations during the San Francisco earthquake. The Southern Pacific spent $3.1 million on rescuing Imperial Valley and although Congress was urged by both President Theodore Roosevelt and his successor William Howard Taft to reimburse the claim in some measure "for coming to the rescue of the Government at the instance of President Roosevelt in a great emergency," as Taft put it, the claim was never honored. The Senate House Committee on Claims in January 1911 reported a bill appropriating $773,000, but it was not taken any further. In 1916 it was claimed that the farmers in the Imperial Valley expected to earn a sum equivalent to the interest on $500 million!

ABOVE BROAD STREET STATION, PHILADELPHIA, IS ONE OF MANY NOBLE STATIONS. THIS VIEW OF THE TRAIN SHED WAS AT ABOUT THE TIME OF ELECTRIFICATION IN 1915.

Railroad Museum of Pennsylvania

To quote Slason Thompson again: "In this splendid piece of rescue work the Southern Pacific simply added to the long list of sacrifices American railroads have made for the communities they serve only to experience the traditional ingratitude of republics."

This is but one instance of a natural disaster seriously damaging to railroads. Another disaster befell the cities, towns and villages in the state of Ohio in March 1913. Floods covered an area of about 315 square miles, with Columbus at its center, when between seven and eight inches of rain fell in four days following wind damage which had already disrupted telegraph and telephone communication. The Pennsylvania Railroad probably suffered most, but other railroads also affected were the New York Central, "Big Four," Erie, Baltimore & Ohio, Hocking Valley, Wabash and other small roads serving the flooded area. This time the direct money loss was estimated at $300 million.

But enough of disasters. To turn now to achievements, the New York Central in 1906 began construction of a tunnel to replace the ferry which for long had been its only way to take trains from Detroit, MI across the Detroit River into Windsor, Ontario. The river is over half a mile wide and in places 50 feet deep with an uneven bottom and a 2 mph current. To avoid steep approach gradients it was decided to construct a tubular tunnel on the river bed rather than a bored tunnel beneath it.

In order to provide a graded bed for the tubes the river was dredged at that point to a depth 74 feet below the lowest surface level. Sections of tube 260 feet long were constructed five miles up stream, loaded on pontoons which were launched sideways, and floated down river to be sunk into position. Supreme accuracy was essential so that sections could be placed and joined to form a continuous tunnel. The internal

St. Louis Mercantile Museum

ABOVE THE 1890S SAW MANY LARGE PASSENGER STATIONS BUILT, AND THIS PICTURE IS OF THE GRAND OPENING OF THE ST. LOUIS UNION STATION ON SEPTEMBER 1, 1894.

diameter of each concrete-lined tube was 23ft 4in, and they were encased in concrete so as to form in cross-section a solid rectangle, the function of which was to completely exclude water.

The tunnel opened on October 16, 1910 and, together with the approaches, measured 2.4 miles in length. To avoid smoke and ventilation problems, trains were hauled through the tunnel between Detroit and Windsor by electric locomotives operating from 600V dc third rails. Six were delivered initially in 1909 from General Electric, which was responsible for the whole scheme. As far as is known, the tunnel has never developed any structural defects.

The new (1910) Pennsylvania Station in New York City has been described as contributing to the monumental edifices of the world. The part visible from the streets was of classical proportions, but the work of reaching Manhattan began across the Hudson at Harrison, in the New Jersey hinterland. The double-track Hudson River tunnels were built at a depth of 97 feet below mean water level, but the line emerged at Manhattan's 10th Avenue to enter the main terminal building. The tracks were about 9 feet below mean water level at the highest point. For the Long Island Line trains there were four tunnels under the East River which emerged on the Long Island shore in Queens.

St. Louis Mercantile Museum

ABOVE THIS PHOTOGRAPH OF ST. LOUIS UNION STATION SHOWS THE GENERAL LAYOUT. ON THE RIGHT ARE WELLS FARGO AND AMERICAN EXPRESS BUILDINGS WHILE ON THE LEFT IS THE POWER HOUSE TOPPED BY THE SIGNAL TOWER.

RIGHT THE TYPE OF TRACK LAYOUT OF ST. LOUIS UNION STATION WAS REPEATED IN A NUMBER OF CITIES WHERE FREIGHT LINES BY-PASSED THE PASSENGER TERMINAL.

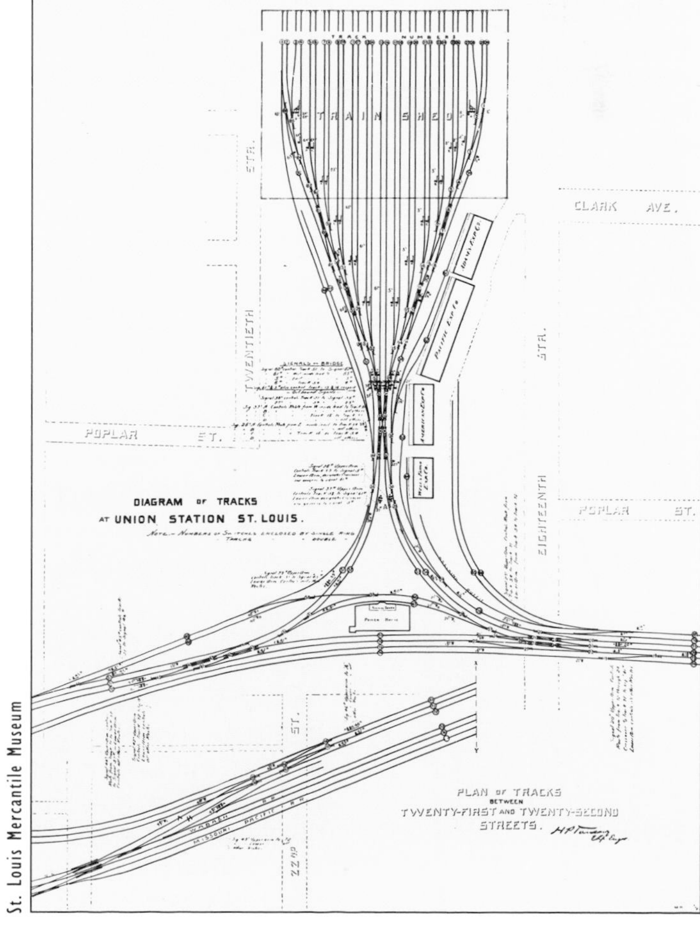

St. Louis Mercantile Museum

The station and yard covered an area of 28 acres with 16 miles of tracks with siding space for 386 cars. There were 21 standing tracks in the station and eleven island platforms. The capacity of the tunnels feeding the station has been estimated at 144 trains per hour. The station was opened to traffic in September 1910, nine years after the franchise was granted by the City of New York. It was demolished in 1966.

Pennsylvania Station was one of a number of great stations built in that era. On June 4, 1911 the Chicago & North Western opened its new station in Chicago on Madison Street and Canal and Clinton Streets, moving its passenger services from the old Wells and Kinzie Street site on the north side to the west side of the City. The total was $23.75 million.

Twelve railway systems united to provide Kansas City Union Station and the list includes all those railroads entering Kansas City in 1906. When the scheme was

J.W. Swanberg Collection

ABOVE THE APPROACH TO SOUTH STREET, BOSTON, MA., SHOWING THE TWO LARGE SIGNAL GANTRIES.

first promoted it included a new belt line around the northern end of the city with the station on an entirely new site. The main buildings and train shed covered 18 acres, an area exceeded only by the Pennsylvania and Grand Central stations in new York. The station was not a terminal as such as the tracks ran right through.

Another grand station to be built was the Union Passenger Station on Massachusetts Avenue in Washington, DC which was completed and opened on November 17, 1907. Built by the Washington Terminal company in agreement with the Baltimore & Ohio RR and a subsidiary of the Pennsylvania, the terminal was for the joint use of the Southern, the Washington Southern, the Chesapeake & Ohio and "such other companies as might be admitted to the use of its facilities and connections." Expenses and revenue were to be charged separately against the tenant companies in proportion to their use. Under Act of Congress all other stations in the city were abandoned, together with their approaching tracks.

In spite of all this apparent opulence, American railroads were being stifled by restrictive legislation. By 1910 the combined efforts of increasing costs of materials and labor together with the restrictive policy of regulation, both state and national, were slowly but surely eroding the railroads' ability to pay their way.

Between 1900 and 1910 everything affecting their operation had increased in price, except that of the one

RIGHT WASHINGTON UNION STATION HAD BUILDINGS IN KEEPING WITH ITS STATUS AS THIS PICTURE OF THE WAITING HALL SHOWS.

RIGHT THE NEW UNION PASSENGER STATION IN WASHINGTON, DC WAS OPENED ON NOVEMBER 17, 1907 AND REPLACED TWO OTHER STATIONS. IT WAS PART TERMINAL AND PART THROUGH STATION AND SHARED ORIGINALLY BY FIVE COMPANIES.

St. Louis Mercantile Museum

St. Louis Mercantile Museum

J.W. Swanberg Collection

B & O Railroad Museum

TOP THE NATURAL DEVELOPMENT OF THE *ATLANTIC* FOR PASSENGER TRAINS WAS THE *PACIFIC*. THIS 1902 4–6–2 WITH 69IN DRIVERS WAS BUILT BY ALCO'S BROOK WORKS. THE TYPE-NAME *PACIFIC* IS THOUGHT TO HAVE ORIGINATED WITH THIS LOCOMOTIVE OF THE MISSOURI-PACIFIC RR.

thing they all had to sell: transportation. This by legislation, was fixed. By contrast all their essential commodities increased by an average of a little over 2 percent per annum. Any other industry would have added these increases to their selling price; but, being unable to benefit by any increases, the actual expenses incurred by the railroads over the decade increased by $250 million. An application to the Commission for increased rates was denied in 1911 owing to a misinterpretation of railroad profits in which dividends were counted twice! There was also an optimistic anticipation on the part of the Commission of heavier traffic which in the event did not materialize. An increase in expenses, however, *did* materialize and the next few years showed a marked shrinkage of net income.

About this time a number of the leading personalities involved with building up the railways died. Alexander J. Cassatt died in 1906 at the age of 66. He was President of the Pennsylvania RR, 1899–1906, and did

ABOVE BALTIMORE & OHIO'S HEAVY FREIGHT WAS HANDLED BY THESE LARGE 2–10–2 *SANTA FES* IN THE YEARS AFTER WORLD WAR ONE WITH SOMETIMES TWO OR MORE AT THE HEAD AND ONE "PUSHING" OVER THE ALLEGHENIES.

A,T & S Fe

ABOVE ENGINE 945, 2–10–2 TYPE, CLASS 900–1600, WERE THE FIRST 2–10–2 TYPES TO BE USED ON ANY RAILROAD. ORIGINALLY EQUIPPED WITH TANDEM COMPOUND CYLINDERS.

not live to see the completion of his crowning glory. He had great foresight and remarkable gifts as a railway engineer and executive. His monument was the great double-track tunnel under the Hudson River and the magnificent Pennsylvania Station, the four tunnels under East River and the Great steel arch bridge over "Hell Gate" connecting with the New Haven road. The monument erected to him in Pennsylvania Station bore the inscription: "Alexander Johnston Cassatt, President, Pennsylvania Railroad Company, 1899–1906, whose foresight, courage and ability achieved the extension of the Pennsylvania Railroad System in New York City."

Edward H. Harriman died in 1909 at the age of 61. It has been said of Harriman that wherever he touched a piece of railroad property the result was an improved and more profitable service to the public at reduced rates. There was one exception to this: the Chicago & Alton RR, which he left rehabilitated and improved – but impoverished. Harriman is perhaps best remembered for his reconstruction of the Union Pacific line, some of which has already been mentioned. The most difficult task facing his engineers was the easing of the gradients on the section of line over the Black Hills. His board had laid down a maximum gradient of 43 feet to the mile, 1 in 123 (0.81 percent). This involved building a new line over all manner of natural hazards to easing the curves either side of Sherman summit, itself lowered 247 feet by the boring of an 1,800-foot tunnel, and the 6,000-foot Aspen tunnel.

He was responsible for the reorganization and consolidation of minor roads south of the Mason Dixon line. This involved bringing together practically all the lines in the South which had suffered in the financial panic of 1893 to make four trunk lines: the Southern, the Atlantic Coast Line, the Louisville & Nashville and the Seaboard Air Line. Together they operated 20,000 miles of track. Harriman also helped to place the Illinois Central in the forefront of railroad progress.

James Jerome Hill died in 1916 at the age of 78. He was a farsighted man and many unconnected with the railroads will long remember him for his thought and foresight. Among railmen he was known as the Empire Builder, a title earned by his work through the whole of the northwest from Lake Michigan to Puget Sound in Washington state. He was deeply involved in two great transcontinental projects, the Great Northern and Northern Pacific railroad systems, and laid the foundations for their eventual consolidation with the Chicago, Burlington & Quincy RR.

Another personality to die in this decade, at the age of 75, was Edward Payson Ripley, President of the Atchison, Topeka & Santa Fe from 1895. He too was one of the great railroad builders. The passing of these men perhaps signified the end of an era.

The light construction of the early roads had its influence on the design of rolling stock and in the way American locomotives and cars evolved. Passenger locomotives had large driving wheels – usually only four or six – while freight locomotives tended to have smaller drivers, and by the turn of the century had six, eight, and even ten coupled wheels.

In the 1860s and 1870s the classic American eight-wheeler (4-4-0) was giving way in passenger haulage to the ten-wheeler and in freight haulage to the "Mogul" (2-6-0) and "Consolidation" (2-8-0) types for freight. Around the beginning of the 20th century these had given way to the "Atlantic" (4-4-2), the "Pacific" (4-6-2) and "Mountain" (4-8-2) types for passenger trains with the "Mikado" and, later, "MacArthur" (2-8-2) and "Santa Fe" (2-10-2) types for freight.

Other wheel arrangements were also used on freight and banking (pusher) locomotives. A two-wheel trailing truck was provided underneath the firebox, which had grown in size, to give a larger grate for more power output. By the 1920s the demand for yet more power resulted in even larger fireboxes which required four-wheel trailing trucks for support. Among the best known designs representing these types were the "Hudson" (4-6-4), "Berkshire" (2-8-4), "Northern" (4-8-4) and "Texas" (2-10-4); their names giving an indication of the roads for which they were first developed.

With the introduction of steel for freight-car frames and the adoption of automatic couplers and automatic

ABOVE ANATOLLE MALLET, A SWISS ENGINEER WHO PIONEERED COMPOUNDING AND DEVELOPED THE ARTICULATED LOCOMOTIVE WHICH HAD A PRONOUNCED IMPACT ON AMERICAN MOTIVE POWER.

FIRST U.S. MALLET–BALTIMORE & OHIO NO 2400 "OLD MAUD"

DESIGNED BY JAMES MUHLFELD	
BUILT BY AMERICAN LOCOMOTIVE COMPANY	
DATE BUILT	1904
WHEEL ARRANGEMENT	0–6–6–0
DIAMETER OF DRIVING WHEELS	56IN
NO. OF CYLINDERS	4
BORE OF HIGH-PRESSURE CYLINDERS	20IN
BORE OF LOW-PRESSURE CYLINDERS	32IN
PISTON STROKE	32IN
BOILER PRESSURE	235LB/SQ.IN
TRACTIVE EFFORT (MAXIMUM)	71,500LB
GRATE AREA	72.2SQ.FT
EVAPORATIVE HEATING SURFACE	5,584SQ.FT
LENGTH OF ENGINE AND TENDER (APPROX)	80FT
WEIGHT OF ENGINE	334,500LB
WEIGHT ON DRIVING WHEELS	334,500LB
TENDER TYPE	8-WHEELED

The absence of "guiding" axles led to an unstable locomotive, and "Old Maud" was confined to pusher work. In the meantime, in 1906/7 Baldwins profited by the experience and produced 30 2-6-6-2s for Great Northern. Five were used as pushers and the remainder were modified for head-end work between Spokane and Leavenworth, WA.

Railroad Museum of Pennsylvania

ABOVE TWO PENNSYLVANIA I.1 CLASS "DECAPODS" LIFT A HEAVY FREIGHT TRAIN OVER THE ALLEGHENIES IN THE EARLY 1920S.

B & O Railroad Museum

ABOVE MUHFELD'S AND AMERICA'S FIRST MALLET COMPOUND. NO. 2400 WAS AN 0–6–6–0 AND WAS KNOWN AS "OLD MAUD" BY FOOTPLATE CREWS. IT WAS HARD ON THE TRACK AND WORKED CHIEFLY AS A "PUSHER" ON THE BALTIMORE & OHIO'S ALLEGHENY GRADES.

air brakes, longer and heavier trains, which suited the American market, became possible. By the early 1900s 5,000- and 6,000-ton trains became the norm on many lines, with trains up to a mile long. With long stretches of road consisting of a single track, it was beneficial to run the longest possible trains between any two points. This called for extremely powerful locomotives.

As train weights increased, so the problem of steep gradients became more acute. Making headway uphill was not the only problem: it was often difficult to stop a long, heavy train on the steepest downhill gradients. Pusher locomotives had been employed since early times on the mountainous lines, and some had been specially developed for that purpose. In 1900 it was quite common to find two at the end of a long and heavy coal train as well as a "helper" at the head. These were invariably of the small-wheeled type, and their number of axles grew as their duties became more onerous. Even with the newer up-graded tracks the weight had to be spread as much as possible. While the pioneering *Stourbridge Lion* of 1829 weighed 8 tons, the *Sante Fé* (2-10-2) of 1903 from Baldwin weighed 287,000lb (143.5 U.S. tons).

About this time, a significant European development

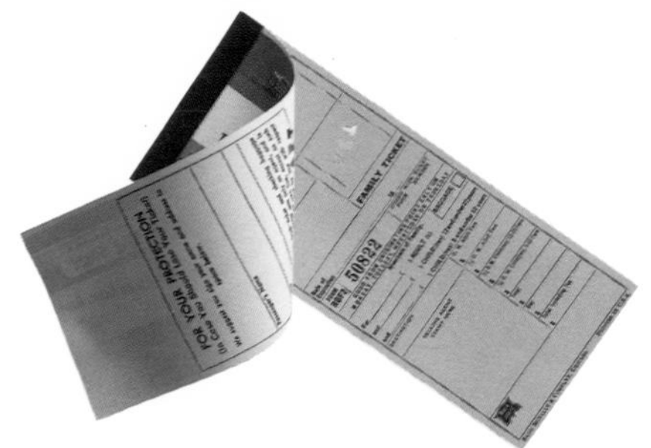

in locomotive design began to interest American engineers. This was the articulated, or duplex, type of locomotive invented by the French engineer, Anatole Mallet and patented by him in 1885.

Briefly the Mallet locomotive may be described as two engine units supplied with steam from one boiler, one engine unit being rigidly attached to the locomotive bed and the other, forward unit, connected to the first by a vertical hinge joint. Mallet's original thinking was to make this a compound locomotive with the cylinders of the rear, fixed unit, receiving steam at boiler pressure and exhausting into the cylinders of the front unit.

The natural conservatism of early 20th-century American locomotive engineers restricted innovation to the addition of more and more wheels fed from larger and larger boilers. Some 10- and even 12-coupled designs resulted. It was J. E., Muhlfeld, the Baltimore & Ohio's superintendent of motive power, spurred on by B & O's president, who introduced the Mallet locomotive to the United States. This was to have far-reaching consequences.

The B & O were working trains of 2,000 tons over the Alleghenies, and for these three "Consolidation" locomotives were needed – one hauling, two pushing – to work such a train over the Sand Patch gradient. Muhlfeld calculated that using a Mallet he could replace two of the locomotives and crews by one and reap the benefits of higher thermal efficiency with compounding. He designed a 0-6-6-0 Mallet and ordered one from the American Locomotive Company (ALCO), which was delivered in 1904 – just in time to be exhibited at the St Louis Exposition. It was at the time (if only briefly) the largest locomotive in the world, and weighed 334,500lb (167.25 short tons).

It incorporated a number of "firsts." It introduced U.S. railroads to the Walschaerts valve gear (until then Stephenson's link-motion had been the normal type); it employed steam-assisted reversing gear; and it was (later) fitted with an early form of mechanical stoker. On test on the Sand Patch grade, No 2400 easily accomplished the task normally undertaken by two "Consolidations" and burned one third less coal. Indeed, one authority on articulated locomotives claims a 38 percent saving between 1905 and 1910.

Having no separate guiding axles, No 2400 – affectionately known as *Old Maud* by its crews, after a fabulously strong strip-cartoon mule of the period – was unstable at speed, so it was confined to pusher work

MALLET ARTICULATED FOR BOSTON & ALBANY RR

BUILT BY AMERICAN LOCOMOTIVE COMPANY – CLASS 2662 C S 354

NUMBER BUILT (ALL TYPES)	1,315
DATE OF FIRST	1915
WHEEL ARRANGEMENT	2-6-6-2 ARTICULATED
DIAMETER OF DRIVING WHEELS	57IN
NO. OF CYLINDERS	4
CYLINDER BORE:	
2 HIGH-PRESSURE	21½IN
2 LOW-PRESSURE	34IN
PISTON STROKE	32IN
BOILER PRESSURE	200LB/SQ.IN
TRACTIVE EFFORT (MAXIMUM)	67,500LB
BOILER DIAMETER	82IN
GRATE AREA	56.5SQ.FT
EVAPORATIVE HEATING SURFACE	4,481SQ.FT
SUPERHEATER HEATING SURFACE	1,082SQ.FT
WEIGHT OF ENGINE	354,000LB
WEIGHT ON DRIVING WHEELS	302,500LB
TENDER TYPE	8-WHEELED
WEIGHT OF TENDER	154,700LB
WATER CAPACITY OF TENDER	8,000U.S. GAL
COAL CAPACITY OF TENDER	12 TONS

This locomotive is only one of many different classes of 2-6-6-2 Mallet compound locomotives built for United States railroads. This particular wheel arrangement was built in the largest quantities of all articulated types. This one was a compound, but later some simple-expansion types were built. The earlier superheated compounds had piston valves on the high-pressure cylinders and slide valves on the low-pressure cylinders.

The compound Mallets were really suitable for road operation only at modest speeds up to about 25 mph with heavy trains. Their power output was impaired when one set of driving wheels slipped without the other and got "out of phase". With simple expansion this did not matter as one "engine" was independent of the other; it just meant the exhaust beats were irregular!

612

J.W. Swanberg Collection

LEFT ONE OF THE FAMOUS PENNSYLVANIA RR K4S *PACIFICS*, NO. 612, AT ASBURY PARK, NEW JERSEY, ON OCTOBER 20, 1957.

until something even bigger came along. It was then relegated to switcher work, where it remained in service until 1938.

Baldwin Locomotive Works was not slow to see the benefits of Mallet locomotives and even profited from a lesson learned from operation of *Old Maud* on the Sand Patch grade. While *Old Maud* clearly demonstrated the potential of the articulated compound-type locomotive for sustained running with heavy trains, it was clear that guiding wheels were needed. In 1906/7 Baldwin built 30 2-6-6-2 Mallets for the Great Northern Railway's Cascade Division through the Rockies. They were designed primarily for head-end service between Spokane and Leavenworth, WA, but five were reserved for helper service.

Next in the field was *Old Maud*'s builder, ALCO, who delivered to the Erie Railroad three of the biggest Mallets ever made. These too had no leading axle, and were 0-8-8-0s weighing 411,000lb (205.5 U.S. tons). So big was the firebox that they were built as camelbacks, with the cab close behind the stack – not appreciated by the engineers. Two firemen had to be provided to feed the 100 square feet of grate, and they rode in a very rudimentary shelter behind the firebox. These locomotives were used on the road up to Gulf Summit grade, east of the Susquehanna, PA.

The use of two firemen was not economic and this gave rise to the invention of the mechanical stoker. It was the Archimedes' screw which provided the answer. Placed in a trough or pipe, the spiral screw was driven by a small steam motor and brought coal from the locomotive tender to the grate. A design of mechanical stoker was developed for the Pennsylvania Railroad in 1905, but it was about 1920 before satisfactory models were in general use. A grate area of about 50 square feet was considered to be the limit of firing for one fireman. One slight disadvantage of mechanical stokers was that only small-size coal could be used, but means were soon provided to obtain the necessary size of coal by grading.

As one road adopted the Mallet, so others with severe gradients soon followed suit and it was not long before even bigger locomotives were being built. Another attraction, of course, was that train weights and lengths could be increased if Mallets were used for head-end power, with another Mallet as pusher on steep grades. The limit to the size of locomotive was the limit placed on the diameter (and length) of the boiler which could be accommodated. Some rather strange beasts appeared, but in the end these gave way to reason. In all, it is estimated, that approximately 3,100 Mallet locomotives were built for service on the American railroads.

The story of the American Mallet is well encapsulated in a book by A. E. Durrant, *The Mallet Locomotive*, published in 1974. The spectacular success of the various Mallet designs to some extent overshadowed the steady progress made in improving the "conventional" steam locomotive during the same period. Boiler efficiency was increased by a number of devices but the invention of the superheater in 1897 by the German engineer Wilhelm Schmidt, was probably the greatest advance in this field.

The steam locomotive at best is not a very efficient converter-of-energy into power, but the superheater enabled much better use of the steam generated in the boiler. The superheater allows the temperature of the steam generated by the boiler to be raised without increasing its pressure and, hence, to expand more in the locomotive cylinders, so producing more work for the same volume of water evaporated. Increases of 25–30 percent in power output over a similar unsuperheated locomotive can be obtained.

The superheater consists of a reservoir divided into two compartments. The first compartment receives steam from the boiler and feeds it through tubes that run back and forth in the boiler flues. Here the heat of the gases increases the temperature of the steam, which is then fed into the second chamber for supply to the cylinders. Schmidt return-bend superheaters were generally adopted from about 1910.

In Europe, locomotives were developed with inside as well as outside cylinders, but the extra complication was never popular on North American railways as it led to more, and often more difficult, maintenance. In the 1920s there was some interest in three-cylinder locomotives, but here, too, the extra complication forced their discontinuance. Mallet locomotives were the exception, but their cylinders were all external. The Mallet compound was an additional complication. It

PENNSYLVANIA RAILROAD – K4-s "PACIFIC"

Built by Pennsylvania Railroad	
Number Built	420
Date of First	1914
Wheel Arrangement	4-6-2
	"Pacific"
Diameter of Driving Wheels	80in
No. of Cylinders	2
Cylinder Bore	27in
Piston Stroke	28in
Boiler Pressure	205lb/sq.in
Tractive Effort	
(85% Boiler Pressure)	44,460lb
Grate Area	70sq.ft
Evaporative Heating Surface	5,020sq.ft
Weight of Engine and Tender	541,150lb
Weight on Driving Wheels	209,300lb
Tender Type	
8-wheeled	

The Pennsylvania Railroad was the only major railroad to have a high degree of standardization. In the main they built their own locomotives and their designs were unique to the PRR, being built in several hundreds in various classes, with continuous development from one class to another.

USRA STANDARD 4-8-2 OF CHESAPEAKE & OHIO

Built by Baldwin Locomotive Works for U.S. Government for C & O RR	
Date built	1917
Wheel arrangement	4-8-2 "Mountain"
Diameter of driving wheels	69in
No. of cylinders	2
Cylinder bore	28in
Piston stroke	30in
Boiler pressure	200lb/sq.in
Tractive effort (85% boiler pressure)	58,000lb
Boiler diameter	86in
Grate area	76.3sq.ft
Evaporative heating surface	4,662sq.ft
Superheater heating surface	1,078sq.ft
Weight of engine	352,000lb
Weight on driving wheels	243,000lb
Tender type	8-wheeled
Weight of tender	194,000lb
Water capacity of tender	10,000U.S. gal
Coal capacity of tender	16 tons

disadvantage: the high and low pressure motors not being coupled, led to "choking" when the two sets of wheels did not synchronize, and so Mallets were never suitable for high-speed haulage.

For most North American railmen, the ideal locomotive should be big, powerful, rugged, and mechanically simple. As the locomotive increased in size, its fuel and water appetite grew – and so did its tender. No steam locomotive is complete without its tender (unless it is a tank locomotive, which carries its fuel and water on the same frame). Originally tenders were kept as small as possible because they were a non-revenue-earning load. The simple tender carried on two four-wheel trucks soon became too small to allow a long-distance train to complete its journey without stopping for replenishment.

The "Pacific"-type locomotive built by ALCO in 1924 still had a double-truck eight-wheel tender, and it could carry 15 tons of soft coal and 10,000 gallons of water. This was a more or less standard size of tender for the era. By way of contrast, the Northern Pacific 2-8-8-4 Mallet of 1928, also built by ALCO, had a tender with a capacity of 27 tons of coal and 21,200 gallons of water carried on two six-wheel trucks. (Of course, a Mallet of that size was almost the equivalent of two "Consolidations".)

By 1917 the number of locomotive builders in the United States had been reduced to three: the American Locomotive Company (ALCO), Baldwin Locomotive Works, and Lima Locomotive Company. The last had its roots in a locomotive builder established in 1880, Carnes, Agather & Company, with a works in Ohio. They also produced sawmill equipment and, as logging railroads had particularly light and rough tracks, they added a special articulated type of locomotive invented by a Michigan lumberman, Ephraim Shay. These were double-truck locomotives, usually with double-truck tenders, with all wheels – including those of the tender – driven through bevel gears from a longitudinal shaft connected flexibly to each end of the crankshaft of a two- or three-cylinder vertical engine. The Shay locomotive was particularly flexible and adjusted itself to the dips and rises of the hastily laid, uneven track far better than any conventional locomotive could.

Lima commenced building conventional locomotives in 1912, from which time they became the company's chief product. When in December 1917 the federal government took over the railroads, representatives of the three builders formed a committee of the United States Railroad Administration (USRA) to develop 12 standard types of locomotive for wartime service. These

RIGHT IN THE EARLY PART OF THE 20TH CENTURY PASSENGER CAR DECOR WAS VERY ORNATE AS TYPIFIED BY THIS *ROCOCO* PERIOD SLEEPER INTERIOR.

A.S.M.E

RIGHT 12-WHEEL CLERESTORY CAR OF PENNSYLVANIA RR IN EARLY 1900S.

Railroad Museum of Pennsylvania

J.W. Swanberg Collection

ABOVE 2-10-10-4 MALLET COMPOUND. THE HIGH PRESSURE CYLINDERS USED PISTON VALVES WHILE THE FRONT LOW PRESSURE CYLINDERS HAS SIDE VALVES.

included a six-wheel switcher, a "Sante Fe," "Pacific," and a "Mountain," and two Mallets – a "light" 2-6-6-2 and a "heavy" 2-8-8-2. The only previous example of a "Mountain" (4-8-2) had been built in 1911 by ALCO's Richmond, VA plant for the Chesapeake & Ohio Railroad.

The USRA locomotives were good and pleasing, well-proportioned designs. They had a large number of interchangeable parts and, being mass-produced, they came off the production lines fast with low unit costs. In less than two years 1,830 were turned out by the three manufacturers. This example of efficient design and standardization made good economic sense – but it was swiftly abandoned when the railways were returned to private control in 1920.

This was the big-locomotive era but at first the pace was slow. It took a good few years to recover from the effects of the panic of 1907. There had been two lean years in 1911 and 1912; then, in 1913, operating revenues grew, aided by a 5 percent rate increase in the Central territory in 1914.

As we have already noted, passenger cars had been of timber construction, but it was the projected opening of the Manhattan terminals approached by relatively deep tunnels which prompted the design of more fire-resistant passenger cars in 1904. The Pennsylvania RR decided to abandon timber cars on grounds of safety; in any case, by this time suitable timber was becoming more scarce and had increased in price dramatically, so the change to steel cars also made a lot of sense economically.

By 1907 a practical design had been developed and tested and large-scale production began. By 1913 no more timber cars were produced for domestic service. Despite this the timber car was slow to disappear; even in 1920 some 60 percent of the nation's car fleet was still made of timber, and a few timber cars remained in commuter service as late as the 1950s.

One result of the introduction of steel cars was a dramatic increase in weight. Cars were longer (up to 80 feet), and although they looked very much like the timber cars they replaced, the designs involved the fitting of massive underframe support sills. Add to this the use of concrete floors for fire resistance, cast-steel end-frames and cast-steel six-wheel trucks with massive wrought-steel wheels, and the result was a very heavy car of 80–90 tons which would (and did) last 50 or more years in service. This all taxed the motive power and increased the fuel bill.

During the 1920s some effort was made to reduce car weights by replacing steel with aluminum, but this was largely confined to commuter cars. Heavy-weight steel cars remained for a long time on long-distance trains.

Freight cars, too, were growing in size and weight. In 1900 the standard open-top hopper car was constructed from riveted steel plates and had a capacity of 50 tons, a weight when empty of 21½ tons and a volume of 2,035 cu.ft. Between 1912 and 1925 the coal car grew from 50 through 70 to 100 tons capacity. The 100-ton car had an empty weight of 30 tons, giving a weight on each axle of 32.5 tons – a punishing load on rail joints, even though freight train speeds were then relatively low, at around 35 mph. A wide variety of freight cars were in use: flat cars, box cars, tank cars, refrigerated box cars, gondola cars, covered hopper cars. Box cars came in various sizes but typically were of 40–50 tons capacity and up to 60 feet long.

Refrigerator cars were already in existence in 1878 and at first used water-ice as the refrigerant. Automated ice-bunker systems had been developed by the early 1900s and could carry a 30-ton load plus 5 tons of ice. A car of this type weighed up to 65 tons.

The first effect of World War One on the American economy was to create a remarkable export boom from

J.W. Swanberg Collection

RIGHT A THREE-TRUCK, SHAY GEARED LOCOMOTIVE WORKING ON THE ST. REGIS PAPER COMPANY'S LINE OF THE K L & L COMPANY IN MARCH 1964.

RIGHT Container cars are not a recent innovation as this one of 1915 indicates. This car of Pennsylvania RR carried five small boxes each with a capacity of 8,500 pounds.

St. Louis Mercantile Museum

St. Louis Mercantile Museum

LEFT The early 1900s freight box cars were still built largely of wood as this ACF box of 1905 shows. The underframe is trussed for strength and the capacity is 60,000 pounds.

RIGHT Meat was transported considerable distances and refrigerator cars were available in the early years of the present century, as this American Car & Foundry (ACF) vehicle of 1917 shows.

St. Louis Mercantile Museum

LEFT THESE TWO ILLUSTRATIONS SHOW THE DEVELOPMENT IN HOPPER CARS FROM TIMBER TO STEEL. THE LOWER HAVING A LADEN WEIGHT IN EXCESS OF 200,000 POUNDS.

which the railways benefitted by way of considerable increases in carriage. In terms of goods exported via the railroads, there was an increase of 260 percent, and a further 37 percent by the time the United States entered the war in 1917.

But the Commerce Law prevented the railroads from reaping the true benefits of this increase in traffic – unlike those profiteers in industry who lost no time in increasing their prices and thereby doubled or even trebled their profits.

During the course of the war the prices of locomotives doubled, the prices of passenger cars rose by 18 percent and of freight cars by 50 percent, while the price of fuel rose by over 80 percent. On August 29, 1916 Congress passed an act authorizing the President in time of war "through the Secretary of War" to assume control of the transportation system. America entered the war on April 6, 1917 and five days later a group of senior railroad executives pledged their co-operation in the war effort and created the Railroad War Board (RWB). Among the problems the board had on their hands were labor difficulties, a rush of employees to join the U.S. Army, and a glut of supplies for the war effort that choked every eastern yard and port.

The RWB's efforts to deal with these problems failed, and on December 28, 1917 President Woodrow Wilson placed the nation's railroads under the control of the Government through the United States Railroad Administration (USRA) agency, appointing his son-in-law, William G. McAdoo, as Director General of

RIGHT THE SO-CALLED FLAT-BOTTOM GONDOLA CARS WERE USED FOR A VARIETY OF GENERAL PRODUCTS. THESE THREE CARS ILLUSTRATE THE INCREASE IN CAPACITY FIRST ON EIGHT-WHEEL CARS AND THEN ON TWELVE-WHEEL CARS.

A.S.M.E

Railroads. McAdoo, at that time Secretary of the Treasury, had some years before built the Hudson & Manhattan RR, now the Port Authority Trans-Hudson (PATH), between New York City, and Hoboken and Newark, NJ.

McAdoo, amongst other acts, discharged all railroad presidents, eliminated all competition and gave a flat increase of $20 per month to all employees earning less than $46 a month. At the same time it was decreed that the railroads should accept the average of their net operating income for the three-year period ending June 30, 1917 "as just and reasonable compensation." The fact that the lean year to June 30, 1915 had been included effectively robbed the railroads of at least $100,000,000 a year while the guarantee lasted. The USRA ordered and assigned to railroads more than 2,000 locomotives and 50,000 freight cars of standardized design.

Much has been written about the shortcomings of federal control of the railroads. Suffice it to say here that it did not do any good. It left them desperately short of rolling stock and locomotives and at the same time increased their labor costs very significantly. When America entered the war there were some 240,000 miles of line. Rolling stock and right of way were being taxed to their utmost and while there was a shortage of some 117,000 freight cars, some 700 miles of double track were added, together with new enlarged freight yards. Federal control of the roads was finally ended on September 1, 1920 when they reverted to fully regulated private operation. The result of nearly three years of Government management was a huge deficit.

Growth of Steam Locomotive 1837–1918

1837

Sandusky built for Mad River & Lake Erie RR in 1837.
Total weight loaded engine & tender 16,000lbs.

1851

"Governor Merey" built for Michigan Southern RR in 1851.
Total weight loaded engine & tender 67,000lbs.

1860

Built for Hudson River RR in 1860.
Total weight loaded engine & tender 108,000lbs.

1880

Built for New York, Pennsylvania & Ohio RR in 1880.
Total weight loaded engine & tender 160,000lbs.

1895

Built for St Louis, Vandalia & Terre Haute in 1895.
Total weight loaded engine & tender 219,000lbs.

1902

Built for Missouri Pacific RR in 1902.
Total weight loaded engine & tender 283,000lbs.

1904

Built for Baltimore & Ohio RR in 1904.
Total weight loaded engine & tender 474,000lbs.

1911

Built for Chesapeake & Ohio RR in 1911.
Total weight loaded engine & tender 493,000lbs.

1918

Built for Virginian Railway in 1918.
Total weight loaded engine & tender 668,000lbs.

A.S.M.E

ABOVE THIS IS AN EXAMPLE OF ONE OF THE EXPERIMENTAL LOCOMOTIVES BUILT FOR THE NEW HAVEN TO COPE WITH HIGHER LOADS AND SPEEDS. IT WAS A TWIN-UNIT WITH FOUR LARGE TRACTION MOTORS AND SIDE-ROD DRIVE.

RIGHT THIS CLASS EP-1 LOCOMOTIVE OF THE NEW HAVEN WAS THE FIRST OF MANY TO USE A HIGH VOLTAGE, 11,000, SINGLE PHASE AC SYSTEM OF ELECTRIFICATION. TO RUN INTO THE GRAND CENTRAL TERMINAL IN NEW YORK, IT WAS ALSO ABLE TO PICK UP 600 V DC FROM SHOES AND A SMALL ROOF-MOUNTED PANTOGRAPH.

The USRA's net operating income for the 26 months of control fell short of the guaranteed payments by $714 million; damage claims were an additional $677 million. One happy legacy, as we have already seen, was the set of 12 standardized locomotive designs to which wartime and postwar locomotives were built – some even as late as 1944.

In 1920 Congress asked the Interstate Commerce Commission (ICC) to prepare a plan for grouping the railroads while at the same time preserving competition and existing routes of trade. The aim was to create some 19 groups from existing railroads in such a way that the cost of transportation on competing routes would be the same – or, to quote the ICC, to "equitably parcel out the weak sisters".

It was 1929 before the commission published its recommendations. Broadly, they were that subsidiaries would remain with their parent companies, short lines would be assigned to the connecting trunk line, and affiliates of the Canadian roads would remain with either Canadian National or Canadian Pacific; a few railroads were assigned to joint ownership of more than one system. The plan would have given the following main railroad companies:

- Boston & Maine
- New Haven
- New York Central
- Pennsylvania
- Baltimore & Ohio
- Chesapeake & Ohio-Nickel Plate
- Wabash-Seaboard Air Line
- Atlantic Coast Line
- Southern
- Illinois Central
- Chicago & North Western
- Great Northern-Northern Pacific
- Milwaukee Road
- Burlington
- Union Pacific
- Southern Pacific
- Santa Fe
- Missouri Pacific
- Rock Island-Frisco

Nobody was happy; and after much agonizing and many proposed changes, some of which were the result

LEFT THE GREAT NORTHERN RR ELECTRIFIED THE CASCADE TUNNEL IN 1909 ON THE 3-PHASE AC SYSTEM WITH TWIN-TROLLEY WIRES. THESE BO-BO ELECTRIC LOCOMOTIVES WERE USED TO HAUL STEAM LOCOMOTIVES AND THEIR TRAINS THROUGH THE ORIGINAL 2.63 MILE LONG TUNNEL.

Dan Pope Collection

of altered circumstances, Congress withdrew its original request in 1940!

Electrification had never played a major part on American railroads (apart from the special tunnel schemes mentioned already) and was confined mainly to mountain sections or urban areas where it could be justified by traffic density.

Following the New York Legislature Act of 1903, the New Haven RR chose to electrify from Woodlawn, NY to New Haven, with alternating current at 11kV, 25 Hz, single phase with overhead conductors. Before the turn of the century the New Haven, which was a heavy-duty,

ABOVE IN 1929 A NEW, LONGER CASCADE TUNNEL WAS OPENED. IN ANTICIPATION THE GREAT NORTHERN RR CHANGED ITS SYSTEM TO 3,000 V DC AND ELECTRIFIED BETWEEN WENATCHEE, MONTANA AND SKYKOMISH, WASHINGTON. THE LAST LOCOMOTIVES TO BE USED WERE THESE MONSTERS, SEEN AT SKYKOMISH, WN IN AUGUST 1955.

A.S.M.E

RIGHT The Norfolk & Western RR was another road to electrify with single-phase 11,000 volts AC. These locomotives had 3-phase motors with regenerative braking which eased handling of heavy coal haulage on 2% grades over the Appalachians.

St. Louis Mercantile Museum

ABOVE Most railroads with prestige passenger trains adopted the "streamlined" image. No. 600 was the first of Norfolk & Western's *Northerns* used on the *Pocahontas* and other trains.

RIGHT Virginian Railway 4–6–2 No. 212, beautifully restored at Roanoke, Virginia, with two 12-wheel clerestory passenger cars in 1957.

Dan Pope Collection

Dan Pope Collection

ABOVE No. 3895 on an enthusiast's special at Dallas, Texas.

high-traffic-density railroad, had electrified some branch lines using low voltage direct current. To work into the NYC terminal their electric locomotives were designed also to operate from 600V direct current third rail. Electric operation commenced in 1907, was eminently successful and later extended.

The Butte, Anaconda & Pacific Railroad was a mining railroad serving the copper mines at Butte, MT. By 1911 it employed a considerable amount of electrical plant in the mines and decided to electrify its rail operations to take advantages of the economy of electric traction. The system of electrification was 2,400V direct current with overhead conductors. It opened in 1913 and continued for many years.

In 1915 the Norfolk & Western electrified 56 miles of line in the region of Iaeger and Blufield, in the southwest corner of West Virginia, to cut out steam operation over 2 percent grades and through the Elkhorn Tunnel, both of which were severe obstacles to steam operation. Electrification enabled the line capacity to be increased and lasted for 35 years, by which time a realignment had obviated the need. The system was alternating current at 11kV, 25 Hz, single phase line.

In 1925 the Virginian RR began electric operation between Roanoke, VA and Mullens, WV, a section noto-

RIGHT AND BELOW

PENNSYLVANIA RR ELECTRIFIED ITS MAIN LINE SOUTH FROM NEW JERSEY ALSO ON 11,000 VOLTS AC AND DEVELOPED ITS ELECTRIC LOCOMOTIVES CONTINUOUSLY. THE "DD-1" WAS ITS FIRST STANDARD LOCOMOTIVE, WHILE THE "O-1" WAS AN EARLY EXPERIMENTAL TYPE.

A.S.M.E

A.S.M.E

riously difficult for steam operation which in 1916 was worked unsuccessfully by the 377-ton 2-8-8-8-4 triple Mallet. Electrification enabled the road to move heavier trains twice as fast as stem. The system was again alternating current at 11kV, 25 Hz, single phase.

Electrification in the mountainous region of the continental divide was an attractive proposition and in 1916, the Milwaukee Road put 30 electric locomotives into service on freight followed by another 12 on passenger trains. The first section, from Harlowton, MT to Avery in northern Idaho was followed by the section from Othello, WA to Tacoma with a northward branch to Seattle. In nine years the Milwaukee Road had savings of $12 million over steam operation. The system chosen in this case was 3,000V direct current.

The Pennsylvania terminal line into New York City was electrified initially (1910 with third-rail direct current at the time principally to conform with that of its subsidiary company the Long Island RR. In 1915 Pennsylvania electrified the line from Philadelphia to Paoli, PA on the alternating-current system at 11kV, 25 Hz, single phase. With electrification from New York to Washington, DC and Philadelphia to Harrisburg, PA in mind, the single-phase system was extended to Wilmington, DE and Trenton, NJ. The line into New York City terminal was changed over to alternating current to meet up with the line from Philadelphia. No further electrification, except for that of suburban services in the New York City area, took place until after World War Two.

Mention was also made earlier of the growth of the interurban railroads in the early part of the century. Some had some success and were enlarged and extended. But the interurban was not the sole competition for long. The automobile and the extension of paved highways began to make inroads into the interurbans' business for short journeys. The majority of interurbans did not last much beyond 1930 – and the automobile then began to eat into the railroad business. Many railroads formed bus and truck businesses; some even entered the airline business. Thus we enter the next era – and the Great Depression.

St. Louis Mercantile Museum

ABOVE THESE EL-2B LOCOMOTIVES WERE THE MODERN VERSION OF THE EARLIER ROD-DRIVE EL-1A LOCOMOTIVES AND NORMALLY RAN IN PAIRS ON HEAVY COAL TRAINS. THEY WERE REPLACED IN 1956 BY THE CLASS E33S WHICH WERE MORE FLEXIBLE AND HAD A GREATER TRACTIVE CAPACITY.

St. Louis Mercantile Museum.

LEFT VIRGINIAN RAILWAY CLASS E33 ELECTRIC FREIGHT LOCOMOTIVE OF 1956. THESE WERE THE FIRST RECTIFIER FREIGHT LOCOMOTIVES AND THE FIRST WITH A ROAD-SWITCHER CONFIGURATION.

Chapter Four

The Pace of Change

The Great Depression hit the railroads every bit as hard as industry generally. Business declined: there was less freight and even fewer passengers. Services were cut, and locomotives and cars were stored (some were even scrapped). The low point was 1933. Many railroads became bankrupt, including major roads such as the Frisco (St Louis-San Francisco), Missouri-Illinois, Milwaukee Road, New Haven and others. The strongest survived but in a very much weakened state. The effects of the Great Depression were to continue throughout the 1930s until after the outbreak of World War Two. By 1939 close to a third of the United States' total mileage of track belonged to companies in receivership.

The Frisco came out of receivership in 1947, its receipts having been boosted by revenues from increased traffic in World War Two. Missouri Pacific acquired control of Missouri-Illinois in 1929, when the latter entered reorganization, and emerged from bankruptcy in 1944, merging with the Mississippi River & Bonne Terre Railroad in 1945.

The Milwaukee Road was reorganized as the Milwaukee, St Paul & Pacific Railroad in 1925, and in 1935 it declared bankruptcy again. Despite this, the 1930s and 1940s saw the railroad involved in several notable developments. One of these was the introduction of the *Hiawatha*, the 100 mph steam-operated streamliner operating between Chicago and Milwaukee and St Paul. The train was a great success and *Hiawathas* were introduced on other routes. Milwaukee's own shops produced the cars for the *Hiawathas*, as they did for most of the company's freight and passenger cars and many of its locomotives. Again the postwar boom brought the Milwaukee Road out of bankruptcy.

B & O Railroad Museum

The New York, New Haven & Hartford Railroad eventually swallowed up nearly all the railroads in Connecticut, Rhode Island and southeastern Massachusetts and primarily connected many places with New York City. It was a heavy-duty, intense-traffic railroad, more on the European style than American. It operated an intense suburban service out of New York and had electrified its main line in the 1920s.

Despite four-fifths of New Haven's stock being owned by the Pennsylvania RR and having an interest in the Boston & Maine, the Depression played its part here, too, with the New Haven entering bankruptcy in 1935. Reorganization involved pruning much of its branch-line network and upgrading plant and rolling stock on the main line. It introduced "piggy-back" services (which entails double-stacking of containers on

Above A 12-wheel Pullman observation car with open platform as used on the *Capitol Limited* in the 1930s. Note the blind which was lowered in inclement weather.

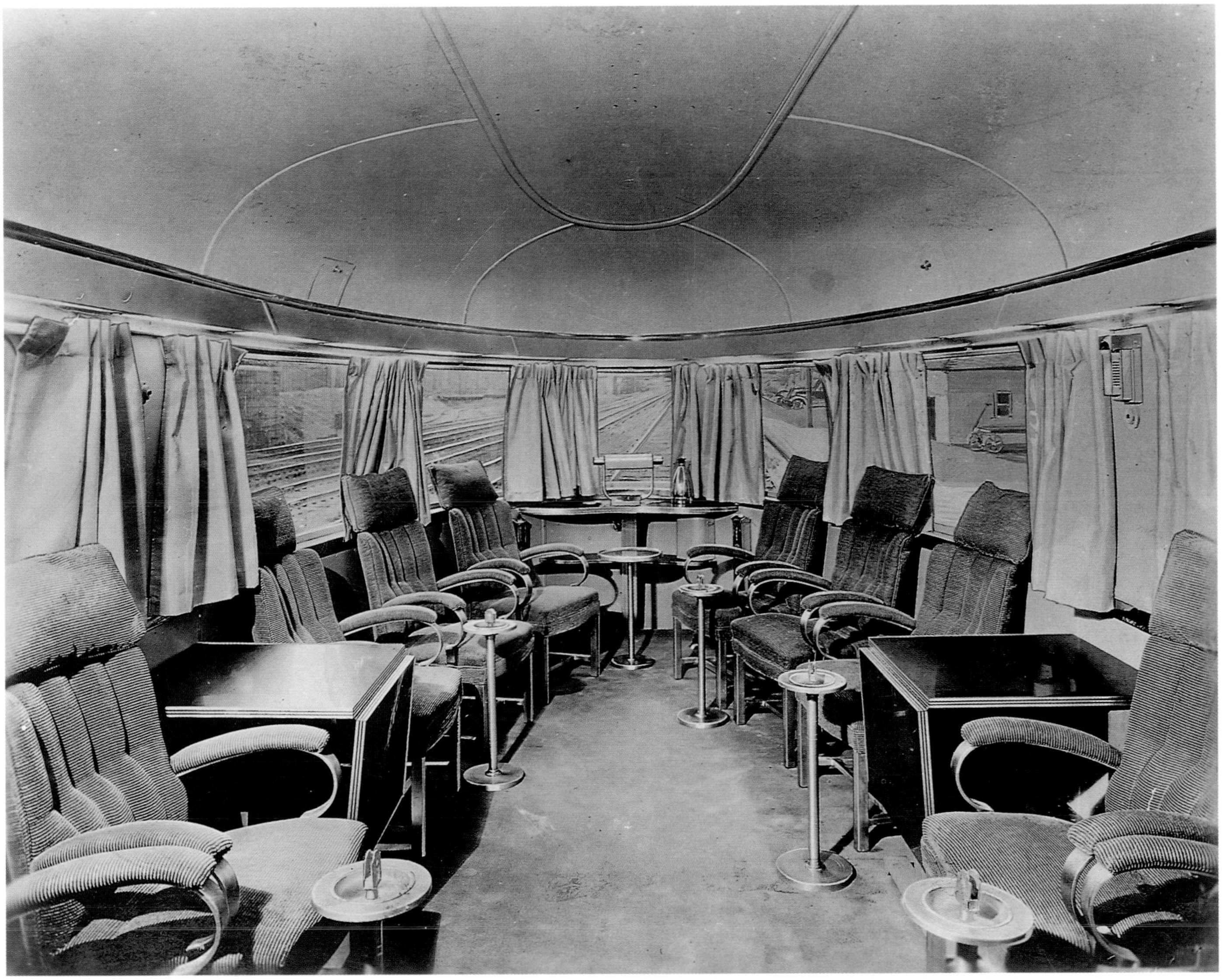

Burlington Northern

ABOVE THE OBSERVATION END OF THE REAR CAR IN THE 1934 *PIONEER ZEPHYR*, CB&QRR.

Dan Pope Collection

LEFT SANTA FE OPEN END, 12-WHEEL HEAVYWEIGHT OBSERVATION CAR AT CHICAGO, ILLINOIS ON JUNE 27, 1970.

BELOW Southern Pacific RR cab-forward 4-8-8-2 No. 4203 passes Glendale Tower, CA with a passenger train in November 1950.

Dan Pope Collection

flatcars) in 1938, and it dieselized many of its main-line trains. Traffic increased considerably in World War Two, but it wasn't until 1947 that the New Haven completed its reorganization.

Hardly had this happy state been reached when in 1948 control passed into the hands of Frederic C. Dumaine, Patrick B. McGinnis and others. The New Haven's fortunes quickly plummeted to new and greater depths. Experienced executives were dismissed and new management came in, leading to turmoil. McGinnis assumed the presidency in 1954; in 1956 he became president (and in 1962 chairman) of the Boston & Maine; and he resigned in 1963.

Many battles raged between stockholders and management, and some dubious accountancy, which had valued the road at more than double its worth, was exposed when McGinnis departed for the Boston & Maine in 1956. It took another six years to get the New Haven back into reorganization and seven years more before it was healthy enough to be involved in merger with the Penn Central. McGinnis' financial dealings culminated in a prison sentence for receiving kickbacks on the sale of B & M's streamlined passenger cars and ended his career in railroading.

Many other railroads were involved in similar financial wrangles, but these examples will serve to illustrate the kind of problems besetting railroads in the late 1930s and the post-World War Two era. On the other hand there were still successful railroads. The Union Pacific, for example, enjoyed impeccable credit in the capital markets throughout the Depression and was able to afford new locomotives and even new streamlined diesel trains. And even among the harder hit railroads the picture was not wholly gloomy: along with the bankruptcies, reorganizations and mergers there were improvements in operating methods, new construction techniques, upgrading of tracks, new signaling and ever larger and more powerful locomotives.

Following the outbreak of World War Two in Europe the American government's Neutrality Act of 1937 was altered to permit war material to be sent to the Allies. At home steps were taken to build up the army and navy. All this increased both freight and passenger traffic, but this time no steps were taken to exercise

Dan Pope Collection

federal control over the railroads. And even when the Japanese bombing of Pearl Harbor on December 7, 1941 brought the United States into the conflict, the railroads remained in full control of their affairs and were able to put their best effort where they were most needed. Overall, freight traffic doubled and passenger business quadrupled, much of the extra freight traffic being the movement of war materials from factories to ports on both sides of the continent. Traffic peaked about the beginning of 1943, then dropped gradually at about 3½ percent a year until 1946. Motive power, particularly for freight, was stretched to the limit, and although there was shortage of steel the War Production Board permitted some new building. However to save valuable time construction was restricted to locomotives of tried and proven designs or, at most, limited developments of existing types.

One design chosen by the Pennsylvania Railroad was the Chesapeake & Ohio's *Texas* (2-10-4) freight locomotive and 125 more were built, shared between Pennsylvania's own Juniata shops and Baldwin's between December 1942 and December 1943. These

ABOVE Southern Pacific RR AC12 No. 4274 with an enthusiast's special at Roseville, CA on November 30, 1969. No. 4294 is preserved at the California State Railway Museum in Old Sacramento.

were regarded by many as the finest freight locomotives ever to have run on the Pennsylvania.

Diesel locomotives will be considered separately but suffice it to say here that the switcher diesel was well-established by the outbreak of war, and the first generation of passenger and freight diesels was already in series production. Production of passenger diesels was halted between 1940 and 1944, but that of freight and switchers was allowed to continue for a time.

Although coal was the normal fuel for steam locomotives, this is not to say there was no interest in oil as fuel, but it was not until the American oilfields began to produce large surpluses in the late 19th and early 20th century that the price became attractive. Railroads with access to the oilfields of the south and west now began to take an interest. Even so, many railroads were slow to adopt oil as a fuel for steam locomotives because it required much more careful handling. The normal steam locomotive firebox could be adapted to burn oil without difficulty, but special burners and firing techniques had to be developed.

On the other hand, some roads had to burn soft coal from local coalfields. One such was the Chesapeake & Ohio, and photographs of many of their trains are notable by the large volumes of black smoke emitted by the locomotives when working hard.

The principle producers of oil in the United States were Texas, California, the Gulf, Oklahoma, and Kansas, and it was the railroads of these areas that turned first to oil-burning locomotives. The Southern Pacific was one of the first roads to turn to oil in the early 1900s; the Santa Fe soon followed.

Were it not for oil, the famous Southern Pacific "cab-in-front" locomotives would not have been possible. In all, 250 cab-in-fronters were built. The first AC-4 was a conversion from a Baldwin 2-8-8-2. Later a 4-wheel truck was substituted to improve curving. There were also some AM 2-6-6-2s. In the class names, "AC" stands for "articulated Consolidation" – the "AC" was conned and "AM" for "articulated Mogul". Both types were Mallet locomotives. They provided an effective answer to the problem of heavy haulage over the "Hill" – the tortuous stretch which climbs the western slopes of the Sierra Nevada in California between Sacramento and

CAB-IN-FRONT – SOUTHERN PACIFIC CLASS AC–10

California State Railroad Museum

Built by Baldwin Locomotive Works	
Number Built	40
Date of First	1942
Wheel Arrangement	4–8–8–2
Diameter of Driving Wheels	63½in
No. of Cylinders	4, simple expansion
Cylinder Bore	24in
Piston Stroke	32in
Boiler Pressure	250lb/sq.in
Tractive Effort (85% Boiler Pressure)	124,300lb
Boiler Diameter	94in
Grate Area	139sq.ft
Evaporative Heating Surface	6,470 sq.ft
Superheater Heating Surface	2,616sq.ft
Length of Engine & Tender	112ft 2in
Weight of Engine	657,000lb
Weight on Driving Wheels	531,700lb
Tender Type	12-wheeled
Weight of Tender (fully loaded)	393,000lb
Water Capacity of Tender	22,000U.S. gal
Oil Capacity of Tender	6,100U.S. gal

This type of locomotive would not have been possible without oil fuel. Visibility from the forward cab was excellent and the crew were never troubled by exhaust fumes in tunnels.

Dan Pope Collection

ABOVE PENNSYLVANIA MOUNTAIN 4-8-2, NO. 6762 OF 1930 BEARS A STRONG "FAMILY LIKENESS" TO THE K4S *PACIFIC*. BUILT BY PENNSYLVANIA RR AT ALTOONA, THIS PRIMARILY FREIGHT LOCOMOTIVE IS AT WILLIAMSPORT, PA IN 1957.

Donner Summit, close to the Nevada state line. This section abounds in a succession of snow sheds – 20 miles of them or more – with a ruling grade of 2.65 percent (1 in 37.7). A similar state of affairs existed on the line through the Cascades between Eugene and Klamath Falls, OR and Redding, CA, where many single-line tunnels exist. Even diesels can get a little short of breath on this line!

The last cab-in-front to be withdrawn from traffic in 1958, No 4294, is preserved in the California State Railroad Museum at Sacramento. It carries a commemorative plate which bears the inscription:-

LAST STEAM LOCOMOTIVE
PURCHASED BY
SOUTHERN PACIFIC

RETIREMENT OF STEAM POWER
ENDED A TRANSPORTATION ERA
THAT BEGAN IN 1855 TO PLAY
AN OUTSTANDING PART IN
THE BUILDING OF THE WEST

BEGAN SERVICE MARCH 1944
DEDICATED OCTOBER 1958

One major road to go through the Depression without going bankrupt was the Pennsylvania. As mentioned earlier, it had begun early to electrify its main artery from New York City to Washington, DC. It completed the conversion of its New York terminal to high-voltage alternating current in 1933, and in 1935 electrification was extended through Baltimore, MD and Washington to Potomac Yard in Alexandria, V A. It was further extended in 1938 from Paoli to Harrisburg with the intention of later reaching Pittsburgh, PA.

The New York Central in 1930 leased the "Big Four" – Cleveland, Cincinnati, Chicago & St Louis – and it too weathered the Depression. The NYC continued to develop its prestige passenger services and its crack train, *The Twentieth Century Limited*, was so popular that it frequently ran in many sections; the record number had been achieved just before the Depression when on January 7, 1929 it ran in seven sections carrying a total of 822 passengers. It now carried sleeping cars, with single rooms, barbers, fresh-and salt-water bathrooms, valet and ladies' maid services, and manicurists. Stock market reports were available, together with the services of a stenographer.

New Pullman cars were introduced with single and double rooms, some with drawing-room accommodation, restaurant cars, club lounge, and a rear observation lounge. An express parcels and post-office car was included as required.

From 1927 motive power for NYC's main passenger trains was provided by a new design of 4-6-4 steam locomotive developed specially by ALCO; this wheel arrangement henceforward became known as the "Hudson". The type was developed with each successive batch built until by 1948 there was a total of 275, all except 10 coming from ALCO. The latter were built by Lima and allocated to the Boston & Albany RR, which had been leased by the NYC in 1900. In 1932 the New York City to Chicago schedule was cut to 18 hours, in 1935 to 16½ hours, and in 1936 to 15½ hours.

Meantime, Pennsylvania's rival *Broadway Limited* continued to prosper and through the 1920s it was hauled mainly by 4-6-2 "Pacifics" of the famous "K.4" class until supplanted by electric locomotives as far as Harrisburg, PA in 1938. In 1926/7 more powerful steam 4-8-4 class "M.1" locomotives, built in Pennsy's own Altoona, PA shops took the express over the Alleghenie between Altoona and Pittsburgh, negotiating the famous Horseshoe Curve. From Pittsburgh a "K.4" would take the train on to Chicago; similarly on the run to New York City, a K.4 would take over at Altoona.

In the depths of the Depression the Chesapeake & Ohio introduced a new all-air-conditioned train, the *George Washington*, between Washington, DC and Newport News, VA and Louisville, KY and Cincinnati, OH. Clearly the heat was on to win as much traffic as

Dan Pope Collection

LEFT K4s *Pacific* No. 3678 outside Juniata Shops, Meadows, New Jersey, on September 18, 1956.

RIGHT AND BELOW GE/Ingersoll-Rand 300 hp demonstrator switcher of 1923. Following a successful tour in 1924, Alco joined the consortium and produced the first ever standardized line of diesel locomotives.

A.S.M.E

A.S.M.E

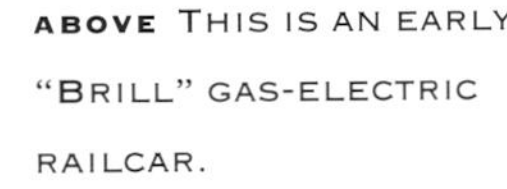
ABOVE This is an early "Brill" gas-electric railcar.

possible. In this period and following the end of World War Two it was fashionable to name the principal trains. Many will remember such names as:-

Panama Limited (Illinois Central RR): Chicago–New Orleans
Overland Limited (Chicago & North Western/Union Pacific Southern Pacific): Chicago–San Francisco
California Limited (Santa Fe RR): Chicago–Los Angeles
The Chicago Express (Erie RR): New York–Cleveland, OH
Super Chief (Santa Fe): Chicago–Los Angeles
El Capitan (Santa Fe): Chicago–Los Angeles
Daylight (Southern Pacific): San Francisco–Los Angeles
Florida Special (Atlantic Coast Line):

Orange Blossom Special (Seaboard Air Line):
The Black Diamond (Lehigh Valley RR):
Erie Limited (Erie RR):
City of Salina (Chicago, Burlington & Quincy RR): Kansas City–Salina, KS
City of Portland (M–10001) (C & NW/UP): Chicago–Portland
City of Los Angeles (UP): Chicago–Los Angeles
City of San Francisco (C & NW/UP): Chicago–San Francisco
California Zephyr (CB & Q/Denver & Rio Grande/Western Pacific): Chicago–Denver, CO
City of Denver (CB & Q): Chicago–Denver
Rocky Mountain Rocket (Chicago, Rock Island & Pacific): Chicago–Colorado
The Flying Yankee (Boston & Maine/Maine Central): Boston–Bangor (ME)
*Twin Cities 400** (C & NW): Chicago–St Paul and Minneapolis, MN
Chippewa (Milwaukee Road): Chicago–St Paul and Minneapolis
Hiawatha (Milwaukee Road):
*400 miles in 400 minutes!

Mention should be made here of the Pullman Company. George Pullman built his first sleeping car in 1864. By the 1920s some 100,000 travelers slept in Pullman beds every night; but at the height of the Depression in the early 1930s the company was losing money heavily. Only under heavy pressure from the railroads did Pullman modify its rigid attitude and concede that it had to change from its very heavy car image. It did introduce private-room accommodation, but it was slower to build lighter vehicles.

In 1940 the U.S. Department of Justice filed a complaint against Pullman's monopoly of the sleeping-car business. The monopoly had been tolerated by the railroads because Pullman's vast pool of cars could be moved around the country to wherever they were most needed. In 1947 Pullman was forced to separate its car-building from its operating division, creating Pullman Inc., Car Builder. The sleeping-car operation, the Pullman Company, was sold to the 57 railroads over which it ran its cars.

Long-distance travel was still in demand, and continued for the next decade; but in 1957 Pennsylvania began operating its own parlor cars and one by one the other railroads pulled out of the Pullman operation. In 1958, when New York Central started to run its own sleeping cars, the first commercial jet-powered airliners, which were to take most business away from Pullman, went into service. At the same time, the interstate highway construction program, funded by the tax-payer, was making inroads into the coach passenger business.

In the 1920s a few roads had experimented with internal-combustion engined vehicles – some with diesel switcher locomotives but many more with self-propelled passenger vehicles (railcars). The self-propelled vehicles were mainly gas-electric passenger cars, one of which could usually replace a two or three-car local train and be operated by fewer crew. There was a saving in maintenance because such a car needed less servicing and was instantly available. By 1930 there were many such cars, the most successful being built by the Electro-Motive Company of Cleveland, OH who between 1922 and 1929 had built around 500. Electro-Motive built the cars and their transmission system, while power was provided by Winton gasoline engines.

Now there arose a need to cut operating costs. With the industrialization of the eastern states and the ever expanding programs of road building and improvement, many passengers opted for personal transportation in the form of the automobile. The first to feel the effect of this were the lighter-loaded branch and secondary lines. The same was not yet true of the less-industrialized states of the Mid West, whose railroads were confident they could continue to attract a commercially viable flow of passenger traffic. They

A.S.M.E

ABOVE THE REAL CHALLENGER TO STEAM'S SUPREMACY ON THE MAIN LINE CAME FROM THE DIESEL ENGINE. THE FIRST SERIOUS ATTEMPT IN NORTH AMERICA WAS THIS 1928 2,660 HP TWO-UNIT 334 TON LOCOMOTIVE WHICH MADE A TRIP FROM MONTREAL TO VANCOUVER IN 1929.

reckoned they could do this if "limited-stop" trains were introduced. But to achieve this, it would be necessary either to increase the water-carrying capacity of existing locomotive tenders or to abandon steam locomotives in favor of internal combustion-engined trains. There was a limit to the former option, while the latter form of motive power needed to be developed.

By 1936 there was a relatively small number of various types of diesel-engined locomotives, ranging from switchers to road diesel units. The first three diesel-electric locomotives in the United States were switchers produced in 1918 by General Electric. One went to the Jay Street Connecting Railroad, one to the U.S. Army and one to an industrial concern in Baltimore, MD. Commercial success came in 1924 following a tour with a demonstrator by GE/Ingersoll-Rand. This resulted in production by ALCO/GE of five locomotives for stock, the first of which, No. 1000, was sold to the Central Railroad of New Jersey in October 1925. This was still in service as late as 1957.

Why were diesel locomotives so desirable? In a sickly industry, where economies of operations were desperately needed, a unit which could run nearly continuously, be operated economically and comply fully with local smoke-abatement laws was seen to be just what the railroad managers needed for switching and transfer work. By 1936 there were 200 such locomotives operating in the United States and Canada.

But if switchers were so desirable, what about road locomotives? The first experimental road locomotives in North America were built by the Canadian Locomotive Company, engineered by Sir Henry Thornton in 1925, for Canadian National. They were powered by 4- or 8-cylinder motors built by Beardmore, of Glasgow, Scotland. In 1929 this twin-unit locomotive made a passenger trip from Montreal to Vancouver to demonstrate the long range capability of this type of locomotive. It completed the 2,937-mile run in 67 hours.

The first diesel-electric locomotives in the United States were two for the New York Central delivered in 1928 and 1929, one for freight and one for passenger haulage in the Putnam division. The first had a succession of failures, but the second performed better, yet neither of these experimental locomotives was wholly satisfactory. Moreover, the railmen, still fiercely loyal to steam power, did not care for them, and there was a lack of adequate service and maintenance facilities.

Perhaps the most important event in American diesel locomotive history came about by the lucky collaboration of Hal Hamilton and Carl Salisbury. The first founded the Electro-Motive Engineering Company of Cleveland, OH and the second was Chief Engineer of the Winton Engine Company, also of Cleveland, which had built the successful gas-electric self-propelled railcars mentioned earlier. A third person was also a significant contributor in the field of electric transmission. This was Richard (Dick) Dilworth, who later had a major influence on the design of diesel-electric locomotives. He became Chief Engineer of the Electro-Motive Company on January 1, 1926 and was an active contributor until he retired in 1952.

General Motors Corporation purchased the Winton

RIGHT UNION PACIFIC RR PROTOTYPE *CITY OF SALINA* OF 1934. THIS WAS A 3-CAR TRAIN BUILT BY PULLMAN STANDARD WITH ALUMINUM BODIES AND AT FIRST POWERED BY A WINTON DISTILLATE ENGINE OF 900 HP.

Burlington Northern

ABOVE THE ORIGINAL 1934 *PIONEER ZEPHYR* 3-CAR ARTICULATED TRAIN OF THE CHICAGO, BURLINGTON AND QUINCY RR.

Union Pacific Railroad

Burlington
Route
9900

LEFT ONE OF THE FAMOUS *BURLINGTON ZEPHYR* 3-CAR ARTICULATED TRAIN SETS, NO. 9900 *LINCOLN*, OF THE FORMER CHICAGO, BURLINGTON AND QUINCY RR, PHOTOGRAPHED IN MARCH 1960.

Dan Pope Collection

Engine Company in June 1930 and, in December 1930, the Electro-Motive Company (which would later become GM's Electro-Motive Division, or EMD). Here begins the story of diesel-electric traction in the United States. Diesel-electric is specifically mentioned as that was the chosen system in the 1930s and has remained the most practical form of motive power for locomotives to this day, despite a number of efforts to introduce alternatives.

In 1933 Ralph Budd, President of the Chicago, Burlington & Quincy RR, visited the Chicago World's Fair and was impressed by the Winton diesel engines he saw powering the Chevrolet model assembly plant. At the time he was engaged in the design of a high-speed, lightweight, self-propelled train and this engine was just what he needed. It was the right size, had a low specific weight and developed the right output.

The CB & Q design was for three-car articulated unit with the cars constructed of stainless steel, and it was intended to run long distances at higher than usual speeds. The train, called the *Pioneer Zephyr*, used a modified design of Winton's 8-cylinder two-stroke engine called the 8–201A and with electric transmission from General Electric was capable of a top speed of more than 110 mph. It was built by the Edward G. Budd Company and delivered to the CB & Q on April 18, 1934.

The three-car *Pioneer Zephyr* weighed only 97½ tons and was immediately successful in drawing the public's attention to a new era. This train is generally considered to be the single most important factor in introducing the diesel-electric locomotive to road passenger service. After a short period of trial, on May 26, 1934 it ran from Denver, CO to Chicago, a distance of 1,015.4 miles, in 13 hours, 4 minutes and 58 seconds – an average speed of 76.61 mph – exceeding 100 mph at several points in the journey. In entered regular service between Lincoln, NE and Kansas City, MO in November 1934. Later, in 1938, a fourth vehicle, a Dinette, was added.

The innovative Union Pacific Railroad had already ordered a three-car streamlined articulated train. This was an even lighter train, which made extensive use of aluminum alloy. It was built by the Pullman Standard

BELOW THE EMD FREIGHT "DEMONSTRATOR", PRODUCED IN 1939 WAS A FOUR-UNIT 5,400 HP CONSIST. ON ITS MAIDEN TRIP IT TOOK 66 FREIGHT CARS FROM KANSAS CITY, MO, TO LOS ANGELES. THE FIRST WERE ORDERED BY SANTA FE AND WERE DELIVERED IN 1941.

A.S.M.E

Car Company in Chicago and weighed 85 tons. Named *The City of Salina,* it made an extensive tour in February, 1934. Apparently it was not quite what was wanted, as shortly after a longer articulated train was built consisting of a power car and six trailers, two of which were sleepers and one a day car. This was also powered by a Winton engine, a 12-Vee 201A of 900 hp; this was later changed to a 16-Vee 201A of 1200 hp. The train was then named *The City of Portland.*

In all there were seven generally similar units built between 1934 and 1936. Only the first had a single engine: the second had a 900 hp booster engine and the remaining five had 1,200 hp booster engines. Another six units followed in 1937, all with a single 1200 hp engine.

Meanwhile, in 1935, the Burlington Road had added two more three-car train sets and two four-car sets. All eventually carried names; *The Flying Yankee,* which ran between Boston, MA and Bangor, ME was probably the best known in the east. All the *Zephyrs* have been preserved in various railroad museums. Gradually, power cars began to lose ground to locomotives. But, in whatever form, diesel-electric power, especially in prestige expresses, began to take a firm hold. Other famous named trains introduced in this period included New Haven's *Comet,* B & O's *Royal Blue,* Santa Fe's *Super Chief,* and Chicago & North Western/Union Pacific's *City of Los Angeles.*

In May 1935 Electro-Motive completed a prototype passenger locomotive with a total rating of 3600 hp. It was a twin-unit, in reality two separate, identical 1800 hp halves coupled. Each unit weighed 120 tons and had two 12-cylinder, 900 hp 201A engines with electric transmission. Although successful demonstrators, they had a short life and were retired in 1938. A similar single locomotive for the Baltimore & Ohio built in August 1935 had much longer life and was used to haul the *Royal Blue,* which ran between New York City and Washington, DC. Beginning with the B & O, one driving cab end was re-styled in 1937 when it went to the Alton, later becoming the property of the Gulf, Mobile & Ohio RR on merger in 1949. It was later restored to its original design and livery.

Electro-motive

ABOVE THE ORIGINAL EMD PASSENGER DEMONSTRATORS, NOS. 511–512, OF 1935. THIS WAS A PAIR OF VIRTUALLY IDENTICAL BOX CABS AND COULD BE RUN SINGLY OR TOGETHER UNTIL SCRAPPED IN 1938, HAVING PROVED THEIR POINT.

Later in 1935 a 3,600 hp twin-unit passenger locomotive was introduced and this really set the scene for the concept of the multiple-unit passenger locomotive which became the standard for many years. They were the forerunners of the E series which were developed from 1,800 hp per unit to 2,400 hp per unit over the next 19 years. In the same year General Motors started construction of its diesel locomotive manufacturing plant at La Grange, IL. Here it developed its own version of the Winton engine, a simplified design, tailored to locomotive work, which became the EMD 567 series of 8-, 12- and 16-cylinder engines.

Diesel locomotives soon showed they could accelerate faster than steam locomotives, take curves at higher speeds, and run greater distances without service stops. It was therefore logical that what was good for passenger trains was equally good, if not better, for freight and attention turned to the development of freight units for long-distance haulage. In 1939–40 the first EMD freight locomotive made a national tour of a number of railroads, including the Santa Fe RR, for testing.

BELOW BALTIMORE & OHIO RR EXPRESS PASSENGER TRAIN CROSSING THOMAS VIADUCT, RELAY, MARYLAND, HAULED BY EMD E-TYPE LOCOMOTIVE, 1937.

RIGHT UNION PACIFIC'S 800 CLASS WAS DESIGNED FOR HIGH-SPEED PASSENGER WORK BUT WERE EQUALLY EFFECTIVE ON FREIGHT AS THIS SHOT OF NO. 823 SHOWS.

B & O Railroad Museum

The freight demonstrator was a four unit 5,400 hp (4x1,350 hp) locomotive. On its maiden trip it took 66 cars from Kansas City, MO to Los Angeles efficiently and economically. Known as model FT, the first were ordered by the Santa Fe and were delivered in 1941. Although wartime restrictions limited production, no fewer than 555 A-units and 541 B-units were delivered by 1945, most semi-permanently coupled as A+B pairs.

The diesel locomotive seemed the answer to the railroadman's prayers. The first railroad to turn to diesels was the Santa Fe. With long drags through desert country it had always had water-supply problems for steam locomotives. Apart from its relative shortage, much of what water there was gave problems with scale and other deposits in steam locomotive boilers, leading to increased maintenance costs and downtime. Diesel fuel was also relatively cheap and diesel locomotive efficiency was high – about three times the typical 6–7 percent efficiency of comparable steam locomotives. So it was not surprising the Santa Fe heralded the purchase of the first 68 new FT models from EMD.

One drawback to diesels was first cost – a little over twice the cost of a comparable steam locomotive. Another was the considerable investment the railroads had in existing steam-locomotive servicing plant, repair facilities, coal depots, and water supplies, not to mention the men and materials needed to keep steam locomotives running. But there was no getting away from the fact that with steam locomotives went dirt and pollution: they threw out large quantities of smoke and cinders. And although to the enthusiast today that is one of its attractions, it didn't help to run the railroads.

The diesel manufacturers began their marketing campaigns well before World War Two. Fuel and

St. Louis Mercantile Museum

18
18
823
823
UNION PACIFIC
823

operating-cost economies were highlighted, as was the reduction in servicing facilities. The high purchase price was countered by the claim that operating savings more than recouped the price difference over a very short period. This could easily be demonstrated with switchers: with their higher availability, fewer diesel locomotives – probably only half the number – would be needed to do the same amount of work. Passengers would be won back by the vision of new, fast, clean motive power which didn't shower the traveler with cinders. The United States, rapidly becoming a nation of automobile drivers, would be attracted back to the railroads.

Some steam roads were, however, sceptical; a few even remained opposed to the very idea of diesels. But soon after the end of World War Two, many of the smaller and most of the larger roads had succumbed. Among the few that held out against diesel was the Norfolk & Western, a coal hauler from the Appalachian coalfields to the port of Norfolk, VA. The company designed and built its own locomotives at Roanoke, and many of those, they claimed, were more than a match for the diesels.

Before the beginning of World War Two other manufacturers besides GM entered the diesel field. ALCO and its Schenectady, NY neighbor General Electric produced a long line of switchers and line locomotives using ALCO diesel engines and GE electrics. Baldwin combined with Westinghouse to build a similar range. Finally, towards the end of the war, Fairbanks-Morse entered the field with its novel two-stroke opposed-piston engines.

Economy and low price went together, and this was understood by General Motors. From the start GM saw the advantage to the railroads of highly standardized products and the flexibility to meet haulage demands by running relatively small locomotives coupled in two, three or four units as the occasion demanded. This was also understood by the ALCO-GE combination, but Baldwin still adhered to the time-honored railroad tradition of custom design, and their products were more costly and often cumbersome.

Fairbanks-Morse also introduced a line of standardized locomotives for all applications; but they were late in the field, arriving in August 1944. Their lightweight opposed-piston engine had been supplied almost exclusively to the U.S. Navy during World War Two. It had been very well regarded by navy engineers, but it was never taken up by the railroads in large quantity.

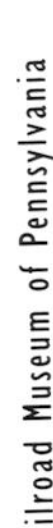
Railroad Museum of Pennsylvania

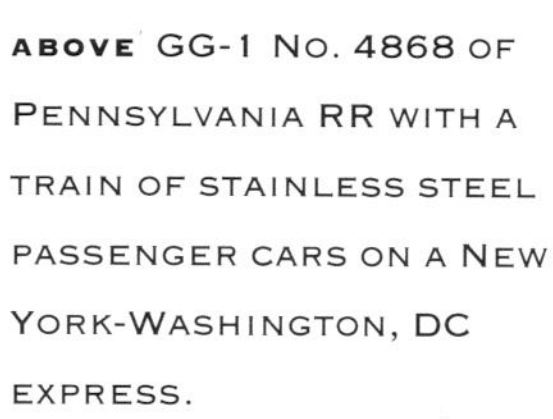
ABOVE GG-1 NO. 4868 OF PENNSYLVANIA RR WITH A TRAIN OF STAINLESS STEEL PASSENGER CARS ON A NEW YORK-WASHINGTON, DC EXPRESS.

LEFT IN 1938, PENNSYLVANIA'S JUNIATA SHOPS PRODUCED THIS 6–4–4–6 RIGID FRAME LOCOMOTIVE. IT WAS TOO LONG AND WAS FOLLOWED BY THE "T.1" CLASS 4–4–4–4S IN 1942 OF WHICH THERE WERE 52.

Railroad Museum of Pennsylvania

Dan Pope Collection

ABOVE PRESERVED EX-NORFOLK & WESTERN RR "A" CLASS 2–6–6–4 NO. 1218 ON AN ENTHUSIAST'S SPECIAL AT ATLANTA, GEORGIA ON OCTOBER, 31, 1987. TWO EXTRA TENDERS ARE ATTACHED TO REDUCE THE NUMBER OF "WATER STOPS."

To go back a little in time, the advent of the *Zephyrs* was at the beginning of what might be termed the "streamlined" era. Railroads of the early 1930s needed to present a new look, and the public associated diesels with state-of-the-art passenger services. But not all railroads could afford the luxury of these fine but expensive train sets.

Publicity-conscious managements began to employ the new breed of industrial designers. Among the most famous associated with railroads of the early 1930s were Henry Dreyfuss, Raymond Loewy and Otto Kuhler, who respectively styled the NYC's *Twentieth Century Limited*, the Pennsy's *Broadway Limited* and the Milwaukee Road's *Hiawatha* in an attempt to give steam power a more modern, sophisticated image in face of the diesel threat. Loewy was particularly associated with the striking appearance of the R–1 and GG–1 electric locomotives, but his talents were also applied to steam locomotives, notably the duplex high-speed "T.1" 4-4-4-4.

Otto Kuhler styled the 4-6-4 "Hudson", with 7ft-diameter drivers, for the Milwaukee Road's *Hiawatha*. For a time this seemed to be an effective answer to the high-speed, light-weight diesel streamliners. These and similar designs of steam locomotives for other roads were used until the last days of steam when diesels replaced them, particularly where grades were encountered with heavy passenger trains.

Much of the so-called streamlining on both diesel and steam locomotives was bogus, being little more than styling to create a new image and paying little attention to aerodynamics. As a result much of it "aged" very quickly – rather as last year's styling gimmick does in the automobile industry – and was soon discarded, particularly if it hampered access for maintenance.

On the other hand, the coming of the diesel led quickly to very pleasing styling, and the basic American diesel locomotive profile was emulated in many parts of the world. It too had its practical aspects: the early slab-fronted diesel locomotives had given skant protection to crews, and the characteristic "nose-front" was adopted to provide crash-protection as well as for aesthetic reasons.

But steam was not standing still. Freight predominated, but the roads continued to woo passengers with still faster steam trains and improved facilities, until World War Two brought more passengers than could be comfortably handled. As freight trains grew in weight, so locomotive power was increased to meet the needs and to avoid double-heading, except where it was necessary to use helpers on severely graded lines. By 1930 the Mallet-type articulated locomotive was well-established as a freight hauler over the more mountainous lines, but perhaps the first popular freight locomotives for heavy hauling at relatively low speeds were first the 2-8-0 then the 2-10-2.

The first 2-10-2s were built for the Santa Fe RR and henceforth the wheel arrangement was known as the "Santa Fe" type. The first 2-10-2s were described in the previous chapter when discussing compounding. The wheel arrangement was then developed both ways: with a four-wheel trailing truck as a 2-10-4, or "Texas",

UNION PACIFIC THREE CYLINDER 4–12–2

Built by American Locomotive Company, Order S–1701	
Number Built	88
Date of First	1930
Wheel Arrangement	4–12–2 "Union Pacific"
Diameter of Driving Wheels	67in
No. of Cylinders	3
Cylinder Bore	27in
Piston Stroke	
– Inside Cylinder	31in
– Outside Cylinders	32in
Boiler Pressure	220lb/sq.in
Tractive Effort (85% boiler pressure	96,650lb
Boiler Diameter	90in (internal)
Grate Area	108.25sq.ft
Evaporative Heating Surface	5,853sq.ft
Superheater Heating Surface	2,560sq.ft
Weight of Engine	515,000lb
Weight on Driving Wheels	372,000lb
Tender Type	12-wheel, cylindrical tank
Weight of Tender	308,880 full
Water Capacity of Tender	18,000U.S. gal
Coal Capacity (semi-bituminous) of Tender	22 tons

Three-cylinder propulsion was not popular because of the restricted access to the "middle engine". These locomotives could not be operated on heavily curved routes owing to their long rigid wheelbase.

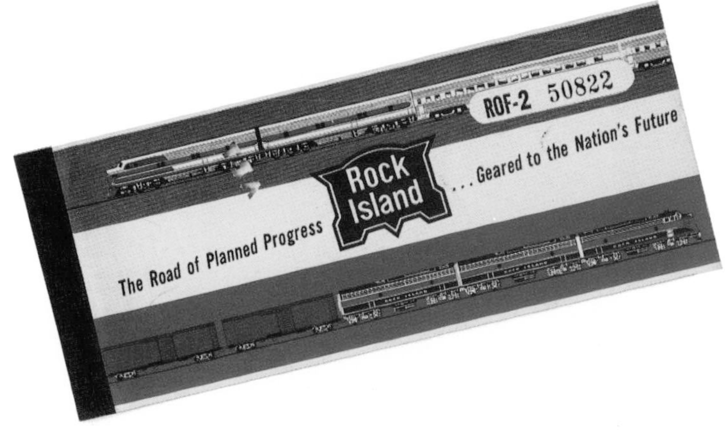

HIGH POWER 2–10–4 – ATCHISON, TOPEKA & SANTA FE

Built by Baldwin Locomotive Works – Construction No 62,162	
Number Built	10
Date of First	1938
Wheel Arrangement	2–10–4 "Texas"
Diameter of Driving Wheels	74in
No. of Cylinders	2
Cylinder Bore	30in
Piston Stroke	34in
Boiler Pressure	310lb/sq.in
Tractive Effort (72.5% Boiler Pressure)	93,000lb
Boiler Diameter	94in
Grate Area	121.5sq.ft
Evaporative Heating Surface	6,053sq.ft
Superheater Heating Surface	2,675sq.ft
Weight of Engine	538,520lb
Weight on Driving Wheels	371,990lb
Tender Type	12-wheeled
Weight of Tender (fully loaded)	393,200lb
Water Capacity of Tender	21,000U.S. gal
Oil Capacity of Tender	7,000U.S. gal

The piston thrust of this engine was the highest ever developed and the power output was the highest available from two cylinders. The 74in driving wheels gave it high-speed capability along with high tractive effort.

to support a larger firebox; and with a four-wheel leading truck for greater stability as a 4-10-2, or "Overland". Some three-cylinder "Overlands" were built for the Union Pacific and Southern Pacific. The last "Texas" built by Baldwin for the Santa Fe RR in 1938 had the highest piston thrust of any steam locomotive, and with 6ft 2in driving wheels it was very capable of reaching high speeds.

A notable and rare type for North America was the S.515 "Union Pacific" type. It was a three-cylinder 4-12-2, of which 88 were built by ALCO for the Union Pacific RR in 1926–30. It was an interesting design for two reasons: it was a rare example of a non-articulated multi-cylinder locomotive; and it represented the limits of a rigid driving wheelbase (30ft 8in). It was also a rare American example of Nigel Gresley's combination valve gear. The long wheelbase restricted its use to roads with only moderate curvature. The "Union Pacific's" were operated for 10 years on main line work and were then relegated to lesser duties.

For general-purpose freight the 2-8-2 ("Mikado" until 1941 and "MacArthur" thereafter) and its development the 2-8-4 ("Berkshire") were built in large numbers. The Louisville & Nashville RR took its final delivery of "Berkshires" as late as 1949.

Articulated locomotives were built mainly to provide greater power for lines with special characteristics, especially heavy grades with severe curvature. They were the largest and most powerful steam locomotives to be built, but there were only about 2,800 of them spread over 22 main-line railroads. The first examples were compounds and were restricted largely to helper or yard work as they were unable to work at acceptable speed on main lines. In articulated locomotives, the rear, fixed engine worked at boiler pressure,exhausting steam into the front, pivoted engine. Not being physically coupled the front and rear engines tended to get out of "phase" and the exhaust from the high-pressure engine was choked by the low-pressure engine.

The later articulated locomotive – 2-6-6-0, 2-8-8-0 and derivations – were capable of road work at speeds up to about 25 mph with heavy trains. The design was expanded to some immense machines, even triple locomotives with six cylinders and 2-8-8-8-2 and 2-8-8-8-4 wheel arrangements, but they had so many practical limitations they were never built in large numbers.

Compound expansion was dropped by American locomotive builders around 1924 because simple expansion was so much more flexible and produced a greater tractive effort at starting. Even so, fewer than 500 4-cylinder simple locomotives were built. The more modern types had larger driving wheels of 67–70in diameter and were capable of operating at over 60 mph, with power outputs of up to 7,000 indicated hp. The best known were Union Pacific's "Challenger" 4-6-6-4s of 1936 from ALCO; the type was named for a passenger train for which its 80 mph speed capability was needed.

RIGHT THIS GRAPH ILLUSTRATES THE RISE AND FALL IN PASSENGER TRAFFIC PARTICULARLY FOLLOWING WORLD WAR II COMPARED TO FREIGHT.

PASSENGER AND FREIGHT TRAFFIC TRENDS IN THE UNITED STATES

REVENUE FREIGHT TON MILES

REVENUE PASSENGER MILES

REVENUE: PASSENGER MILES (BILLIONS)

80
70
60
50
40
30
20
10
0

REVENUE: FREIGHT TON MILES (BILLIONS)

800
700
600
500
400
300
200
100
0

30 34 38 42 46 50 54 58 62 66 70 74

YEAR

BELOW RESTORED SOUTHERN PACIFIC RR *DAYLIGHT* ENGINE NO. 4449 WAS REBUILT IN 1975 FOR THE *AMERICAN FREEDOM TRAIN* AND HAS RUN EVER SINCE. IT IS SEEN HERE ON MAY 12, 1981 AT LOS ANGELES.

Dan Pope Collection

Dan Pope Collection

ABOVE THE SANTA FE *NORTHERN* OF 1944 WAS THE HEAVIEST OF THE 4–8–4 WHEEL ARRANGEMENT EVER BUILT, PARTLY DUE TO WARTIME RESTRICTIONS ON THE USE OF LIGHTER, STRONGER MATERIALS. NOTE THE VERY LARGE TENDER.

Union Pacific operated 105 "Challengers" and a further 149 were built for six other roads until the early 1940s. While they were sometimes used on passenger trains, their main duty was to haul heavy freight trains at near passenger speeds. One UP "Challenger" has been preserved in running order and is used on long-distance excursions from time-to-time.

The ultimate in articulated steam locomotive design was reached with the aptly named 4-8-8-4 "Big Boy". This was a 1941 design, also for Union Pacific, and again from ALCO. Over the next three years 25 of these immense locomotives were built, and they were the largest conventional steamers of all – more than 130ft long, 16ft 2½in high, and (with tender) weighing 552 tons and developing no less than 7,000 hp. The "Big Boy" was an express freight locomotive, designed to run up to 80 mph, and to take 100-car trains over the formidable Sherman Summit. At times, trains were so heavy that two were needed to maintain speeds in the region of 40 mph up "The Hill."

To satisfy their large appetites, these and the later "Challengers" were provided with 14-wheel tenders of a novel design, carrying 28 tons of coal and 24,000 gallons of water. They were intended principally for the long, heavy drag from Cheyenne, WY, up through the Wasatch Range in Utah and on to Salt Lake City. The "Big Boys" cost $265,174 each, could develop a starting tractive effort of 135,375lb and, with tender, weighed 552 tons – the tender alone weighing more than 150 tons. Today a few have been preserved and reside in railroad museums for all to see the awe-inspiring ultimate in steam locomotive size and power.

To quote from Henry B. Comstock's delightful book *The Iron Horse*: "The engines were deliberately 'overbuilt' to withstand the punishment of eighty miles per hour speeds, and during World War Two they occasionally topped seventy with heavy troop trains. However, they were at their vocal best when they drummed up Weber Canyon out of Ogden [UT.], punc-

St. Louis Mercantile Museum

LEFT A UNION PACIFIC *BIG BOY* ON A VERY LONG AND HEAVY FREIGHT TRAIN OF THE 1950S.

tuating each beat of their exhaust with a towering black exclamation mark."

Pennsylvania Railroad and USRA apart, standardization of design was almost non-existent in the steam era. Most railroads considered their own designs were necessary to meet their own particular requirements. To quote E. Thomas Harley from an article published by the American Society of Mechanical Engineers (ASME) in 1979: "It has been said, with some overstatement, that the steam locomotive standard was 'N.T.A.' (no two alike). Be that as it may, American Railroads and Builders provided what the U.S. required, locomotives that were relatively crude and simple, yet powerful and reliable. Nevertheless the U.S.A. built the largest and most powerful steam locomotives ever produced."

The steam locomotive fleet reached its peak at 70,000 in 1924 and this steadily dwindled from that time onward. There were 40,000 in 1944 and only 29,000 by 1949, when commercial steam locomotive production in the United States ceased. The last steam locomotive in regular service on a road carrier dropped its fire for the last time in 1960. Of the 29,000 in 1949, only 8,000 had been built after 1925, indicating that the diesel mainly replaced worn-out steam locomotives at or near the end of their economic lives, and not a large number of modern high-capacity steam locomotives as has sometimes been suggested.

At the end of World War Two, in the summer of 1945, railroads breathed a sigh of relief. They had weathered 15 difficult years, first with the Depression and then with the war. They had done a magnificent job moving men, supplies and munitions, all the while handling passengers and freight at home. In the public eye the railroads' role had been amply reinforced by war as the backbone of transportation. Most people assumed – as did the railroads – that this situation would remain, at least for the foreseeable future.

Returning servicemen, having made sacrifices overseas, saw it differently. Their dream was a job, a family and an automobile. Automobile manufacturers, released from wartime restrictions, responded and automobile sales soared. Pressure put on the legislators for highway improvements was seen by politicians as a vote catcher and they underwrote a boom in highway construction. Tax funds for new highways became plentiful, and truckers took to the new highways, capturing short- and medium-haul business from the railroads whose deliveries were generally less favorable.

Internal air traffic also began to increase and aircraft manufacturers, who had benefitted from advances in technology enforced by the war, produced airliners like the Douglas DC-7 and the Lockheed Constellation, both developments of highly successful wartime transport planes. The cost per passenger seat fell below that of pre-war prices, and flying now took on a "popular" image. Meantime, truckers' success with short and medium haul encouraged them to enter the long-haul business, particularly for the carriage of light manufactured goods using articulated (tractor and semi-trailer) vehicles. Gasoline was cheap and this cheapness, made possible by the vast production of the Texas, Oklahoma, Louisiana and California oilfields, plus the newly tapped reserves of the Middle East, helped truckers and airlines to lower their rates and become highly competitive with rail.

The effect on the railroads was dramatic. In 1944 railroads handled nearly 80 percent of passenger-miles between cities. By 1950 this had dropped to 47 percent and by 1960 to 29 percent. Freight did not fare quite so badly; nonetheless, it was down from 69 percent in 1944 to 44 percent by 1960. What had gone wrong?

There were a number of factors. With the end of the war in sight railroad managers had made smug assumptions that business would continue more or less as usual.

Union Pacific Railroad

RIGHT UNION PACIFIC *BIG BOY* NO. 4003 ON A HEAVY FREIGHT TRAIN IN WEBER CANYON. THIS WAS THE ULTIMATE IN STEAM LOCOMOTIVES. *BIG BOYS* WERE BUILT FOR FREIGHT, BUT IN WORLD WAR TWO, WERE USED ON HEAVY TROOP TRAINS.

X4003
UNION PACIFIC
4003

BIG BOY – UNION PACIFIC RAILROAD CO

BUILT BY AMERICAN LOCOMOTIVE COMPANY, ORDER NO S–1844

NUMBER BUILT	25
DATE OF FIRST	1941
WHEEL ARRANGEMENT	4–8–8–4
DIAMETER OF DRIVING WHEELS	68IN
NO. OF CYLINDERS	4, SIMPLE EXPANSION
CYLINDER BORE	23IN
PISTON STROKE	32IN
BOILER PRESSURE	300LB/SQ.IN
TRACTIVE EFFORT (85% BOILER PRESSURE)	135,375LB
BOILER DIAMETER INSIDE	95IN
GRATE AREA	150SQ.FT
EVAPORATIVE HEATING SURFACE	5,889SQ.FT
SUPERHEATER HEATING SURFACE	2,466SQ.FT
LENGTH OF ENGINE AND TENDER	133FT
WEIGHT OF ENGINE	762,000LB
WEIGHT ON DRIVING WHEELS	540,000LB
TENDER TYPE	14-WHEELED
WEIGHT OF TENDER (WITH ⅔ FUEL 7 WATER)	342,200LB
WATER CAPACITY OF TENDER	24,000U.S. GAL
COAL CAPACITY (SOFT COAL)	28 TONS

This was the ultimate steam locomotive, yet it was easily capable of speeds of 60 mph and over – indeed one at least is credited with 88 mph drawing a heavy troop train. It was a superb performer with few problems.

Investment in track, locomotives and rolling stock had not kept pace with demand: the locomotive fleet, in particular, was in the main old and worn out and represented a major cost sink which the war had exacerbated. Very few locomotives had been built between 1942 and 1945.

Now coal prices were jacked-up by strikes in the Appalachian coal fields. This increased fuel costs for railroads from the east through the Mid West, the latter having higher haulage costs to add to the higher fuel bill. Railroad workers demanded higher wages and every railroad union bargained for higher pay, with walkouts in most grades. By 1951 there were still almost as many railroad employees as in 1944; yet, although railroad revenue had fallen steadily during this period, employees' wages had risen by as much as 53 percent. Something had to change.

Attitudes and employment levels had, in fact, not altered much since the early years of the century. In spite of the universal use of reliable continuous brakes, the numbers of trainmen differed very little in 1950 from 1905, and the same applied in other fields. Now the diesel locomotive loomed as a serious challenge to steam. Many roads were quick to see diesel's advantages; others would fight almost to the death to keep steam. The big locomotive builders were, in the main, in the latter category, even though ALCO then had a lucrative arrangement with GE for diesel-electric work, and Baldwin in 1950 acquired Lima Locomotive Works.

There could be no doubt that a wholesale switch to diesel power would bring sweeping changes. It would offer greater flexibility in operation, and much less labor-intensive servicing and maintenance work. It also promised much greater standardization in locomotive design and manufacture. As we have seen already, many railroads stuck to the conviction that they were best served by locomotives designed specifically for their needs. This was undoubtedly true with steam locomotives – but for diesels it was quite another story.

In the road diesel field the Electro-Motive Division (EMD) of General Motors created for itself a virtual monopoly for a number of years. They researched railroads' needs very thoroughly and came up with a very flexible concept: the relatively low-powered unit which could be coupled to one or more similar units to form one high-powered locomotive, and operated *by one crew*. A great deal of experience had been obtained during the war and it had amply demonstrated what diesels could do!

It was probably the Santa Fe's President, Fred Gurley, who was the diesel's greatest salesman. In a speech in 1946 he declared of the diesel: "Time does not permit a discussion of all its virtues; sufficient to say it is the best which man's ingenuity has produced for our service." *Life* magazine took this up in 1947 and, with a big photo-spread, made the observation: "Last year 90 percent of the locomotives ordered by railroads were diesels." Except for the Norfolk & Western, which continued building its own steam locomotives until 1953, the last steamer on United States railroads was ordered in 1947.

The diesel protagonists, however, had a big battle on their hands. The change to diesel would affect not only machines but people and their jobs. In the eyes of the American locomotive industry, General Motors was an outsider. How could they possibly know what the railroads really needed to run their business? But GM, with an outsider's eye, could see very well what was needed to pull the railroads out of their doldrums. They rejected design collaboration, refusing to be a party to the traditional railroad-company/locomotive-supplier relationship. Indeed on one famous occasion, when one railroad wanted to help in the development of a diesel locomotive, GM refused its offer to underwrite the cost of testing. When asked why, GM's reply was: "So you fellows won't tell us how to build it."

Standardization in high-volume production – GM's basic manufacturing credo – would be impossible if each individual customer wanted a different locomotive design. High volume meant efficient production methods, low production costs, low material costs – and low prices to customers. EMD had already shown that, with the flexibility electric transmission conferred, a good general-purpose diesel-electric locomotive could successfully handle a much wider variety of traffic over a wide variety of different routes, grades, etc, than any steam locomotive. That being the case, customized design was no longer necessary.

One episode famous in American railroad history calls to mind Henry Ford and the Model "T", of which he is alleged to have said, "You can have it any color you like so long as it's black". A certain railroad persisted in asking for a series of design alterations to the diesel they wished to order so that GM finally delivered the following ultimatum: "We'll build you a locomotive. You tell us what color you want it painted and we'll be responsible for everything else. We'll send you the locomotive without charge, with one of our men in it to supervise . . . You run the locomotive for six months. At the end of that time, you send us either the locomotive or the money." Six months later the railroad paid – and ordered five more locomotives of a standard EMD specification.

The big three locomotive builders all went into the diesel locomotive business. Baldwin – now known as BLH following its merger with Lima and Lima-owned Hamilton in 1950 – now built standardized diesel-electric switchers with mainly Westinghouse electrical equipment. BLH ceased building locomotives in 1956, by which time they

A T & S F CLASS 2900 "NORTHERN" TYPE

A.S.M.E

Built by Baldwin Locomotive Works	
Number Built	30
Date of First	1944
Wheel Arrangement	4-8-4 "Northern"
Diameter of Driving Wheels	80in
No. of Cylinders	2
Cylinder Bore	28in
Piston Stroke	32in
Boiler Pressure	300lb/sq.in
Tractive Effort (70% Boiler Pressure)	66,000lb
Boiler Diameter	902in
Grate Area	108sq.ft
Evaporative Heating Surface	5,312.5sq.ft
Superheater Heating Surface	2,366sq.ft
Weight of Engine	510,150lb
Weight on Driving Wheels	293,860lb
Tender Type	16-wheeled
Weight of Tender (⅔ oil & water)	369,690lb
Water Capacity of Tender	24,500U.S. gal
Oil Capacity of Tender	7,000U.S. gal

This was the heaviest "Northern" ever built and the reason was partly due to the use of "wartime" materials which alone accounted for an excess of approximately eight tons over similar locomotives built earlier. The tender is also unique.

Dan Pope Collection

Above Three General Electric U25Bs of Rock Island Railroad at Lincoln, Nebraska in August 1963. After 1965 the single piece windshield was replaced by a split front windshield.

Right A trio of new 2,800 hp New Haven GE U25B road switchers of 1966 build on a freight at Hopewell Junction, New York in September 1966.

J.W. Swanberg Collection

J.W. Swanberg Collection

ABOVE DIESELIZATION OF CERTAIN NEW HAVEN PASSENGER TRAINS LED TO THE PRODUCTION OF 60 OF THESE EMD FL9 BO-CO LOCOMOTIVES WITH THIRD RAIL PICK-UP TO WORK INTO NEW YORK. HERE A PAIR ARE AT NEW HAVEN, CONNECTICUT IN MAY 1962.

had built around 3,000 locomotives for the American market. They fell into the trap of trying to satisfy the demands for custom design, and did not survive.

ALCO, on the other hand, understood the need for a high degree of standardization and, while its arrangement with General Electric for transmission equipment endured, it became an effective competitor to EMD. ALCO saw the need for high horsepower units and pioneered the 2,000 hp locomotive, which could be used singly or in multiple for both main freight and passenger service.

The first was put into service on the New York, New Haven & Hartford RR in 1941, working the Shore Line between Boston, MA and New Haven CT. The New Haven had been one of the pioneers among eastern roads in the use of diesel locomotives, putting its first switcher into service in 1931. This was the first 600 hp switcher to be manufactured by ALCO-GE.

General Electric broke off its partnership with ALCO in 1952. And although ALCO continued using GE electrical equipment for a time, together with its off-shoot, Montreal Locomotive Works (MLW), it built its last diesel in 1969.

The last diesel builder to enter the field was Fairbanks-Morse in 1944. They had built gasoline-engined railcars early in the century, but now launched an opposed-piston diesel engine with a good power/weight ratio of particular interest to railroads. They built complete diesel-electric locomotives with GE or Westinghouse electrical equipment in their shops near the Illinois state line at Beloit, WI. Their first 1,000 hp switcher went to the Milwaukee Road on August 8, 1944. F-M built both switchers and road diesels for a number of years, but dropped out of the United States market in 1958.

GE had been early in the market but concentrated chiefly on the smaller industrial switcher market, being well occupied otherwise with electric locomotives and multiple units. They produced a four-unit test set which operated on the Erie RR as a test laboratory in 1954–9, after which it was sold to Union Pacific. Two of the units originally had 1,200 hp engines and the other two 1,800 hp. For UP service all were equipped with 2,000 hp engines.

GE did not enter the large locomotive field seriously until 1959, with their U25B road switcher of 2,500 hp,

California State Railroad Museum

having sold 10 road switchers of 1,800 hp to Mexico in 1956. Today they are the only serious competitor to EMD.

By 1960, it is estimated, approximately 34,000 diesel-electric locomotives had been built for United States railroads, with a further 3,500 for Canada and Mexico.

The diesel locomotive was probably the catalyst for a host of changes which railroad managements knew had to be made. The cost of labor to operate trains remained high. Steamers required a crew of two for each locomotive used on a train; fuel and watering facilities were needed at frequent intervals on every line, and each had to be manned; and servicing and repairing was much more labor-intensive for steamers than for diesel-electrics. The switch from steam to diesel would be revolutionary, not least in its effect on the size of the workforce. There was much hardship, and there would have been even more if train crews had been reduced still further. The Unions fought tooth and nail to keep communities together where the livelihoods sometimes of whole townships were bound to the railroads.

Passenger Car Evolution

Earlier there was reference to heavyweight passenger cars, built like tanks and with a life of 50 or more years. In the 30 years covered in this chapter change was forced on the railroad carbuilders by the need to cater for higher speeds with more comfort over longer distances.

The advent of the experimental diesel trains in the early 1930s showed that passenger cars could be made from something other than ¼-inch thick steel plate. Lightweight aluminum alloy and stainless steel, together with carefully designed trucks, brought weight down. However, the provision of amenities such as air-conditioning and its power supply left the new cars for the streamliners still in excess of 60 tons apiece. Large-scale introduction of air-conditioning began in 1930 and by 1936 there were some 5,800 cars equipped with it.

Other new devices began to appear in the 1930s but were not generally adopted until the 1950s. A notable example was the disc brake, which the Budd Company began marketing in 1938–9, but which was not in

LEFT AND BELOW THE MOST DURABLE AND EXPENSIVE CARS WERE BUILT OF STAINLESS STEEL. THE BUDD COMPANY FABRICATED THE WHOLE STRUCTURE OF THIS CAR OF THE 1933/8 PERIOD. CARS LIKE THIS ONE WERE USED ON THE SANTA FE *CHIEF*.

Dan Pope Collection

general use until the mid-1950s. Disc brakes are not only quieter than shoe brakes but save on wheel wear.

No other major innovations appeared until the 1950s. While 3,000 new cars had been ordered in 1945–6, they were essentially copies of earlier models, and even by 1950 only 15 percent were lightweights. Economic conditions did not yet favor a full-scale replacement of cars, and as passengers deserted the railroads in favor of the automobile and air travel, few new cars were ordered.

Among many attempts by the roads to lure passengers back was the dome car, from which passengers could enjoy traveling through the most scenic parts of a route. They were, however, few in number as were the Santa Fe's "Hi-level" cars. By 1955 the passenger market had collapsed generally; new car construction was stopped and obsolescent vehicles retained. It was a dismal picture symbolized at the end of 1960 with the American Car & Foundry, quitting the market altogether.

Freight traffic, although it could have been better, held up fairly well, with bulk traffic, the kind of haulage well-suited to rail, retaining a fair market share. Again, steel had replaced timber in the early 1930s, and welded steel structures were being designed and adopted for hopper cars to reduce dead weight. As a result, it was possible to increase the payload from 70 to 82 tons within the gross rail load limit of 210,000 lb in force at the time. Since then there has been a gradual increase in load as rail load limits have been raised in the wake of stronger tracks.

High-capacity flat cars were introduced in 1933, enabling road vehicles to be transported great distances. From the 1950s the flat car grew to a length of 89 feet; at the same time auto-rack and piggyback carriers were introduced. Boxcars, too, grew to a length of 86 feet. Various devices were introduced to cushion loads from shunting and other knocks.

Many other special-purpose cars have been introduced, with tank cars particularly reaching a capacity of 12,000 gallons by 1960. The range of special-purpose freight cars is interesting in its diversity. There are cars

1322
2322
3322

LEFT A POPULAR INNOVATION WAS THE INTRODUCTION OF "*DOME CARS*" IN THE 1960S. FOUR CARS WITH SHORT DOMES ARE INCLUDED IN THE CB&Q *ZEPHYR* SERVICE BEHIND TWO F-8A LOCOMOTIVES IN 1970.

Dan Pope Collection

Dan Pope Collection

ABOVE A *STAINLESS STEEL DAY CAR, NEW GEORGIA,* SPONSORED BY COCA COLA AT ATLANTA, GEORGIA IN 1988.

for hauling hot metal, steel billets, poultry, pickles, vinegar, milk, livestock (horses, cattle, pigs), military equipment of all kinds, atomic waste, and bridge components.

As an illustration of what happened to rail traffic in the 30 years to 1960, the accompanying graph is of interest. Summarizing, passenger traffic movements in 1930 were 32 bn, which fell to 19 bn in 1933, rose to a peak of 71 bn in 1943, then fell to 64 bn in 1946, to 32 bn in 1950, and to 21 bn in 1960.

Freight, on the other hand, began at 42 bn in 1930, fell to 28 bn in 1933, rose to a peak of 65 bn in 1943, and seesawed mainly between that figure and 58 bn in 1960, with a low of 52 bn in 1949.

1960 saw the last steam locomotive retired and diesel reigning almost supreme (there was still a significant amount of traffic operated by electric traction). Passenger traffic receipts were falling but the pace of fall had slowed. Freight receipts were holding up fairly well. The implications were obvious. Rail as a passenger-carrier seemed to be in terminal decline, but freight was in fair shape, with the possibility even of increasing its share of the market. We shall see in the next chapter how the inevitable changes affected the shape of America's railroads.

CHAPTER FIVE

MERGERS, DEREGULATION, AND RENAISSANCE

By 1960 diesel-electric locomotives had changed the face of railroad operation – but so, too, had the automobile and the jet airliners. With reduced passenger traffic and the fall in receipts as lines closed down, managements had to merge to survive. Big was beautiful, or so it seemed to many railroads struggling to compete with other modes of transport as well as with each other.

The merger era had really started earlier than 1960 – some say in the late 1940s, when six roads merged to form three. These were the Gulf, Mobile & Ohio with the Alton; the Denver & Rio Grande Western with the Denver & Salt Lake; and the Chesapeake & Ohio with the Pere Marquette, a small road mainly in Michigan. Then there was the merger in 1957 of the Louisville & Nashville Railroad with the Nashville, Chattanooga & St Louis Railroad.

Dan Pope Collection

ABOVE Amtrak AEM7 No.919, EMD development of Swedish RC-4, is pictured at New Haven, Connecticut in June 1981.

At first only the smaller, regional roads began to disappear. Then in 1963 the Chesapeake & Ohio acquired the celebrated old Baltimore & Ohio; and in 1973, together with the Western Maryland it became a subsidiary of the Chessie System. In 1964 the Norfolk & Western acquired two smaller roads and leased two others. But the big news of the year was the announcement that the arch-rivals Pennsylvania and New York Central were to merge to form Penn Central; the merger was completed in 1968. Penn Central traded for just two years before becoming the biggest single bankruptcy in United States history, and from its wreckage and that of several other smaller roads the federal government formed Consolidated Rail Corporation (Conrail) on April 1, 1976. Conrail began to show a profit four years later.

All of these and other failures had to be considered by the ICC, and its bureaucracy made the proceedings very protracted. The fate of the Chicago, Rock Island & Pacific is a case in point. In 1964 the chairman of the Chicago & North Western, Ben Heineman, proposed a merger with the Rock Island (1964 was Rock Island's last year of profitability) and the Milwaukee Road into an Upper Midwest system, selling the lines south of Kansas City, MO to the Santa Fe. Union Pacific made a counter proposal which would give UP access to Chicago.

The proposal began the longest, most complicated merger case ever handled by the ICC. Other roads west of Chicago protested, some petitioned for inclusion, some asked for a piece of Rock Island. In 1973 the ICC proposed a restructuring of the railroad systems of the west around Union Pacific, Southern Pacific, Burlington Northern and Santa Fe. The railroads involved in the merger other than the two principals, Union Pacific and Rock Island, petitioned to dismiss the case and begin again.

The merger was approved by the ICC in November 1974, but several conditions were attached. Union

Dan Pope Collection

Dan Pope Collection

ABOVE A TRAIN OF EARLY PENNSYLVANIA ELECTRIC MU CARS AT SOUTH AMBOY, NEW JERSEY ON A COMMUTER TRAIN IN JUNE 1957.

LEFT A TRAIN OF PENNSYLVANIA CLERESTORY ELECTRIC MULTIPLE UNIT CARS AT MEDIA, PA IN 1972.

Dan Pope Collection

ABOVE Locomotive-hauled double-deck commuter cars on a Chicago Regional Transportation service behind F40PH No. 123 in December 1978.

Pacific said the merger now needed re-evaluation as the Rock Island of 1974 wasn't the Rock Island of 10 years before. Rock Island filed for bankruptcy on March 17, 1975 and on August 4, 1975 Union Pacific withdrew its offer. ICC dismissed the case on July 10, 1976 and that was the beginning of the end of the Rock Island, which ceased operation on March 31, 1980. This was the first time the railroad industry had seen an abandonment of such magnitude. In 1978 Rock Island had operated 7,021 miles of track!

Railroad Classification

The ICC divides United Sates railroads into three categories. Class I railroads are, today, those having income in excess of $251.4 million per year; class II have operating revenues of between $20 million and $251.3 million; and class III are those with less than $20 million. The last are mostly "short lines", but some are nominally independent subsidiaries of class I roads. Today there are ten Class I railroads and these are of course all of the large operators.

Major recent mergers are the Southern with Norfolk & Western to form Norfolk Southern; Atlantic Coast Lines with Seaboard Air Line to form Seaboard Coast Line, then with Louisville & Nashville to form Seaboard System, and finally with Chessie Systems to form CSX; Union Pacific-Western Pacific-Missouri Pacific; and Burlington Northern with Santa Fe to form BNSF.

With the general demise of long-distance passenger travel, many roads no longer operate passenger services. In 1970, therefore, the federal government again stepped in to form an organization to cater for inter-city passengers. Amtrak was set up by Act of Congress in 1970 as a government-funded private corporation to operate inter-city passenger trains. Twenty individual railroads elected to join Amtrak, and four of those hold common stock. All preferred stock is held by the U.S. Department of Transportation. Amtrak currently operates passenger services over some 24,850 miles of route, of which it owns 780 miles in the northeast corridor, plus areas in New York State, Michigan and Illinois.

Amtrak also operates commuter trains under contract in Boston, the Baltimore–Washington area, Connecticut,

Dan Pope Collection

ABOVE A PAIR OF F40PH LOCOMOTIVES, NOS. 100 AND 101 OF CHICAGO REGIONAL TRANSPORTATION AUTHORITY ON THEIR FIRST COMMUTER RUN, SEPTEMBER 29, 1977.

northern Virginia and California for various authorities and state agencies. It also has 345 miles of line electrified at 12.5kV 25 Hz ac, single phase. In 1993 Amtrak recorded 22.1 million passenger journeys, averaging 280 miles. The corporation owns 65 electric locomotives, 281 diesel locomotives, 29 electric multiple-unit cars, and 1,706 passenger cars.

Conrail was created by an Act of Congress and began operations in 1976. It comprises major portions of the Central of New Jersey, Erie Lackawanna, Lehigh & Hudson River, Lehigh Valley, Penn Central and Reading railroads. Conrail is the largest freight carrier in the United States northeast and operates in 12 states plus the District of Columbia as well as in the Canadian province of Quebec. It owns 12,700 miles of track, 2,200 diesel locomotives and 57,800 freight cars.

At the time of writing the following are the 10 class I railroads:–

Amtrak
Burlington Northern-Santa Fe (BNSF)
Chicago & North Western
Conrail
CSX Transportation
Illinois Central
Kansas City Southern
Norfolk Southern
Southern Pacific Lines
Union Pacific

The merger of the Atchison, Topeka & Santa Fe (to give it its full title) with Burlington Northern was agreed in 1994 and received final approval from the ICC on July 20, 1995. The combined railroad will be known as the Burlington Northern Santa Fe Corporation and will own 4,400 locomotives, 92,000 freight cars and have a combined workforce of almost 41,000 people operating 31,000 miles of track. The justification for this, the biggest merger in the history of United States railroads, is increased service with the expansion of several railroads in certain areas.

The Santa Fe was one of the original railroads of the southwest and it serves many of the principal cities from Chicago, south to the Gulf of Mexico and then west to the Pacific at Los Angeles, Oakland and San Francisco. It was one of several rail routes to the Pacific completed in the 1880s; Santa Fe's own route across New Mexico and Arizona was completed in 1883. Chief traffics are motor vehicles, grain and intermodal.

J.W. Swanberg Collection

LEFT The EP-5 Co-Co electric locomotive was the last design of the New Haven and the first to have DC motors fed by Ignitron rectifiers. Of dual voltage capability No 4072, in Penn Central colors, is working from the DC third rail outside New York.

Burlington Northern Inc is a 1970 creation from the merger of the Chicago, Burlington & Quincy, the Great Northern, the Northern Pacific and the Spokane, Portland & Seattle. In 1980 the St Louis–San Francisco (Frisco) was also absorbed by BNI, while in 1981 subsidiaries including the Burlington Northern Railroad Company were created. This took in the Colorado & Southern RR in 1981 and the Fort Worth & Denver in 1983. BNI serves 25 states and two Canadian provinces. Principal traffics are coal, grain, and forest products.

On August 3, 1995 Union Pacific announced its intention to buy Southern Pacific in a $3.9 billion cash-stock deal. If this goes through it will make Union Pacific the biggest railroad in the United States.

Outside of the United States there is an impression that the country's railroads are slowly disappearing. This is patently not true, as perusal of a list of operating railroads will show. While many miles of uneconomic track have been abandoned by the larger railroads, many so-called regional railroads have been created – these carry freight as of their own right – as have new "short lines". Others have acquired new trackage and have become quite substantial networks. In addition to the 11 (soon to be 10) class I railroads, the list includes a total of over 475 class II and III railroads, though some of the latter are very small.

Regional Railroads have been defined by the Association of American Railroads (AAR) as those operating at least 350 miles of route and/or earning annually at least $40 million in revenue. Most are members of the American Short Line Railroad Association or Regional Railroads of America. Short lines (also known as local railroads) provide local freight connections; some run seasonal passenger train excursions, and a few maintain regular public passenger services.

The other category of railroads we have not so far included are the commuter railroads. Some 20 urban authorities operate commuter railroads; several operate a number of lines (Chicago, for instance, has nine). These are in addition to the growing number of rapid transit lines, of which perhaps the best known is the New York Transit Authority, which operates the New York Subway and its feeder lines. Owning 5,803 cars, it operates 230 miles of track and carries around one-thousand million passengers each year.

So in spite of the manifold crises forced upon them by the automobile, the truck and the jet airliner, United States railroads are still very much a force to be

Dan Pope Collection

ABOVE A former Virginia Railway 3,300 hp E33 of 1956 made surplus when electrification was abandoned in 1962. They went first to PRR, then to New Haven and have since become Conrail property.

reckoned with and continue to provide a great deal of color and fascination. As we have seen already, the diesel revolution put new life into American railroads and created a new drive for efficiency. In 1960 27,000 diesels replaced some 40,000 steam locomotives in the United States. Canada, too, retired its last steam locomotives in 1962. Steam maintenance facilities disappeared fast, steam workshops were quickly converted to diesel repair shops or shut down entirely. Whole communities were affected. In 1947 some 1,400,000 people were employed by railroads: by 1962 that figure had been cut by half.

There were other cost-cutting strategies, too. Centralized Traffic Control (CTC) had been introduced before 1950, but now much more efficient operation was possible by despatching centrally. By 1965 CTC was at last accepted as the safest form of traffic control then available. By clearing signals and operating switches directly from his desk, the dispatcher had complete control of a train's progress. Commands were transmitted almost instantaneously and the machines themselves were provided with interlocks which eliminated conflicting movements, such as clearing opposing train movements onto the same track.

CTC enabled the reduction of the number of running lines on busy roads, such as the former New York Central from four to two and in other cases from two to one, thus saving the railroads considerable sums of money in taxes and in maintenance. It was so much better for a two-man crew to sit in a control center with a large illuminated board which displayed every switch and every signal on a 300-mile (or more) stretch of track, with colored lights indicating the shifting location of every train on the route. Faster trains could be switched around slower ones so they could have a virtually unobstructed high-speed run.

Today the radio and computer have added another dimension to railroad operation. Two-way radio communication between train crews and control towers is now normal. Today there must be many railfans who own portable radios tuned to RR frequency bands.

BELOW AN E33 ELECTRIC NO. 1 WHEN NEW IN VIRGINIAN OWNERSHIP AT MULLENS, WEST VIRGINIA, JANUARY 1957.

Dan Pope Collection

A well-known computerized system for location of cars and vehicle maintenance is "Tops" (Total Operations Processing System) – an invaluable tool. Car and locomotive numbers and other identifications are read by sensing devices and the information is sent to computers over telephone lines. Information relating to cars, trains and locomotives can be read off as and when required and vehicles picked off for maintenance or other attention at the nearest convenient location.

By 1962 freight ton-miles had reached their lowest ever since the Depression. Passenger-miles plummeted even faster and kept falling until the creation of Amtrak in 1971. Freight fortunes began to turn around in 1963 and slowly but surely they have climbed until today, when the levels are at an all-time high.

This did not happen without a minor revolution. Psychological as well as economic depression hit the railroads in the 1960s and early 1970s. Track maintenance deteriorated – it was particularly bad in the eastern and mid-western states – passenger-car maintenance was shoddy, railroad stations were ill-kept, even decrepit. One of the most serious problems was operating costs, particularly the size of train crews. Also there were too many miles of track, too many maintenance facilities, too many yards. To increase operational efficiency railroads had to merge, as we have already seen; but also the individual roads involved in such mergers had to slim down.

The parlous state of railroads in the 1970s led even to talk of nationalization. Such proposals got nowhere owing to strong conservative opposition; and almost every other proposal put to Congress had some feature which some senators or representatives threw out. But, clearly, planning and action at national level were needed. And the January 1974 Act which created Conrail also created a new entity, the United States Railroad Association (USRA) to do the planning.

Conrail began operation in 1976. Many miles of line owned by the former companies were either sold off or reserved for sale to short-line companies or for operation under the state authority. After many trials and tribulations the new railroad, managed by L. Stanley Crane, recently retired President of the Southern Railroad, was able to adopt a new approach to railroading. He tackled the train-crew problem by avoiding the traditional management posture of confrontation. The unions co-operated, and by adroit negotiation and bargaining a new labor structure was worked out.

Another of Crane's initiatives was to encourage new marketing techniques that focussed on the most important commodities: grain, coal, automobiles, intermodal, etc. Trains must run on time and operation be thoroughly reliable. In a relatively short time, Conrail began running at a profit and Congress was persuaded to authorize the sale of its stock to the public. Conrail had shown that railroads could be a profitable, successful and exciting business.

As we have seen, railroads had been hamstrung by regulating legislation since the 1880s. In the 1970s President Jimmy Carter had partly deregulated trucking and the airlines. This put additional pressure on the freight railroads, and they demanded parity of treatment. In 1980 this was at last granted by the passing of what came to be known as the "Staggers Act", Rep Harley Staggers (West Virginia) being chairman of the House Commerce Committee at that time.

The "Staggers Act" significantly altered the terms under which railroads and shippers could set freight charges. Now railroads could offer volume discounts,

BELOW In 1976–7 a Swedish State Railways Ro4 locomotive was evaluated in the North-East Corridor and found satisfactory. In January 1978 a license was granted to General Motors to build US models for Amtrak. No 950 is one of 67 class AEM7 4250 kW 125 mph locomotives.

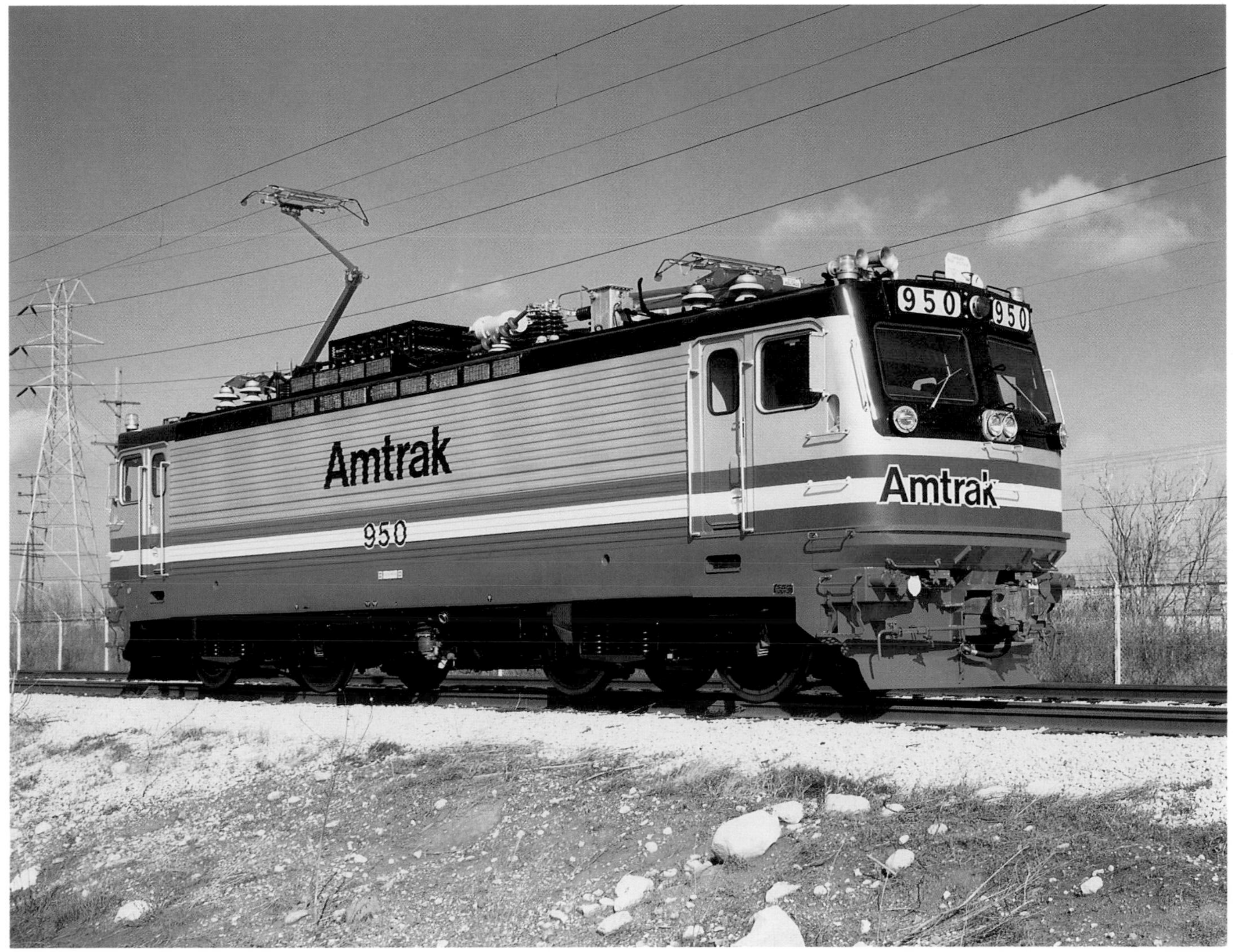

Electro-motive

RIGHT THE EARLIEST APPLICATIONS OF INTERNAL COMBUSTION ENGINES ON NORTH AMERICAN RAILROADS WERE ALL SELF-PROPELLED TRAIN CARS. IN RECENT YEARS MANY OF THESE BUDD-BUILT RDCS HAVE FOUND USE ON SECONDARY LINES. HERE THREE FORM A TOURIST TRAIN ON BC RAIL AT TUMBLER RIDGE, BRITISH COLUMBIA IN SEPTEMBER 1987.

J.W. Swanberg Collection

ABOVE AMTRAK AEM 7 NO.938 LEAVING NEW HAVEN WITH A TRAIN FOR NEW YORK ON 31 DECEMBER 1991.

which formerly had been prohibited. The ICC lost many of its teeth but would still oversee the process; now railroads and big shippers could negotiate their own contracts: an entirely new process. Now, too, there was provision to raise any rate that fell below 160 percent of out-of-pocket costs – all without ICC approval.

Following this new freedom, the railroads began to regain their financial footing. In 1960 railroads carried 44 percent of all inter-city ton-miles; by 1980 this had slipped to 37 percent. The picture is not quite what it seems: in fact the total ton-miles of freight carried by the railroads was increasing year on year – but the increases were overwhelmed by greater increases in tonnages carried by trucks, river boats, and pipelines.

The 1980 deregulation enabled the railroads to expand their carriage of coal and grain, automobiles and intermodal containers; but still their share held

J.W. Swanberg Collection

steady at 37 percent throughout the 1980s. Efficiency has increased remarkably and today railroads use little more than half the hardware used in 1930 and they achieve more than double the ton-miles on 290,000 miles of track compared to the 429,900 miles in 1930.

It was deregulation which was responsible for the creation of a whole new class of railroads – the class III regional and short-haul. The new companies could take on lines with low flow densities and operate them profitably because many of the old high-cost rules no longer applied. Nor, in fact, are they all short. The Wisconsin Central, for example, is a class III road that operates over 2,000 miles of track, and has 115 locomotives and 5,135 cars. Wisconsin Central was formed in 1987 by purchase of the former Lakes States division of the Soo Line. Its main line links Chicago with Minneapolis and extends into Ontario, Canada.

Elsewhere, in the Mid West in particular, roads with household names such as Illinois Central, Kansas City Southern, and Chicago & North Western, have undergone varying degrees of decline and have had to prune money-losing lines. In some cases there have been major abandonments; but each of these companies have come out resuscitated and in good health.

What of Amtrak? The corporation is now 25 years old. In its first 10 years it did even better than its planners had hoped. New rolling stock had replaced the worst of the old, and the better was being extensively rebuilt in their shops at Beech Grove, near Indianapolis, IN. Most Amtrak locomotives were new at that time, so schedules on the one third of the passenger services remaining after the takeover were more reliable and they attracted many more passengers.

Amtrak was given some of its own track. Congress

Dan Pope Collection

Left Budd RDC car No 9918 of B&O RR at Pittsburgh on 5 January, 1974.

Dan Pope Collection

Above Budd RDC Car No.34 of the New Haven RR at New Haven depot in April 1963.

New Jersey Transit

LEFT NEW JERSEY TRANSIT OPERATES STAINLESS STEEL ELECTRIC MULTIPLE-UNIT TRAINS OVER FORMER PENNSYLVANIA AND ERIE LACKAWANNA LINES FROM HOBOKEN, NJ.

authorized transfer of the former Pennsylvania electrified lines between Washington, DC and New York and the main line from Philadelphia to Harrisburg, PA. It also runs the passenger services over the former New York, New Haven & Hartford RR, although it was intended originally to abandon these electrified lines. These have been retained and improved, although only recently have the schedules of passenger trains been brought up to former New Haven standards.

A rolling "Northeast Corridor Improvement Project" was funded to rebuild the former Pennsylvania line to its proper standard. Amtrak received funding for the purchase of new electric locomotives. Then came the new administration of President Ronald Reagan, which began a concerted effort to kill Amtrak's funding.

Amtrak fought back. Congress had originally laid down that Amtrak must cover at least 50 percent of its total operating expenses from fares. Amtrak reached and exceeded the goal in 10 years. But this wasn't good enough for the Reagan administration, and Amtrak was fingered as an example of "Government waste". Amtrak's president vigorously defended the federal investment in the rail passenger business before Congress, overhauled the management, improved services and increased the revenue/cost ratio. In another 10 years he had so improved revenue as to cover 79 percent of operating expenses – a higher ratio than was found in most rail passenger systems elsewhere in the world. In 1992 Amtrak carried 42 million passengers, half on the national system and half on contract commuter operations.

Now Amtrak is in trouble again! It is currently (October 1995) at the center of a debate on the national budget. Like many similar operations, it is underfunded and is constantly criticized by politicians and the press, who seem to have forgotten that Amtrak was originally created to relieve private railroads of the mandate to run passenger trains.

We have already talked of the improvement to passenger and freight cars up to 1960. The decline in passenger traffic had put a severe brake on further improvements to passenger cars for many years. In 1960 there were still many of the older "heavyweight" cars around – indeed, they were built to last and last they did. It was a "Catch 22" situation: as more travelers took to their automobiles, more trains were withdrawn and ever more surplus rolling stock became available.

Car builders either stopped making passenger cars or went out of business. American Car & Foundry left the passenger-car business for good in 1961. Pullman and Budd held on for a little longer, mainly building to a limited rapid-transit car market.

The Pullman Company's sleeping-car operation, controlled by a group of operating railroads since 1947, finally ended in 1968. By this time the American passenger car had been reduced to a collection of veteran to vintage rolling stock. The Santa Fe had gone out of the passenger business and sold its cars to the privately operated Auto Train Corporation. Amtrak acquired its Metroliner cars new in 1969 because it felt it needed a modern image if it was to succeed.

In 1973 federal funds were provided to buy new cars

Below Pennsylvania RR introduced high speed electric multiple-unit trains on the New York–Washington "Metroliner" services. They were not an unqualified success due to problems with bad riding. They have been replaced by AEM7 electric locomotives hauling de-electrified multiple-unit coaches.

J.W. Swanberg Collection

Dan Pope Collection

Left In 1978/1980 Southern Pacific tried four rebuilt U25Bs with Sulzer (Swiss) engines, seen here on the right with rival EMD locomotives.

modeled on the *Metroliner* service on the New York City to Washington, DC route. They were stainless steel cars arranged as coaches and coach-cafes and ran on excellent light-weight trucks of a 1956 design. These cars are still around. More new cars were built in 1975–6 by Pullman. They were hi-level cars with rather more luxurious fittings than the *Metroliner* type, and they filled Amtrak's desperate need for new sleepers and diners.

To quote John H. White from a paper published by the American Society of Mechanical Engineers in 1979: "While both groups (of cars) will be welcomed by rail travelers, neither represents a departure from design or fabrication techniques established nearly forty years earlier. Perhaps this is for the best, since the new generation of transit cars produced by the forward-thinking aerospace industry have proved to be something less than a remarkable success, despite their technical innovations and futuristic styling."

It goes without saying there were one or two disasters with such cars which led to a rethink about the safety of plastic materials used in aircraft quite apart from transit and subway cars. Bay Area Rapid Transit – BART – of San Francisco was a case in point.

Above AEM7 No 916 is seen leaving Pechan Bay, NY, on a "Metroliner" service in May 1981.

Amtrak entered the 1990s with new cars, new locomotives, and some new routes. New designs of low-maintenance truck have improved ride and cut costs, while the introduction of electropneumatic braking with disc brakes gives additional safety. Heating is supplied from the locomotives via a three-phase train line and provides a more cost-effective system than with steam.

So far little has been said about the commuter lines. Following deregulation, the main line railroads ceased direct involvement in loss-making commuter and suburban passenger operations. Local government and state agencies have had to become increasingly involved in the provision of these services. In most cases the operation remains in the hands of the railroads on a contract basis, with the authority providing the funds for improvements, new rolling stock and promotion. In some cases agencies own the rights-of-way and operate the trains themselves; in other cases, commuter lines are controlled by authorities combining the role of provider of all types of urban public transport – buses, subway, rapid transit.

BELOW FOUR-CAR TRAIN COMPOSED OF *ARROW II* "A" & "B" CARS OF NJT ARRIVING AT MADISON, NJ ON A HOBOKEN-MORRISTOWN, NJ SERVICE.

New Jersey Transit

ABOVE 4-CAR TRAIN OF *ARROW II* "A" AND "B" CARS ON NEW JERSEY TRANSIT SERVICE FROM HOBOKEN TO GLADSTONE NJ ARRIVING AT BERNARDSVILLE NJ.

In some cases the authorities have their roots in systems which were established in the early part of the century. An example is the Metropolitan Transportation Authority (MTA) of New York City, which is a public benefit corporation of the state of New York. Created in 1965, it is responsible for almost all public transport in the New York City area. It has five subsidiaries which operate the city's bus, subway, commuter rail (Long Island and Metro North) suburban buses, two tunnels and seven bridges.

There are about 20 commuter railroads, eight of them all or partly electrified, and operating mainly over lines of former main-line railroads. Some of them are quite extensive systems. To take an example, New Jersey Transit Rail Operations Inc. (NJT) operates over 440 miles of line, 310 miles of which it owns, having taken over lines and passenger operations from Conrail (which is now predominantly a freight operation). These lines were formerly owned by such illustrious roads as Erie, Lackawanna, and Central of New Jersey. Today NJT operates modern EMU cars on many routes, with push-pull trains worked by electric and diesel locomotives on others.

As we have seen, some stretches of main line were electrified in the earlier part of the 20th century. The advent of diesel-electric locomotives gave railroad operators a great deal of flexibility plus haulage capacity which at least equalled the ageing electric locomotives, many of which were overdue for replacement. Diesel-electric working meant that locomotives did not have to be changed at the beginning and end of an electrified section. Before electrification was abandoned on one or two routes, special arrangements had to be made for tunnel ventilation before the use of diesel locomotives could be permitted.

In most cases electrification had been provided to meet a specific need: to improve haulage of heavy trains on long, steep grades, to work long tunnels with smoke problems, and so on. Exceptions were the electrification of the Pennsylvania Railroad in the 1920s and 1930s from New York City to Washington, DC and Philadelphia to Harrisburg, PA, and the New York, New Haven & Hartford RR. On these, traffic densities were

Dan Pope Collection

A consist of three Milwaukee Road 2 Bo-Bos headed by No. E298 at Butte, Montana, not long before the abandonment of electric traction.

comparable to some of the busiest European routes and electrification was seen more as an investment of faith towards a better service rather than as a cost saver.

In Europe electrification had usually been a response to an increase in traffic density rather than an attempt to increase haulage capacity. In the United States the capital for electrification could not easily be recouped, and when the diesel-electric locomotive arrived on the scene it offered a much quicker return on capital. One by one the electrified sections disappeared – the only significant exception being the north-east corridor with its high speeds and (relatively) high traffic density.

Another early electrification was the Butte, Anaconda & Pacific RR. Despite its grand title, it consisted of only 69 miles of line connecting copper mines at Butte, MT with a smelter at Anaconda. It was electrified in 1913 and electric operation continued until 1967, by which time all but two of its 30 locomotives were 54 years old! Between 1958 and 1967 B,A&P electric locomotives worked over the Northern Pacific (ex Great Northern) line from Butte to Durant.

There are other lines which have been, and still are, electrified. Two of these are quite recent additions. The Black Mesa & Lake Powell RR in northern Arizona has a single route, 78 miles long, opened in the early 1970s for hauling coal. It was electrified on the ac single-phase system at a pressure of 50 kV, justified economically because its length required only one substation.

The Muskingham Electric RR of the Central Coal Company in Lancaster, OH has a line only 20 miles long and is electrified at 25 kV 60 Hz. Coal is transported from mine to power station and there is again only one substation. An interesting facet is that this operation is semi-automatic: the two electric locomotives are operated by remote control and not normally manned.

The long freight hauls typical of many American roads do not lend themselves to electrification as the trains are too infrequent to render the high capital cost viable. Electrification of the Virginian RR was abandoned in 1962, that of the Milwaukee Road in 1972 and 1974, of the Norfolk & Western in 1950, of the Great Northern in 1956, and of the Northern Pacific in 1967.

This conveniently brings us to freight traffic and its operation. Freight cars were improved continuously through the 1950s and 1960s, but there were still many cars with outdated features. One factor limiting the length or weight of freight trains is the strength of the drawgear; another was the long-continued use of timber in underframe construction. While improvements had been made over many years, a point was reached where train lengths and/or weights could be increased over heavily graded lines only by cutting-in locomotives down the train. This was not necessarily a serious drawback with steam operation, as changes of locomotive and replenishment of fuel and/or water involved a stop anyway, and the trains could be re-marshalled at the same time.

The introduction of diesel-electric locomotives with increased tractive capacity provided the need to improve draft gear strength. They did not need the frequent servicing stops required with steam either. The

RIGHT A South Shore Line (Chicago, South Shore, and South Bend) *Little Joe*, No.802 on freight train at Hegewisch, Illinois on 14 October, 1950.

Dan Pope Collection

BELOW A Milwaukee RR freight descends from the Rockies headed by two 2-6-6-2 electrics and an SD40 diesel, December.

Dan Pope Collection

J.W. Swanberg Collection

ABOVE A HIGH-NOSE SOUTHERN PACIFIC "GEEP" – EMD GP9 NO. 7553 ON SWITCHER DUTY AT MOUNTAIN VIEW, CALIFORNIA IN NOVEMBER 1963. AROUND 4100 OF THIS POPULAR MODEL WERE BUILT 1954–1963.

first big freight diesel developed 5,400 hp: today it is possible to have as much as 25,000 hp at the head of a train. Where necessary, as on long, steep grades with long trains, another 10–15,000 hp can be cut in anywhere from 50–100 cars back and operated from the front unit by remote control.

Diesel-electric locomotives not only have a high tractive capacity but are also capable of acting as braking units on down grades. The traction motors are used as generators and driven by the wheels from the momentum of the train. The power so generated is absorbed in resistances and dissipated as heat. This is called dynamic braking and saves wear and tear on brake blocks and wheels. It also means that the draft gear between the leading car and the locomotive has to transmit the force provided by the trailing load and this force is almost equal to the tractive force required to haul the same load up the same gradient.

Draft gears have been strengthened through the years to accommodate increasing train weights. Freight cars, too, are heavier and carry heavier loads, particularly for bulk cargos such as coal or grain. Oil tankcars are now very long and heavy and run on special four-axle trucks. A typical tankcar now has a capacity of 150–200 tons and can be as much as 89 feet long.

With the generous dimensions possible on most United States railroads it is possible to double-stack containers about the size of a typical truck container. Double-stacking was an innovation of the 1980s pioneered by Southern Pacific. It is now the standard method of shipping manufactured goods long distances. This method began with piggy-back traffic – that is, the carriage of road trailers on flat cars. The modern containers are termed "intermodal": they are interchangeable between the three principal modes of surface transport – sea, rail and road.

A familiar vehicle to disappear in the 1980s was the caboose (or way car) – the vehicle at the rear of the train which originally carried the three or four men of the train crew. By agreement freight trains now run with two- or three-person crews and these now travel in some comfort on diesel-electric locomotives. To ensure

Dan Pope Collection

ABOVE IN THE 1960S AND 1970S PASSENGER TRAINS WERE MAINLY IN THE HANDS OF THE EMD "E" SERIES LOCOMOTIVES. *THE CITY OF MIAMI* IS ABOUT TO LEAVE CHICAGO BEHIND E8A AND E9AS ON APRIL 18, 1971.

RIGHT A HIGH-NOSE GP7 NO. 411 OF LOUISVILLE & NASHVILLE RR. OVER 2,700 OF THESE WERE BUILT, SOME AS "BOOSTERS" WITHOUT DRIVING CABS.

Dan Pope Collection

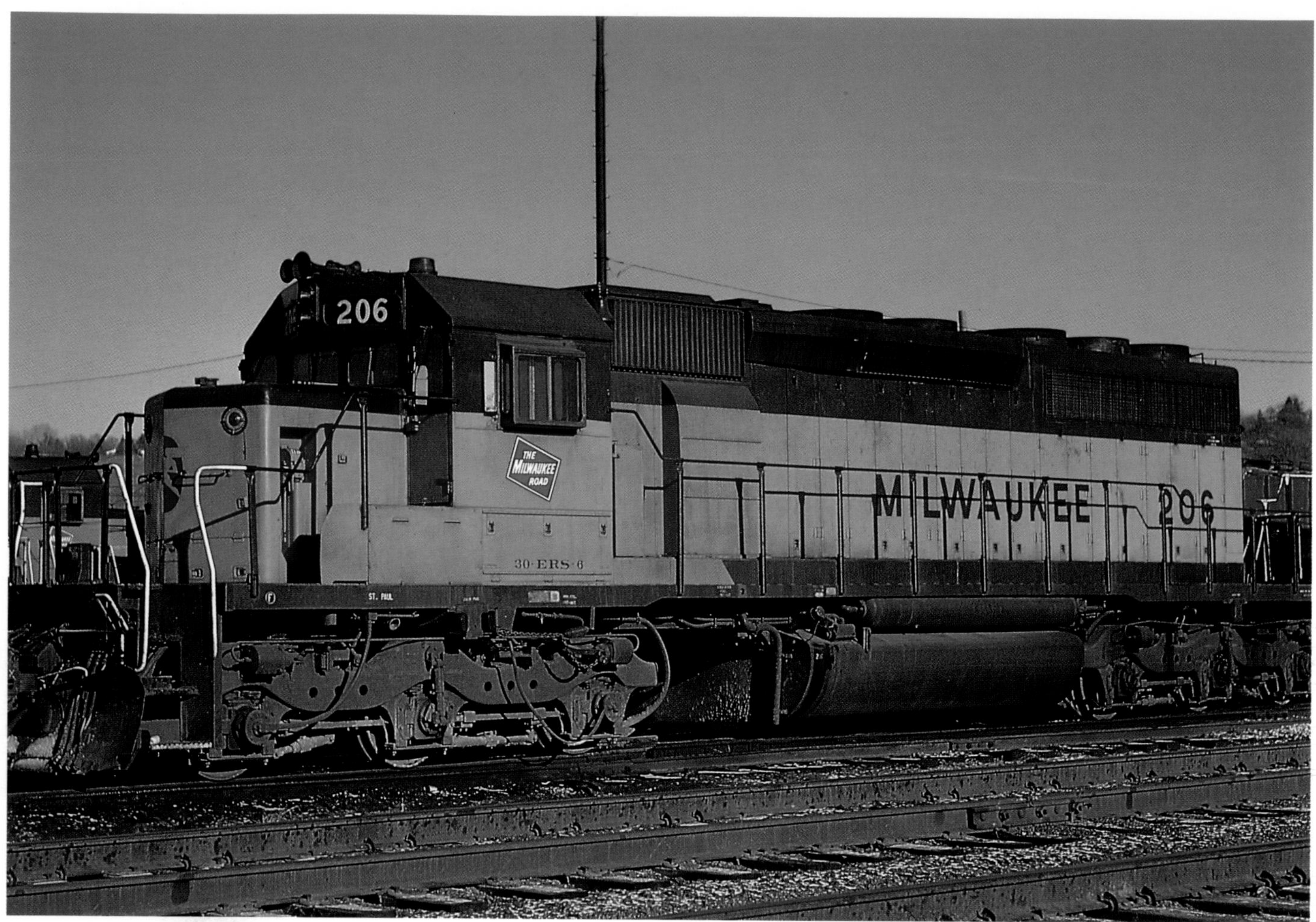

Dan Pope Collection

ABOVE THE POPULAR ROAD SWITCHER FOR FREIGHT IN THE 1970 AND 1980S WAS THE SD40. MILWAUKEE RR NO. 206 IS AT ST PAUL IN OCTOBER 1986.

that the last car of a train really *is* the last car an End of Train Device (ETD) is attached to the rear car, usually on the rear coupler. The ETD incorporates a flashing red strobe light, a motion detector and an air-brake-line monitor. Information on air-brake pressure and motion are automatically transmitted to a receiver in the locomotive cab, helping the driver (engineer) to handle trains one mile or more long more smoothly and safely than ever before.

An important facility to aid development is the Transportation Test Center near Pueblo, CO. This was set up about 20 years ago by the Department of Transportation and is operated under contract to the department by the Association of American Railroads.

The center has specialized test facilities and was originally set up to develop high-speed surface-transport vehicles. The facilities are now available for a number of test purposes. There is a rail dynamics laboratory, a 15-mile ac-electrified test track for main line use; a 10-mile track equipped with third-rail dc and light-rail-type catenary for urban applications. In the early 1980s a great deal of work was done on magnetically levitated applications.

The story of American diesel-electric locomotives has been well documented and in some detail. So far we have dealt with the diesel locomotive only up to its later first-generation state. Here we can do no more than summarize the various stages of development.

From the start diesel engine manufacturers sought to develop and improve their engines. From 1950, four-stroke engines with individual outputs for traction of 2,000 hp from 16 cylinders were available; by 1960 this had reached 2,400 hp. The 16-cylinder EMD 567 two-stroke engine had reached 2,000 hp by 1959 in its turbo-charged form, and 2,500 hp by 1963. Fairbanks-Morse also had a 2,400 hp two-stroke opposed-piston engine as early as 1953. This was a development of their successful marine engine, but was never as suitable as a railroad prime mover as the others.

Switchers had traditionally been built as "hood" units, with a single cab at one end, while road passenger and freight units were of the carbody type, whether driving (A-type) or booster (B-type), until about 1949. The

Dan Pope Collection

majority, whether with four or six axles, had four traction motors. There were exceptions – Fairbanks-Morse was one, but it was never a major builder.

It is generally agreed that the year 1949 saw the first of what were termed general purpose locomotives introduced into road service. Based on the traditional switcher format, but with a nose ahead of the driving cab, these were dubbed road switchers. First in the field was ALCO, with its famous RS-2 of 1,500 and later 1,600 hp. Probably the best known, however, was the EMD 1,500 hp GP7, introduced as a general-purpose unit chiefly for secondary lines which, together with the later GP9, numbered over 6,000 for United States railroads alone.

The hood design proved to be well adapted to the visibility requirements of yard and road operation. The accessibility of the propulsion system components was enhanced by the design of the superstructure. The purely functional bi-directional design provided cost advantages over the full-width carbody types.

Given the relatively low speeds of freight trains in the United States, the theoretical reduction of profile drag offered by the full-width carbody design and streamlined nose was unimportant. As a result the road switcher

ABOVE In 1963 General Electric brought out their 5,000 hp U50 and built 23 for Union Pacific and 3 for Southern Pacific between 1963 and 1965. These locomotives had two FDL-16 engines and were virtually a double U25. No. 43 is seen here at Denver, Colorado in 1972.

RIGHT IN 1978, SOUTHERN PACIFIC RR AGREED TO MAKE AVAILABLE TO MORRISON-KNUDSEN OF BOISE, IDAHO FOUR U25B LOCOMOTIVES WHICH WERE REBUILT WITH SULZER 12-CYLINDER ASL25/30 ENGINES OF 3,000 HP. NO. 7031 HEADS A CONSIST AT OAKLAND, CA IN JULY, 1978.

J.W. Swanberg Collection

J.W. Swanberg Collection

ABOVE SOUTHERN PACIFIC RR HAS BEEN PREPARED TO TRY NON-STANDARD PRODUCTS. IN 1961–3 21 LOCOMOTIVES WERE IMPORTED FROM KRAUSS-MAFFEI, GERMANY WITH HYDRAULIC TRANSMISSION. TWO OF THE 1963 ROAD-SWITCHER TYPE ARE AT SAN JOSÉ, CALIFORNIA IN AUGUST 1965. THEY HAD A SHORT LIFE.

form became the accepted second generation standard for freight operation and, with minor changes, it remains so to this day.

General Electric entered the road switcher market only in 1959, but when they did it was with single-engine locomotives of 2,500 hp against the 1,800 hp then available with the EMD's designs. ALCO had entered the field in 1946 with a design of similar power to EMD's. The popularity of the road switcher grew rapidly and the carbody locomotive dropped out of production with the last E9A/B in 1963.

Around the same time certain railroads had become disenchanted with what they regarded as the manufacturers' small-locomotive policy. In Europe there were one or two examples of locomotives in the 3,500-4,000

BELOW UNION PACIFIC TOOK DELIVERY OF 47 OF THESE IMMENSE 6,600 HP DO-DO TYPE DD40AX LOCOMOTIVES BUILT TO SPECIAL ORDER. NAMED *CENTENNIAL* FOR THE 100TH ANNIVERSARY IN 1969 OF THE "*GOLDEN SPIKE*" CEREMONY AT PROMONTARY, UTAH. NO. 6936 IS AT SPEED, WYOMING IN OCTOBER 1985.

Dan Pope Collection

hp range with high-speed engines and hydraulic transmissions. Between 1961 and 1963 Krauss-Maffei of Munich, Germany exported 21 high-power diesel-hydraulic locomotives, each with two 2,000 hp engines and hydraulic transmissions. Three of these went to the Rio Grande and 17 to Southern Pacific.

American conditions uncovered a number of problems and these locomotives were soon retired. There were other attempts by European manufacturers to break into the American market and one, Sulzer Brothers of Winterthur, Switzerland, sold a few 12- and 16-cylinder engines of 3,000 and 4,000 hp (traction) to three United States railroads through Morrison-Knudsen of Boise, ID in 1979–80. These went to Southern Pacific, Burlington Northern and Union Pacific. While operation was reasonably successful, the proposed licensee in the U.S. did not take up the license.

One limitation on increased engine power, apart from suitable engines, was the direct-current generator, which had reached its limit at an input of about 2,800 hp. In the early 1960s silicon rectifiers had been introduced into railway traction and development was fast so that by the mid-1960s devices were small and reliable enough to enable three-phase alternators to be substituted. This removed the restriction on input power and paved the way for more powerful prime movers and, hence, single-unit locomotives.

In May 1966 GE handed over two U28Bs to the railroads for trials, and from 1966 all high-horsepower GE locomotives had alternators. EMD followed suit with

Dan Pope Collection

ABOVE EMD COWL UNITS WERE INTRODUCED IN 1967 AT THE REQUEST OF SANTA FE FOR A MORE ACCEPTABLE APPEARANCE ON PREMIER PASSENGER TRAINS. SIMPLY A WEATHER SHELTER, A COWL MAY OFFER LESS AIR RESISTANCE AT HIGH SPEEDS. HERE AMTRAK FP40 NO 210 IS AT BRANFORD, CT IN 1991.

2,000 hp GP38s and S38s in 1971, offering alternators as an alternative to dc generators. From January 1972 EMD began production of its Dash 2 range, all of which had alternators as well as other high-reliability innovations.

The pattern for the future had emerged with both four- and six-motor designs. Single-engine locomotives of up to 3,600 hp were available by the late 1960s. Theoretically, fewer units per train were needed but, with the strengthening of couplers and increased speeds over better tracks, three, four and even five units could be found on very long and heavy trains.

Union and Southern Pacific, because of their steeply graded lines over the Sierra Nevada and the Rockies, persuaded both EMD and GE to break with tradition and produce some unique locomotives to their specific requirements. EMD DD35s were originally to be "B" units to work between pairs of GP35s. These were 5,000 hp locomotives riding on two four-axle trucks and each had two 16-cylinder 567D3A engines. Some 30 were produced in 1963–4. In 1965 a further 15 were produced for Union Pacific with cabs.

The crowning glory was the DDA40X of 6,600 hp, built from 1969 to 1971. A total of 47 were built for Union Pacific and were known as "Centennials" in honor of the 100th anniversary of the Golden Spike ceremony of 1869. These, too, were carried on four-axle trucks and had two 16-cylinder 645 E3A engines and "safety cabs."

The GE equivalents were of two designs. Between 1963 and 1965 26 eight-axle locomotives classified U50D were built, but these rode on four two-axle trucks with the draft-gear mounted on the truck. Each had two-16 cylinder FDL-16 engines with a total of 5,000 hp. They had a GE version of the full-width safety cab. A second batch was a six-axle design weighing 208.5 tons (the heaviest six-axle locomotives in the United States), still of 5,000 hp but with two 12-cylinder FDL-12 engines.

The next change to outline came in 1967–9 with the introduction of the so-called "cowl" design. Cowl units were originally produced for Santa Fe RR to provide a more acceptable appearance than the typical road

Dan Pope Collection

ABOVE THREE BURLINGTON NORTHERN RR *SD70MACS* – EMD AC DRIVE, STATE-OF-THE-ART 4,000 HP LOCOMOTIVES, AT FORTH WORTH, TEXAS IN MAY 1995.

switcher for locomotives used on premier passenger trains. It was designed to create an air-tight carbody which permitted trouble-shooting and even maintenance en route, although that need had largely disappeared by then. Ironically, with freight trains now traveling at speeds up to 80 mph, there was renewed interest in reducing air resistance in order to improve fuel consumption. At the same time the design permitted the use of a wider safety or "comfort" cab.

Unlike the earlier carbody locomotives, cowl units are built on the road switcher principle, with a separate underframe; the cowl merely serves to create an airtight carbody. The safety cab has also been applied to hood-type units, but with disadvantages.

The road switcher provides an ideal locomotive for bi-directional working singly. The cowl configuration does not, and it requires turning at each end of a run when used alone. They are common performers on Amtrak passenger trains and it is not unusual to see two cowl units facing the same way at the head of a train – which is inconvenient when the terminal is reached and one or both have to be turned.

New developments for high reliability and less maintenance have been introduced over the years. We have already seen the rapid increase in power per locomotive unit which occurred after the introduction of alternators. As power ratings increased, so did the complexity of electrical controls to obtain optimum performance. To offset this, functions were grouped into discrete modules, and systems were devised to incorporate self-checking features to improve reliability.

Now, with the rapid development of electronic devices, another goal has been reached. Until the early 1990s the direct-current traction motor had dominated the field. It was familiar, highly developed and pretty reliable. But it had a snag: it was maintenance-rich. It has a commutator and brushes which need maintenance; also it is sensitive to overspeeding and requires sophisticated anti-spin protection. Electronics have changed all that. It is now possible to employ alternating-current motors with ideal characteristics which are virtually maintenance-free.

Early in the field in the United States was EMD with

Dan Pope Collection

LEFT SD70 MAC FOR BURLINGTON NORTHERN LEAVES THE MANUFACTURER'S PLANT.

the F69PH-AC, a joint development between EMD and Siemens AG of Germany. Two locomotives were delivered to Amtrak in 1989, based on the well-known F40PH cowl-type unit. The main changes were the engine, now a 12-710G3 of 3,000 traction hp, four asynchronous 3-phase traction motors, microprocessor techniques for the control system and a potential top speed of 110 mph.

Following on the success of these prototypes, EMD introduced its S70MACs (Big MACs) based on the same control system, and to date 235 have been delivered to Burlington Northern. Although a number of roads have been slow to accept the change, clearly 3-phase drive is here to stay.

Today's standard freight locomotive, whether from EMD or GE, is a hood type with a full-width nose and a safety cab designed with special attention to crew safety and comfort. The wide nose caught on in 1990, and now it is the exception if any new road unit is delivered with a standard cab.

This, of course, is not the whole story. Apart from diesel locomotives, the 1970s and 1980s saw the return of fixed-formation self-propelled vehicles in the shape of turbo-trains. They had some initial success, but the turbo-trains, based on French technology, did not come up to United States standards crashworthiness, and a later batch (produced by Rohr Industries) are heavier and not so economical. Others built in Canada by MLW, the so-called LRC (Light, Rapid, Comfortable) trains, had many operational problems and were finally discarded.

Now Amtrak has been looking again at European technology for high speed trains, with French, German and Swedish designs being considered and both German and Swedish trains being tried in the northeast corridor. In 1993 Amtrak borrowed a Swedish X2000 trainset and ran it between Washington, DC, New York City and Boston, MA. With diesel haulage it was also taken for a nationwide tour. More recently a German ICE trainset has been run over the same route and been given the same nationwide treatment. The French TGV and Spanish Talgo have also been studied, and one of the latter is now operating between Seattle, WA and Vancouver, British Columbia, as the *Mount Baker International.*

It has since become clear that a single off-the-shelf train would not suit Amtrak. None of the trains so far examined meet all of the performance, aesthetic and safety criteria. Amtrak is seeking a 3-hour New York City–Boston running time, and this could be met only by a train with tilt technology, but the well-established Swedish X2000 tilt-train, with radial axles, does not have sufficient power for Amtrak's requirements.

Nationalism, moreover, demands an all-American approach and Amtrak is seeking to establish its own identity with such a project. Already its designers have collaborated with the Henry Dreyfuss design firm to produce models of what they would like the American high-speed passenger train to be. It was hoped a contract based on the approved model would be awarded, before the end of 1995, to one of three manufacturing consortiums to build 24 electric trainsets and two fossil-fueled versions for use elsewhere.

J.W. Swanberg Collection

Above In 1973–5 11 5-car Gas Turbine powered lightweight trains were imported by Amtrak and Via Rail of Canada. In 1976 14 more were delivered by Rohr Industries and one of this is seen here at Poughkeepsie, New York on June 24, 1989.

What of the future? There has been much talk of "High Speed Rail" (HSR) projects for passenger services. Already studies have been completed in 17 states and the Clinton administration has encouraged planning, provided the necessary funds are also committed by the relevant states. Texas has its own High Speed Rail Authority, established in 1989 under the Texas High Speed Rail Act. In 1992 the authority awarded the Texas TGV Corporation a franchise to build a 590-mile network of high-speed lines linking Dallas, Forth Worth, Houston, Austin and San Antonio, which would exploit the technology of the celebrated 186 mph French Train à Grande Vitesse. The franchise was cancelled in 1994 owing to difficulty in securing the rights-of-way required and the failure to raise sufficient non-government funds.

There are other schemes, too, and one at least is looking at the possibility of using unconventional land transport. A bi-state governmental commission of California and Nevada looked into the possibility of a high-speed link between Los Angeles and Las Vegas. This was to have been a Maglev system, which in 1980 aroused a great deal of enthusiasm. Maglev (magnetic levitation) was being promoted very actively in the 1970s and 1980s as a means of traveling over land at speeds as high as 300 mph.

The system employs a guideway (usually of concrete) rather than rails, with the train "floating" with a clearance of up to one inch on a magnetic field requiring no power expenditure, with no noise, and no need for maintenance. Frictionless forward motion is provided by a linear motor using the track's permanent field for its excitation.

Major experiments in this technology have been carried out for more than a decade in Germany and Japan using various forms of maglev, and some very high speeds have been attained. However, there has not been any general acceptance so far of either system as a practical or commercially viable high-speed, high-density people-mover.

Electrification has been taken up elsewhere in the world for a variety of reasons: relatively low costs of electricity generation, availability of hydroelectric power, non-availability of liquid fuel or its high cost compared to other fuels, and so on. Electrification of urban railroads makes a lot of sense. From the point of view of pollution alone clean rapid transit can be provided only by using electricity, and it is probable that more electrification of urban routes will take place.

Today in the United States the diesel-electric locomotive is king, and we have seen how it transformed the railroads in the 1950s and 1960s to the extent that it forced the closure of most of the electrified lines except those in the northeast corridor. Probably the particular strictures under which United States railroads had to work played its part: we have seen how investment and maintenance suffered in the struggle of many roads to remain profitable. All this has changed and the railroads have once again turned a corner. But electrification seems as far off as ever, except for any new high-speed lines which may emerge in the future.

There is little doubt that the inflexible regulation imposed on the American railroads in the late 19th century and the power given to the Interstate Commerce Commission did much to discourage investment. Other industries were free to adjust their charges in line with economic circumstances so as to maintain investment capital; the railroads were not. The coming of the automobile led to pressure to improve highways, and later

RIGHT ROHR INDUSTRIES 6-CAR GAS TURBINE UNIT IN AMTRAK COLORS, ON A MONTREAL-BOUND TRAIN AT CROTON NORTH, NY, ON 2 AUGUST 1980.

Dan Pope Collection

mtrak
Power Coach

TURBO

J.W. Swanberg Collection

LEFT AND BELOW THE FIRST LIGHT, RAPID, AND COMFORTABLE (LRC) TRAIN SETS WERE PRODUCED FOR UNITED AIRCRAFT BY PULLMAN STANDARD IN 1967 FOR THE DEPARTMENT OF TRANSPORTATION. AFTER TESTS THEY WERE PUT ON NEW YORK TO BOSTON SERVICES BUT WERE RETIRED IN 1975 AFTER POOR RELIABILITY. HERE ONE IS SEEN AT NEW HAVEN CT IN 1972.

Dan Pope Collection

the vast program of highway and freeway building, financed by governments, coupled with the still highly restrictive regulation led to a rapid and ultimately catastrophic loss of traffic. A similar picture was seen in other countries, too.

Now, at last freed of much of the restrictive regulation by the "Staggers Act" of 1980, railroads have been able to shed much of the unremunerative traffic for which, prior to the act, they were obliged to cater. The ICC still oversees the present processes of charging, but it has lost most of its teeth. It are still responsible for considering the merits or otherwise of mergers and line closures, but today its role is essentially advisory.

To many, the railroads are a relic of the past; but without them the flow of heavy goods and materials would be exceedingly difficult to achieve. Pipelines can take liquids; rivers, canals and coastal shipping can carry bulk loads, but are slow. The modern American railroad system moves vast quantities of a range of commodities speedily and efficiently. Railroads, moreover, are considerably more fuel-efficient than most other modes of transport, and today they create relatively little pollution. With high traffic densities, far less land is employed, and trains have become much more responsive to modern needs. American railroads have entered a new and extremely interesting era.

Appendix for Railfans
Railroad Memorabilia

J.W. Swanberg Collection

• As might be expected in a country as vast as the United States, with a railroad system as large as it was in the 1930s, there is a very large following of railfans. While the steam locomotive had disappeared from the roads by 1960, there are many enthusiasts all over the country who remember it with affectionate admiration, and fortunately many examples have been saved from the scrapyards and hungry jaws of the open-hearth furnaces of the steelmakers.

• There is not only a large following for steam: many railfans have a special interest in the earlier first- and even second-generation diesel locomotives, and these too are preserved at various locations. Moreover, it is not only locomotives which attract the attention of railfans: there is also a very large number who are collectors of railroad memorabilia. Add to that the number of railroad museums all over the United States, and you have a big business for railfans.

• If you pick up any American railroad magazine and turn to the advertisements section you'll find ads for T-shirts, caps, jackets, badges, builders' plates, tickets, lanterns, posters, timetables, calendars, maps, track charts, train journals, dining-car china and cutlery, wax sealers, rail union membership cards, and much else. Many items of railroadiana are offered at auctions; sometimes whole collections go under the hammer. But probably the examples of memorabilia giving the fullest insight into local railroad history are those to be found in local and specialized railroad museums.

• Undoubtedly a good moneyspinner is the sale of memorabilia in the shops or on excursion trains run by the many preserved railroads throughout the country, while much of the early railroad history is to be found in museums such as the B & O Railroad Museum in Baltimore, MD. The Smithsonian Institution in Washington, DC has a Railroad Hall in the National Museum of American History where there are a number of full-size exhibits.

• On the West coast a visit to the **California State Railroad Museum** at Sacramento is a must. The Central Pacific passenger station has been reconstructed to look like it was in the 1870s and there is a large book store and gift shop with many reproductions of railroadiana. Probably the most interesting exhibit is the last Southern Pacific cab-forward 4-8-8-2 No. 4294 steamer; but there are many other examples of West coast locomotives and cars.

• Perhaps best of all there is the **Steamtown National Historic Site** at Scranton, PA, which had its formal opening on July 1–4, 1995. Steamtown is a part of the U.S. National Park Service with its own collection of steam and diesel locomotives. It includes trackage of portions of the old Delaware, Lackawanna & Western RR and runs excursions between Scranton and nearby Moscow. Its day-to-day business is the running of a national park, and it was described by William L. Withuhn, of the Smithsonian Institution, as a museum "not for railfans, but for the American citizenry."

• Trips into railroad history can be made on various tourist lines from the Yukon, Canada, through Colorado to Florida and up through Michigan to Massachusetts. Even some of the so-called "short lines" run steam or diesel excursions in the summer months. Practically all of them have memorabilia of some kind for sale. And we should not forget the miniature railroads, both public and private, with gauges from 7½ to 18½ in, with excellent models of steam locomotives of the past and not so distant past, built by enthusiasts and model engineers to very high standards.

• At the last count there were some 350 tourist railroads, railroad museums and other railroad attractions in the United States, Canada and Mexico. There is something of interest to the railroad enthusiast from the mundane to the development of Pennsylvania Railroad steam locomotives, from "Americans" to the *Zephyrs.*

• The following is a small sample of museums and tourist lines.

• **Durango & Silverton Narrow Gauge Railroad** is one of two remaining portions of the former extensive Denver & Rio Grande Western's narrow (3ft) gauge network and runs from Durango, in southwest Colorado to Silverton, 45 miles to the north. Built originally to transport ore from the mines around Silverton, the line was isolated by the closure of the section from Antonito, CO through to Farmington, NM in 1968. The line was re-opened in 1981 as a private venture. About one third of the trip is through a broad portion of the valley of the

LEFT A DURANGO & SILVERTON TRAIN CLIMBS THROUGH THE ANIMAS GORGE IN COLORADO.

OPPOSITE A TOURIST TRAIN OF THE RESTORED DURANGO & SILVERTON SCENIC RAILROLAD HAULED BY FORMER DENVER & RIO GRANDE 3FT OIN 2-8-2 NO. 48.

Animas River. From Rockwood the valley narrows to a canyon and this is followed by the railroad, in some places high above the river, in others almost at water level. The canyon widens to a broad valley just before Silverton. Motive power is provided by eight former D&RGW 2-8-2 steam locomotives; three are ALCOs and the remainder are Baldwins. Souvenirs are available for sale on the trains.

• **East Board Top Railroad**, at Lincoln Caverns, Raystown Lake, southeast of Altoona, PA, was the last 3ft gauge common carrier east of the Mississippi. Its principal business was carrying coal and it ceased operation in 1956, the locomotives and cars being stored on the property. In 1960 the owner was approached to see if the line could be re-activated to help in the celebrations of the bicentennial of the nearby town of Orbisonia. As a result the East Broad Top re-opened as a tourist railway in August 1960 with the original locomotives, cars and facilities. There are three steam locomotives and three gas/diesels and visitors are offered a 50 minute round trip over the 5 miles of track.

• **Grand Canyon Railway** was formerly a branch opened in 1901 off the Chicago–Los Angeles road of the Atchison, Topeka & Santa Fe RR. The Grand Canyon branch left the main line at Williams, AZ, 30 miles west of Flagstaff. Sleeping cars between Chicago and Los Angeles made the 64 miles each way detour due north to the Grand Canyon.

• Passenger services ceased in 1968 but freight continued to 1974. The line was purchased and re-opened in September 1989 and has gone from strength to strength. Five steam locomotives and two diesel-electrics are operated, while passengers travel in refurbished Pullman-built Southern Pacific commuter cars.

• **Illinois Railway Museum** is one of North America's largest and is noted for its collection of diesels, interurbans, Chicago streetcars and rapid-transit cars. Locomotives include a "GG1", 4-8-4s from Grand Trunk and Milwaukee Road and a Norfolk & Western 2-8-8-2.

• The museum opened in 1953 and moved to its present site on the eastern edge of the village of Union, midway between Rockford and Elgin in northern Illinois. The site covers 50 acres and includes, bookshop, gift shop, and a loop of track taking streetcars around the area. Steam and diesel trains also operate on a three-mile track along the roadbed of the former Elgin & Belvidere Electric Railroad, parallel to a line of the Chicago & North Western.

• **Manitou & Pike's Peak Railroad**, in central Colorado, is not strictly a tourist railroad as it is a rack mountain railroad – the highest in the world and one of only two in the United States. From Manitou Springs, a suburb of Colorado

Manitou & Pike's Peak

LEFT SWISS-BUILT 2-CAR DIESEL-RACK RAILCAR SET OF MAITOU AND PIKES PEAK RAILWAY IN COLORADO. THIS LINE CLIMBS TO AN ALTITUDE OF 14,110 FEET ABOVE SEA LEVEL.

J.W. Swanberg Collection

LEFT A STEAM TRAIN OF THE VALLEY RR IN ESSEX, CONNECTICUT ON 4 SEPTEMBER, 1972. THE TRAIN IS HEADED BY BEAUTIFULLY RESTORED BALDWIN 2-6-2, NO. 103.

Springs, the railroad climbs to the summit of Pike's Peak, 14,110 feet.

• The diesel-powered rack railcars were built in Switzerland and there are single cars as well as twin-car units. The total length of the line is 9 miles and the 18 mile round trip up and down the eastern flank of the mountain takes about 3¼ hours. The scenery is spectacular. At the Summit House are a gift shop, information desk and concession counter. There is also one steam locomotive, and this is steamed up occasionally.

• **Valley Railroad** is the southern portion of a rural branch line running alongside the Connecticut River from Hartford to its outlet at Long Island Sound at Old Saybrook, CT. New Haven RR abandoned the branch in 1968. The Valley Railroad was chartered and the state purchased the line in 1969 and began operating excursion trains from Essex northward to Deep River in 1971. These were extended a couple of miles up river to Chester in 1973.

• The trains consist of well-restored, well-maintained coaches and a parlor-car hauled by steam locomotives. There is one Chinese 2-8-2, purchased new in 1989, and two 2-8-2s from ALCO of 1920/4 vintage. Excursion trains connect with boat cruises at Deep River and the train ride takes 55 minutes; alternatively the train-boat combination takes 2 hours 10 minutes.

• Essex is about 30 miles east of New Haven and 40 miles south east of Hartford. Other attractions for railfans nearby include the **Shore Line Trolley Museum** operated by the **Branford Electric Railroad Association**, a few miles east of New Haven. This has an interesting collection of working street and rapid-transit cars.

• **Pennsylvania Railroad Museum** at Strasburg, between Lancaster and Philadelphia, has a notable collection of motive power and rolling stock. In addition to steam locomotives, there are several electric and diesel locomotives. Notable exhibits are *The Tahoe*, an 1875 wood burner; No 1187, the oldest existing Pennsylvania Railroad locomotive; a 4-4-0 and a 4-4-2 of 1905 and 1902 respectively, retired in 1990 from excursion work; and "GG1" electric No 4935.

• Close by is the **Strasburg Rail Road**, the oldest railroad in the United States operating under its original charter and one of the first railroads to seek viability in the tourist business. Chartered in 1832, it operated until 1957 when storm damage resulted in suspension of services.

• Freight and excursion passenger services were re-started in 1959 after a group of enthusiasts purchased the line. Trains make a 45-minute round trip from Strasburg through lush farmland and woods to a junction with the Amtrak Philadelphia-Harrisburg line (formerly Pennsy's main line) at Paradise (or Leman Place, as the railroads call it). There are four steam locomotives and a variety of gas and diesels.

INDEX

Page numbers in *italics* refer to picture captions.

PICTURE CREDITS

Please note that the author and publishers have made every effort to identify the copyright owners of the pictures used in this publication; they apologise for any omissions, and would like to thank the following:

American Society of Mechanical Engineers (A.S.M.E.), pp 29, 43, 44(tl), 44(tr), 45(t), 46, 53(t,b), 55, 56(t), 57(t), 60–61, 88, 104(t), 109, 110, 112, 113(t), 114(t), 116, 125, 127, 132, 147.
Atcheson, Topeka and Santa Fe Railroad Company, p 95.
The Baltimore & Ohio Railroad Museum, Inc., pp 8, 9, 10(t), 11(t), 31, 73, 94(b), 98, 118, 134.
Burlington Northern Railroad Archives, pp 119(t), 129(t).
California State Railroad Museum, pp 10(b), 11(b), 17(t,b), 23(t), 30, 35(t,b), 37, 40, 54, 56(c,b), 57(c,b), 59, 68, 69, 70, 71, 74, 77(b), 79, 80, 122, 150.
Conrail, pp 187. C.P.Limited, pp 6, 33, 63, 64, 65, 66, 67, 76.
Dan Pope Collection, pp 7, 113(b), 114(b), 115, 119(b), 120, 121, 123, 124, 130, 138, 141, 142, 148(t), 151, 152, 153, 154, 155, 156, 157, 158, 159, 160, 164, 166 (t), 167, 170, 171, 173, 174, 175, 176, 177, 178, 179, 180, 181, 183, 185.
Electro-Motive, pp 133, 161.
J.W. Swanberg Collection pp 72, 84, 92, 94(t), 100, 105, 107, 148(b), 149, 158, 162, 163, 172, 175, 181, 184, 186, 187, 189.
Manitou & Pikes Peak Railway Company, pp 188.
New Jersey Transit pp 165, 168.
Railroad Museum of Pennsylvania (PHMC), 39, 83(t), 85, 89, 97, 104(b), 136, 137.
St. Louis Mercantile Museum, pp 12–13(t), 16, 48, 77(t), 91(b), 93(t,b), 117, 135, 143 (all courtesy Barriger Railroad Library), pp 58, 82–83 (Pennsylvania Railroad, Barriger Railroad Library), 90, 91(t) (Bertram Allen Atwater, Barriger Railroad Library), 114(c), Norfolk & Western Railway, Barriger Railroad Library, 117(t), General Electric Co. (U.S.) Barriger Railroad Library), and 108.
Union Pacific Museum Collection, pp 78, 81, 128–129(b), 144.
Westinghouse, Air Brake Co. (W.A.B.C.O.), pp 42, 49, 50, 51, 52.

The publisher would also like to offer special thanks to the following, for providing artworks and illustrations:
Julian Baker, pp 13, 15, 17(l), 21(b), 22, 24, 26, 32, 41, 75, 86, 87, 96, 111.
Thomas Bailey, pp 14, 21t), 25, 27, 38–39(t), 46–7(t).